READY
FOR THE RETURN OF
JESUS

HOPE AND COMFORT FOR THE END TIMES

READY
FOR THE RETURN OF
JESUS

The Handbook of Preparing for the Return of Jesus

STEVE CAREY

Info Strategies
Mission Viejo, California

Copyright © 2011, 2016 by Steve Carey

All rights reserved

Version 1.2

For updates and more resources visit

www.heartsready.com

Softcover ISBN 978-1-935912-16-3

Hardcover ISBN 978-1-935912-12-5

Library of Congress Control Number 2010913074
Library of Congress subject heading:
Religion
Philosophy
Self Help
End Times

Scripture noted NIV are taken from the Holy Bible, New International Version®, NIV®. Copyright © 1973, 1978, 1984 by International Bible Society. Used by permission of Zondervan. All rights reserved worldwide.

Scripture noted AMP are taken from the Amplified Bible, Copyright © 1954, 1958, 1962, 1964, 1965, 1987 by The Lockman Foundation. Used by permission.

Scriptures noted NASB are taken from the New American Standard Bible®, Copyright © 1960, 1962, 1963, 1968, 1971, 1972, 1973, 1975, 1977, 1995 by The Lockman Foundation Used by permission." (www.Lockman.org)

To the Lost Sheep . . .

To the children and youth of every nation on earth, whom all heaven and hell wage war over. To the young men and women lost and desperate to find a way on life's true path, blocked miserably by the world's thorns and briars of distraction, sin, charade, and heartache. To the old and grey of the hour who your whole life have cried in your heart, "There must be more."

The Great Shepherd Jesus, unwilling any should be lost, hunts for the soul and life of you all.

To those who say, "Life has eluded and passed me by," Jesus sends his Spirit and his ministers to you with good news and hope, now, while there is yet a little time, at the twilight of life and of history, before the great and dreadful day of the Lord.

> *But the day of the Lord will come like a thief. The heavens will disappear with a roar; the elements will be destroyed by fire, and the earth and everything in it will be laid bare. Since everything will be destroyed in this way, what kind of people ought you to be? You ought to live holy and godly lives* (2 Peter 3:10-11, NIV).

Contents

EXPLANATORY NOTES 1

PART I: THE RETURN OF JESUS

Chapter 1   Love Fulfilled Forever 5
Chapter 2   Fight for Your Inheritance 15
Chapter 3   The Return of Jesus Is in You 23

PART II: IMMORTALITY WHEN JESUS RETURNS

Chapter 4   Eternal Life Is Imminent 37
Chapter 5   Characteristics of His Return 47
Chapter 6   Misinterpreting the Revelation 55
Chapter 7   Glory of the Latter House 67

PART III: ONLY JESUS . . .

Chapter 8   Satisfies Your Heart's Desire for Love 73
Chapter 9   Reconciles You to God 83
Chapter 10   Ransoms You From Sin 89
Chapter 11   Lives within Your Heart 95
Chapter 12   Fulfills Scripture as Savior 103
Chapter 13   Created the Heavens and the Earth 107

PART IV: HOW TO BE READY

Chapter 14   Protect God's Dwelling 113
Chapter 15   Keep Your Heart Holy 119
Chapter 16   Maintain Sexual Purity 131
Chapter 17   Forgive Everyone Always 149
Chapter 18   Embrace Emotional Healing 155
Chapter 19   Follow the Shepherd 165
Chapter 20   Obey God in Spirit and in Truth 173

PART V: SCRIPTURE REFERENCES

Background to Scripture References 181
Table of References 185

Explanatory Notes

Much has been written and spoken concerning the end times. Plentiful material, sermons, and financial thesis abound with variations of theories and assertions. Generally, the predictions expire making way for new guesses. This is not the way of peace, but rather, an anxiety-invoking cycle appealing to an almost esoteric desire of the flesh. True salvation inward (not just an outward profession lacking true regeneration) through Jesus Christ is the message of the end times.

The intent of this book is for you to be personally blessed and to experience a love you have never known but have always longed for. You will find within these pages words to facilitate an authentic experience of God's love if you are a new Christian and a deeper, more fulfilling exchange of his satisfying love and affection if you are a seasoned believer.

Created to assist you in being prepared for the return of Jesus, this manual suggests areas in your life to work on in order to be and remain ready. Scriptures are ultimately your governing manual and provide first priority instruction in the conduct of your life and preparation for the return of Jesus.

Divided into five parts, each part is accessible in any order and collectively builds a complete treatise, helping you prepare for his return and maintain an authentic Christian life. All twenty chapters within the first four parts are substantiated by the Scripture references in the fifth part. This biblical reference section in Part V has been designed to foster a more accessible and ongoing experience of the Scripture. The verses are arranged both in support of the material in each chapter and as an easy topical reference.

The easiest ways to access the references are to first note the citation number, such as [2.3] within the text and then refer to Scripture notation 2.3 in Part V; and second, review the Part V Table of Contents to find the topic you would like to read about.

Instruction steeped in biblical Scripture helps you draw close to God, develop a closer walk with Christ, and become or continue as a victor, ready for his return.

PART I

THE RETURN OF JESUS

CHAPTER 1

LOVE FULFILLED FOREVER

The return of Jesus is an imminent supernatural change that will occur within God's people, his true sons and daughters, changing them to be like him.[1.18] According to Scripture, all of creation groans and travails for this event.[5.3] At that time, immortality will come to those who are ready and eternal loss and separation from God's presence will come to those who are unprepared or have rejected Jesus. Simply claiming you are a Christian, but not having his Spirit inside of you, does not make you ready for his return.[31.19]

The enemy of Jesus is actively working to steal your inheritance of eternal life and destroy your soul. You must overcome this adversary.[39] Your victory is assured if you will trust, surrender to, and serve Jesus Christ and his Holy Spirit.

His return is at hand—a change that will happen in a moment—in the twinkling of an eye and forever transform your physical and spiritual condition and relationship with the Lord. His return will be an entirely new move of God and the fulfillment of the Christian dispensation of grace—the current era in God's plan, which is known as the New Testament period. Your priority must be to prepare and be ready for the end of this time period and the return of Jesus.

There is a waiting place—a condition you can be in, always ready and watching to rise above the storms of life and evil. This condition will make you a witness to the world as a light and the salt in the earth. Love is your place of safety, peace is the fruit it produces, and eternal life is the coming glory that Jesus will reveal in you. Neither death nor life, neither powers nor anything in all creation can separate you from God's love, which is in Christ Jesus our Lord.[15.8]

Love is the authentic desire of every person. Jesus Christ meets and fulfills your need for God's love and his Savior's love, now and forever. It is a loving, personal relationship with God; one in which you receive love from him into your heart and soul and respond by extending your love to him in devotion to Christ. This love is eternal. It will fulfill your heart's greatest need and prepare you for the return of Jesus.

The spirit of God pleads with all mankind in every generation to receive his gift of love while each individual still has time. God's love is above earthly love. It produces and maintains the way of holiness within you. Living a life in an exchange of love with God is a life that is holy unto the Lord. It is a life born again from the old carnal nature. It puts on the new nature and spirit of Christ. The flesh—the old man—has been crucified and, in the new nature, you serve God in surrender to his will and obedience to his commands.

The new person—born anew, redeemed in Christ, having put on Christ's Spirit, and turned away from the world—is the life and establishment of righteousness where the love of God flourishes. This is your place of peace and safety, a habitation resisting all the storms and trials of life. A condition and dwelling covered by the love and protection of God, nourishing your heart and dispelling fear and doubt. This inward spiritual house stands in the land of the redeemed and is occupied by those who hear and obey his voice and enter into his reward. This is the heritage of those who know their Lord and God, Jesus Christ.

Have you experienced God's love? Are you, or would you like to be, in a daily, two-way exchange of love with Jesus? Your deepest need and lifelong desire to experience this true love can be continuously satisfied in an intimate relationship with your Creator. Experiencing and exchanging love with God is his gift to you. In fact, it is so important to him that his first commandment is to love him with all of your heart.[25.2] This gift is yours. If you have never experienced this love, it is offered to you freely. If it has been stolen from you, it is time to take it back and enter into love's peace and fulfillment. Do not procrastinate. Be diligent to receive this love and if you already are experiencing it, refuse to let anything come between you and God that would diminish this love. Time is short. The return of Jesus will happen when people are completely unaware. It will be as sudden and unseen as falling into a trap.

Placed along the path of the habits and pattern of the daily routine of the hunted, traps are set to spring and capture when least expected. Often, bait is used as an enticement to lure the unsuspecting prey. In the same way, Jesus warned us that the end would come on the whole earth like a trap.[8.33] He taught we must be ready because the Son of Man will come when we do not expect him. Peter, the apostle, described the day of the Lord as coming like a thief.[8.105] In other words, Jesus's return will have the characteristics of stealth. It will be unexpected, occurring in an unplanned appearance, hidden from sight beforehand.

The quickness of this pending event is described by the apostle Paul as occurring in a moment, the twinkling of an eye.[2.3] God's people who are prepared, watch and hope for the return of Jesus, looking for their heavenly reward at his appearing. The promise to bring the consummation of the ages swiftly and God's reward to his faithful is also recorded by Isaiah in the Old Testament. Isaiah prophetically describes the expression of God's love and splendor of his reward in the following verse, which prophesies of the soon-coming day and its impending nature:

> The sun will no more be your light by day, nor will the brightness of the moon shine on you, for the Lord will be your everlasting light, and your God will be your glory. Your sun will never set again, and your moon will want no more; the Lord will be your everlasting light, and your days of sorrow will end. Then will all your people be righteous and they will possess the land forever, they are the shoot I have planted, the work of my hands, for the display of my splendor. The least of you will become a thousand, the smallest a mighty nation. I am the Lord; in its time I will do this swiftly (Isaiah 60:19-22, NIV).

What about you? Do you have the hope that God will be your glory and your days of sorrow will end? Are you confident you will be found watching and the day of the coming of the Son of Man will not catch you off guard? You can have the love of God that will make him your glory and your everlasting light. It's time to turn to him, and allow him to be Lord of your life, the one you pour out your love to.

As you extend your love to God, you may find your love relationship with him is hindered by a variety of circumstances inhibiting a continuous experience of the love of the Father. Identifying these obstacles and understanding how to overcome them when they appear equips you to have an increasing exchange of love with God and others.

Take a moment and consider your current spiritual condition. Be true to yourself. Evaluate if any of the following love-restricting obstacles that impede both Christians and non-Christians are present in your life:

- » Earning love by seeking approval from God for performing religious activities instead of accepting his unconditional love.

- » Believing God no longer offers power and a personal experience to his people, but instead requires some sort of education, organization, membership, penitence, ritual, or favor earned through performance.

- » Choosing to believe God doesn't exist or that Jesus is not the exclusive way to be saved (have eternal life with him forever)

- » Confident you know what truth is; considering yourself to be philosophically enlightened or too sophisticated to believe the gospel of Jesus.

- » Indifference about God because you have been enamored, preoccupied, or beaten down by the world.

- » Turned off to religion and spiritual pursuits because of the scandals, abuses, and insincerity you see.

- » Fearful of, or running from, God because of your sins, your failing to live up to his expectations, and/or the way you live your life. You feel he cannot love you or forgive you.

- » Feeling that he doesn't care about you personally, is inaccessible, or unavailable to you.

- » Afraid your reputation will be damaged, you will be thought less of by others, or the community or belief system you are currently in will reject you.

- » Hiding from God's love because of shame, risk of being hurt, closed feelings, and relational unworthiness.

No matter how many obstacles stand in your way, you can experience God's transforming love and power. Encounters through prayer, encouragement, kindness, ministry from others, surrender, vulnerability, and trust in Jesus are opportunities for experiencing his love. Choosing to yield to his Spirit, trusting him with your vulnerability, and allowing yourself to experience the love of God is an important step in developing your life in Christ.

Please give yourself the chance to personally feel the love that God tangibly offers. You can begin right now by praying to receive, feel, and exchange the embrace of God, asking Jesus to reveal his love to you. If you don't feel worthy, ask him to forgive you, and tell him you want to experience his love. Quiet down. Be still, and wait expectantly. The gain outweighs the risk. It's okay to not be sure. Just be willing to open the door to your heart, test and try God's love, and see if it is real. He will never let you down.

Perhaps you feel unqualified because of your sins. You feel uneasy because of the things you have done that you know he disapproves of and for which you carry guilt and shame. You still have God's invitation and permission to enter into, to test, and to feel the embrace of his mercy and forgiveness.

You might be skeptical. You have probably read a lot of material arguing against the existence of God, and so you try to tell yourself that there is no God. Do you have the courage to give yourself another chance to prove what you believe, weigh the truth, allow your heart to test if he exists, search for, and feel his love? God's desire is for everyone to experience his love and receive life eternal through his Son, Jesus—if they only believe.

Maybe you have been avoiding the need to address and change your true relationship with Christ. Whether or not you realize it; while you are procrastinating, your heart is hardening. Having a hardened heart dangerously places you in jeopardy of losing eternal life. Your time on earth has a purpose and destiny in God. Pursue this destiny and subordinate your own plans and desires to God's plan for your life. Even though it is not God's will for you or anyone else to perish and be separated from him forever; in the end, only a remnant, a small portion of believers, will be saved and receive eternal life.[10.4] Your time to determine who you will serve is now.

If you have any doubt that Christ does not rule your heart, pause right now for a moment and ask him to be the Lord of your life. Tell him, "God, show me and let me experience your love for me!" Sincerely declare that the blood of Jesus cleanse you and bring you into relationship with your God. Pray to Jesus to forgive you for resisting him and his Holy Spirit and tell him you repent and want the salvation he offers. Ask him to apply his precious shed blood upon your troubled soul, to blot out your sins, and save you for eternity. Tell him you would like him to fill you with his Holy Spirit. Be still and feel his love like fragrant oil flow into your heart and determine to serve him for the rest of your life.

Trust Him. Jesus Christ is God and you can experience him. He will fill you with his Holy Spirit and change you forever, rendering you, and making you born anew. This is the first and essential step preparing for his return within his followers. Value Christ's salvation and the will of God above all of the world's temptations and enticements, and make Jesus your life's greatest treasure, your pearl of great price. Determine never to sell out. Make it your life's mission to follow in the love and will of God. Nothing rivals God's love for you. Fulfillment of the destiny God has for you and your desire for his love cannot be accomplished without surrendering to Christ.

The love of God is extended to all creation, pleading with mankind to receive his salvation through his Son. As it was in the days of Noah, so is it now. An unbelieving, unprepared, antagonistic, pleasure-seeking, preoccupied humanity is resisting Christ's spirit and is in pending danger of perishing when the door to safety finally closes.[7.13] Don't accept the forfeiture of your soul. You must allow Jesus to own your heart. Become obedient to his Spirit and allow him to empower you to overcome this temporal world.

Stay alert! Don't be careless and distracted. Turn from your path full of traps and temptations along the broad road of destruction. Steer onto the narrow path that leads to the one who ransomed your soul, delivers you from death, and promises you eternal life.[9.11] Press into Jesus. Find, experience, and maintain his love in your life.

Take the time away from the daily distractions that keep you from pressing into your walk with God. Whether praying alone, singing, listening to worship music (music that honors and gives glory to Jesus), or participating in a service at a Christ-centered church, let the Lord minister to you so that you can increase your love relationship with him. You will not regret a thing. Jesus Christ is and gives the true bread of life that will captivate your heart and meet the deepest desires of your soul.

Be found watching for his appearance. Believe in, hope for, and prepare for his promises to be fulfilled. As surely as the sun rises, he will appear. Determine to go all the way. Surrender now to Christ, while there is still a little time left. Trust him completely in everything. Prepare, watch, and be ready for the return of Jesus.

SUMMARY POINTS

» Being ready for the return of Jesus is an ongoing relational exchange of love with God and Christ.

» Godly love is the waiting place and inward foundation from which obedience and doing his will flow.

» Love is expressed in hearing, obeying, and doing the will of the Father.

- » A loving relationship with the Father and the Son dissolves fear concerning the end of all things.
- » The Holy Spirit helps you identify and remove barriers to love.
- » Power exists in and is evidenced in the love of God.
- » His love empowers us to use our individual talents and gifts in completing our calling and destiny.
- » The love of God sees us through life's hardships and provides peace for all trials and tribulations.
- » Christ fulfills our need for love forever.

CHAPTER 2

Fight for Your Inheritance

Consider for a moment your current belief system. Do you have the inward peace and assurance that your spiritual condition is prepared? Do you genuinely feel you are ready for Christ's return? Are you willing to risk being wrong? Can you afford to continue to ignore self-examination of your heart's status with Christ? It's time to allow God to open your eyes and draw you into a deeper place in him; he is calling out to you and desires good things for you.

You are the temple of God.[21] Jesus established the current New Testament gospel dispensation you now live in. He made the way with his sacrificial atonement for us on the cross and since then, God no longer dwells in physically-constructed temples made with hands as in the Old Testament covenant. Instead, he now chooses mankind—his sacred creation—as his temple. The Lord lives in those who believe in his gospel; and upon his return, he will appear in fullness in his temple, changing their body and soul into immortal. When the Lord returns, he will suddenly come to his temple, his own in Jesus Christ, and you must be ready.

Warfare for your soul is within you, where the Holy Spirit dwells and the light of Christ contends for Jesus to be worshiped in spirit and in truth. The enemy of your soul assaults your salvation in an effort to steal your reward of eternal life. He distorts and marginalizes truth, particularly every aspect of believing Jesus Christ alone is the exclusive Savior of mankind. The Devil imposes spiritual slavery and requires worship at his altar of false premise, attempting to deceive you into compliance. All the distractions the world has to offer—an endless array of temptations, desires, pleasures, philosophies, and troubles—are deployed to prevent you from making Christ the pearl of great price, your most revered possession and purpose in your life.

Our Lord Jesus was tempted by the Devil in every way yet remained faithful to God. The kingdoms of the earth and all their glory were offered to him if he would bow down and worship Satan. Jesus refused, declaring, "Away from me Satan! For it is written: Worship the Lord your God, and serve him only."[31.36] Jesus won the victory for us, offering himself as a living sacrifice for our sins. He bought our atonement with the shedding of his blood on the cross. He has ransomed you with a price. Do not allow this marvelous gift of salvation to be stolen from you!

Jesus taught the path to salvation is a straight and narrow way with few found thereon it.[9.11] Since so many follow the broad road to destruction, is it any surprise the majority of people and the world do not promote the gospel? The world is antagonistic to spirit-filled worship of Jesus in spirit and in truth. You must not be pressured into silence and compliance with the world's views, which are the cultures and mentalities ruled by the Devil, the Prince of the Power of the Air. Fight for the inheritance Jesus bought for you on the cross. Contend for and take the reward and inheritance Jesus entitles you to. Be an overcomer by allowing his Spirit to rule your heart and by being obedient to his will.

Our fleeting sojourn on earth offers little time to overcome. Scripture compares our lives on earth to a vapor that quickly passes away. Rejecting Jesus during your brief moment on earth in order not to offend the world is an eternal rip-off. The world is perishing and is in need of a Savior. Philosophies of self-will, religious heroes, idols, cults, false practices, esoteric teachings, and all the religions in the unregenerate condition of the heart oppose your entering into the promise of Jesus Christ. Would you be indignant if someone tried to steal your house? How much more should you oppose and resist anything attempting to steal your eternal inheritance and dwelling place that Jesus is preparing for you?

Rebellion against God is the condition of those forfeiting their inheritance. The marketing of an infinite variety of enticements and enlightenments preventing you from salvation is pervasive and appealing. The temptations are compelling. The glamour and excitement of your time will ultimately turn to terror if you serve the world—and the Devil—and choose to ignore Christ. Accepting distortions of truth and trusting in and promoting your own will rather than God's will are destined to result in unspeakable eternal separation from God.

A sober example of the consequences of rebelling against God is found in the book of Jude, which describes angels who lost their status with God because they rebelled and are even now being kept bound until judgment: "And the angels who did not keep their position of authority but abandoned their own home—these he has kept in darkness, bound with everlasting chains for judgment on the great Day."[9.33] The time of judgment is imminent; you can and must be ready before the end of time comes or before your days on earth expire.

Truth will set you free. Lies will make you a slave to a deceiving master. The god of this world, the Devil, will beat you, cheat you, and steal your inheritance of eternal life in Jesus Christ. The world, today, as in Christ's time on earth, chooses a thief and a robber—the flesh, the worship of the fallen will, which is the beast (metaphorically)—to be its guiding principal instead of the Christ: "Away with this man and release for us Barabbas," the mob cries out for one thrown in prison for insurrection and for murder (Luke 23:18).

Overcoming the adversary by the love and power of God is freely available to every man, woman, and child. God the Father extends incomparable love to you through the saving power of his Son, Jesus. His is the mountain above all other mountains and will break every power and authority for time and eternity. Choose to align with this power, which is the spirit of Jesus, his Holy Spirit and overcome the world, which is the devil and his temptations. Receive life and peace. Be a victor and enter into the reward of the God who created you and knew you before you were born. The true guiding principal is the Holy Spirit who will lead you out of worships in the fallen will and be your teacher to guide you into truth. He will help you resist and overcome the Devil and his promotion of unbelief and rebellion against God.

For instance, do you say or are tempted to believe there is no God? Examine your precepts to see if you are influenced by elaborate theories explaining why it is not possible for an original creation by the hand of an almighty God. Denying that the earth and humans were created by a loving God requires significant energy and rebellion against God. Truth is what defines scientific fact and both are from God. The creation issue is further discussed in chapter thirteen, which emphasizes that the Holy Spirit will lead you and guide you into all truth if you will allow him. Your soul is eternal and Jesus beckons you to choose life and live forever.

Your only safe choice is Jesus, who will return to be admired in all who believe in him. At that time, his people will be changed to be like him. The faith you need to believe you will participate in this change and to believe his return is pending comes from the Holy Spirit. Faith is a gift of the Spirit, which establishes hope in your heart and the power to believe and trust in Jesus. As you draw closer to Jesus, you will become more aware of faith and more alert to conflict in the spiritual realm that seeks to diminish your faith. The Holy Spirit fights for you, and Christ's faith always prevails over the lie of despair from the Devil.

Fidelity to God and his Spirit is your soul's place of safety and rest. Abraham obeyed when he was called to go out to receive his inheritance even though he didn't know where he was going. He was a stranger to the foreign country he dwelt in as he waited for the city whose builder and maker was God.[12.8] In the Old Testament, the Lord designated to his people a land of their own, described as flowing with milk and honey, a metaphor of a nourishing and sustaining community to dwell in, desirable, and sweet to human life. A land with cities of contentment fulfilling men and women's desires and needs and providing rest, peace, and joy.

Requirements to enter this Promised Land had to be met. God's people first had to have the faith and belief they could achieve the promise and could trust God to provide the means. During Moses's time, captive Israel, upon exiting Egyptian slavery, faced a foreboding desert wilderness that stood between themselves and their rewards and destination. Foreign occupants presenting a fearsome challenge had to be conquered and eliminated both along the way and within the lands promised. In the natural, the odds were against God's people to achieve these prerequisites. Supernatural power was required and provided by the Lord to enable his people to enter into their land and reward.

The overcomers (those who believed in God's promise and trusted in his power) entered the land victorious, yet a substantial portion perished in unbelief and infidelity. You, also, must absolutely resolve and determine to trust God's supernatural power in your life so that you can go all the way, enter your promised eternal life, and receive your reward and inheritance!

Power will be given to you to accomplish your journey into the promised city of God. The kingdom of God is within you. Crowning Jesus ruler of your heart and receiving the baptism of the Holy Spirit in your soul entitles you to live in the spiritual kingdom today and prepares you to live in the coming spiritual New Jerusalem.[12.12]

Called the holy city, the New Jerusalem and the bride of the lamb are declared in the last book of the Bible, the Revelation, to be descending now. This descending symbolically and metaphorically describes the advancement of God's plan for its final spiritual destination. The completeness of the promises of God, immortality, and an eternal city are soon to be realized by his people.

The deep desire of humanity's heart is for a place of safety and community where love flows in purity and the watchful love and protection of the Father is ever present. Do you feel this desire? Or has the flame of hope for it dimmed? Open your heart to Jesus and be transformed into an heir of God. Prepare to become a resident of the city where the light of the sun and the moon are obsolete because Jesus is the light, and God dwells and shines throughout its streets.

Throughout all of Christianity's ages, God's children have yearned for the spiritual city where death is abolished and a final everlasting abode established. Having been born again and filled with the Holy Spirit, they dine at a spiritual table the rest of the world's residents are unaware of. They live now in the kingdom of God incompletely and are preparing to occupy it fully when it comes down as the New Jerusalem descending from heaven.

The building, houses, and cities you see around you with your natural eye are temporal habitations. The spiritual holy city that will be ruled by Christ and prepared for those who love him will be established at his return. The natural world is a temporary, fallen dwelling place Christ calls you out from, so that you can live inwardly in fellowship with him and the Father, who is preparing for his people a new heaven and earth where righteousness dwells. His power enables you to overcome the world and the burdens and cares of life. It entitles you to enter into the spiritual promised land—a city where death no longer bereaves the inhabitants and God wipes away all tears from your eyes.

You may not be ready for the return of Jesus, but he will still return when least expected, within, and to be admired in those who are his. The vast majority of people will be unprepared and forfeit eternal life with unprecedented anguish. God is not willing that any should perish, but rather, is longsuffering that all people would come to salvation through his Son, Jesus.

An end is coming to the time in which his grace and mercy is offered through his Son for the forgiveness of sin and reconciliation with himself. He is coming in fire, taking vengeance on all that do not know God and that have not obeyed the gospel of the Lord Jesus Christ. He will punish them with everlasting destruction from his presence and his glory when he comes to be admired in all who believe.[7.19] Time is short. You must believe, prepare, and be ready.

Courageously fight with spiritual weapons to obtain your inheritance in the heavenly city.[35.2] Though you live in the flesh (the natural world), you cannot conduct warfare for your soul and others using human weapons. Your weapons are not physical. They are divinely powerful, allowing you to demolish strongholds and refute theories and pretensions opposed to God.[35.2] His weapons allow you to keep your thoughts obedient to Jesus.

Individually, you will have to experience your own relationship with Jesus Christ and God the Father. As you grow in the Holy Spirit and surrender to the will of God, knowledge and wisdom will come uniquely to you. Tranquility you never conceived obtainable will expand in your heart and soul from the love, joy, and peace of the presence of the Holy Spirit in your life. No one can take this from you; it is a gift from God in the form of a direct connection with him. You cannot trust in or lean on any earthly man, woman, or belief system for this. There is only one true mediator between God and mankind—Jesus Christ. Let him empower you to overcome even as he overcame. Pursue your inheritance, fight against the enemy of your soul in the power of the Spirit, assume your position as sons and daughters of God, and be found ready when he returns.

SUMMARY POINTS

- » Most Christians are not prepared.
- » Christ's death on the cross purchased an eternal inheritance for you.
- » To receive your reward, you must receive Jesus into your heart and live a life that overcomes.
- » Skeptics, atheists, sinners, the proud, and backsliders are urgently called to get prepared before it is too late.
- » Those that are prepared live in peace. They have a love relationship with God and his Son, Jesus.
- » The sun is setting on the opportunity to be ready; the call is urgent.
- » Powers antagonistic to Jesus Christ work to destroy your relationship with Jesus and steal your eternal life.
- » Jesus has overcome all power and authority and enables you to overcome and enter into his reward.
- » Jesus gives you his Holy Spirit to teach you and help you overcome.
- » Fight for your inheritance and be found ready when he returns.

CHAPTER 3

The Return of Jesus Is within You

Do you feel the changes in the spiritual winds? Like flashes of lightning penetrating your distracted conscience, do you sense the passing of the harvest, the conclusion of summer, and a multitude—possibly including yourself—not saved and ready?[6.13] Have the cares of this world, a distracted, lustful, prideful heart, or the addictions of a frenzied and rebellious mankind numbed your alertness to his appearance? The return of Jesus is imminent and is within his sons and daughters. Are you prepared?

> He shall come down like rain upon the grass before mowing, like showers that water the earth. In His days the righteous shall flourish, and abundance of peace, until the moon is no more (Psalm 72:6-7, NKJV).

The moon will be no more because we will no longer see a reflection of Jesus; we shall see him as he is. The Spirit of God is falling like rain from heaven in an urgent plea to allow his son to change us into his image by his Holy Spirit.

Beyond comprehension is the wonder of Jesus's glorious plan. Indescribable glory and fulfillment of your heart's desire will be soon realized. Christ triumphantly paid the price for this glory to be available to everyone who would receive him. Unfathomable in splendor, unrivaled in glory, his return will bring peace and fulfillment to the deepest longing of your heart's desire for his love. Nothing past or present can compare to the majesty of Christ's soon return and appearance within his people.

Christ in you is the hope of this glory, a change you will put on when he appears again to be admired in all that are his.[1.12] This change will only take place for those who are ready. It will be an apparent, visibly noticeable presentation of Christ within his people resulting in immortality and the redemption of their physical body. It is the hope of coming glory that the Bible urges Christians to anticipate. Currently we are mortal, subject to death, but Scripture declares this mortal must put on immortality when Christ appears again.[5.4]

Eternal life will be realized by the return of Jesus within his people. These believers in Jesus Christ, who have been saved by his atonement and have his Spirit, will experience the fulfillment of all things when Jesus appears again in all of those who believe, changing them into his nature and likeness and redeeming their bodies.[2] The redemption of the body is a supernatural, physical change into an immortal status similar to Adam's state before the fall, yet even more infallible.[5] It is not fully revealed exactly what we will be like, but the transformation will include an incorruptible, immortal body and the glory of Christ within us.[2]

Culminating over two thousand years of the current New Testament dispensation is this event—the Christian hope of glory, Christ in you.[1.12] His coming is as planned and certain as the dawn. According to Hosea, the prophet, it will revive us in Christ's salvation on the second day (this time of the new testament) and on the third day (the coming new dispensation) to full restoration so that we may live in his presence forever:

Come let us return to the Lord. He has torn us to pieces but he will heal us; he has inured us but he will bind up our wounds. After two days he will revive us; on the third day he will restore us, that we may live in his presence. Let us acknowledge the Lord; let us press on to acknowledge him. As surely as the sun rises, he will appear; he will come to us like the winter rains, like the spring rains that water the earth (Hosea 6:1-3, NIV).

Thirsty Christians, look up and press in to your first love! Do not lose hope. Let the fire of your passion for Christ be rekindled. Nominal or non-Christians, now is your time to receive your life's and heart's desire—the love and presence of Jesus Christ in your life. God has not forsaken you. He will come as surely as the sun rises. Press on to know him and to receive your reward. He is coming like the spring rains to satisfy your yearning desire for him and to restore your famished soul. One day soon, you will see him as he is. He will be admired in all who believe in him and, if you are ready, you will be changed to be like him.[8.59]

God's ultimate purpose for you, whom he created in his image, has been unfolding for over six thousand years. You were known by him and established by him before the foundation of the world, and now you are working out your own destiny with God during your time on earth. God's plan is for you to be conformed to the image of his Son, Jesus, because you were created to ultimately inherit all things and rule together with the Lord Jesus Christ as joint heirs.[4.1] Jesus declared that whoever would overcome would be granted the right to sit with him on his throne (or position of authority with God).[39.22] Only the children of God become heirs of God.

Throughout history, God has been revealing his plan for how men and women on earth are to be completed as his sons and daughters and rightful heirs of the kingdom. Jesus Christ is the only way God established for you to be accepted as his child. Through obedience to the Holy Spirit, which is the Spirit of Christ, and by allowing Christ to reign in your heart (submitting your will to his), you are prepared to enter the next phase of God's plan—growing up into the fullness of the stature of Jesus Christ, unto a perfect person.[1.10]

Your determination and partnership with the Holy Spirit is essential to overcome and inherit all things. Christianity is not passive; it is a call to fidelity and obedience to Jesus Christ. Choose life. Serve and worship Jesus Christ through whom all things were created. Allow no person, system, achievement, addiction, or unrighteousness to rob you of your inheritance as a child of God.

To watch and be ready is the admonition from Jesus. When speaking of the time of his return, he emphasized two things. First, no man knows the hour in which he will return; only our Father in Heaven knows.[6.4] Second, he instructs us to be ready.[20] Missing the return and opportunity for relationship with God will result in incomprehensible anguish. You must be ready now and have a love relationship with Jesus, making him Lord of your life, so you, too, will be changed into his image at his appearing. Allow the Holy Spirit to make you an overcomer. Worship God through Jesus Christ and live a life of holiness, walking in the Holy Spirit.

Action is required to overcome. Participation in the inheritance involves your individual will and determination to submit to the Holy Spirit. Having head knowledge about Jesus, without your soul being transformed and filled with his Spirit is not enough. Relying on an event or an organization and its rituals will not prepare you. Preparation is based on your spiritual relationship with Jesus Christ now. The fight is and has been raging for your soul. Worship God and the Lord Jesus Christ while there is yet a little time, before the end comes or your time on earth expires and you have no more time to prepare for God's final judgment.

Many Christians consider themselves ready because they believe in an event at Jesus's return called the rapture. There are many variations of rapture teachings, the most common version teaches Christians will be caught up and removed from earth before the coming judgment or tribulation (a term used for interpreting the judgments in the book of Revelation, the Gospels, etc.).

The soon-coming change—when Jesus transforms Christians to be like him—could also be termed a "rapture." This definition of rapture shares commonality with more traditional rapture descriptions, such as when Christians are caught up to meet the Lord in the air and this mortal puts on immortality.[1.14] This occurs at the appearance of Jesus when he comes back to be admired in all of his people.

Maybe a rapture is what you believe regarding the return of Jesus, but nothing—including the rapture—can help you if your heart is not ready. The ark of safety that assures you will receive eternal life at the return of Jesus is to be saved and born again by accepting him as your savior, putting on his will and Spirit in a love relationship with him. Only he can apply to your heart his sacrifice and forgiveness for you on an ongoing basis. He alone is your true safety.

False religions reject the provision of Jesus as the exclusive means of salvation and relationship with God. The truth is that all things were created through Jesus and there is no other way to be saved than through the blood of Jesus. The God of this world, the Devil, disputes this exclusivity. The Devil isn't opposed to you talking about Jesus as long as you reject the power and Spirit of Jesus—his Holy Spirit—and as long as you do not worship Jesus in Spirit and in truth.

Separation from the spirit of the world, including the carnal mind of the flesh, is a normal characteristic of an authentic Christian. This means to walk in the spirit and crucify the flesh, to let your will die and replace it with Christ's will. This basic requirement of the Spirit-filled and Spirit-led Christian is radically different from the standards set by nominal Christianity. Any outward profession of Christ without inward regeneration of the heart by his Spirit is an ineffective Christianity.

The kingdom of God is within you. The return of Jesus is within his own who have allowed the Holy Spirit to crucify the flesh (bring the fallen nature into subjection to the Spirit of God) and live holy lives unto God. Preparation is inward and requires obedience to the Spirit of Christ. As you obey, you will grow in Christian maturity, but at all times you will only be saved by the blood of Jesus and his Spirit dwelling within your heart. God's love will provision your soul's hungry desire for him on a daily basis.

Many Christians have been tempted to settle in spiritual deserts and have experienced the gradual decline of their first love—the presence of Jesus in their lives. In this condition, Christian activity and ministry promoting the gospel can become wearisome when the anointing of the Holy Spirit (provision of empowerment from God) diminishes. Substituting programs, rituals, and personalities for the non-routine order of Spirit-led church meeting can bring spiritual deadness. Veteran and seasoned believers can starve in a church environment offering no spiritual nutrition for mature Christians.

The answer for today is the same hope the first Christians were admonished to have. Pressing in by faith for the hope of glory, Christ in you, reignites the fire of the dry and thirsty Christian. Restoring and clarifying the vision and hope for the soon-coming return of Jesus within his people turns their countenance to gladness in anticipation and renews their zeal for being prepared.

Your spiritual journey on earth was never intended to be a permanent camp in heathen territory. Just like Abraham, you are a stranger and pilgrim in this world, journeying toward the city whose builder and maker is God.[12.8] As a Christian, you must overcome as Christ overcame. You must overcome the obstacles and live your life in faith to enter into your promised inheritance and take it for yourself.

There is much more waiting for you than your natural circumstances suggest. All of creation groans in anticipation, waiting for the manifestation of God's people and the redemption of the physical body into immortality.[5.3] We do not fully know what followers of Christ will be like when changed at his return, but you have the promise you will be changed to be like Jesus.

Weary Christians, let the power of Jesus Christ and the promise of his reward at his coming lift your faith and flood you with joy in anticipation of his soon return.

Let God replace your reliance on a philosophy of the rapture, other people's theories, or your good works with focused assurance, Holy Spirit-led preparation of your heart, and readiness for the fulfillment of all things when Jesus returns in his people in a moment and twinkling of an eye. Being enamored with end-time seminars, prophecy theories, rapture stories, setting dates that expire, and Armageddon predictions have a tendency to appeal to and feed the carnal and religious nature, but they distract and do not genuinely prepare you for Christ's return. Pray for the Holy Spirit to reveal what he wants you to understand regarding the end of all things. Determine to allow God to lead you to his truth instead of being a part of the guessing, fear, and anxiety (see chapter six for further discussion of the end times).

This unsettled condition is produced by speculating different theories, declaring dates for the rapture or the end of time, interpreting political events, and predicting or selecting the current generation's Antichrist. The fact is that any spirit that denies Jesus is the Christ is an antichrist spirit. Instead of worrying about or trying to control future events, keep your mind and thoughts on things that are pure and lovely and full of the hope we have in Christ to redeem this body and bring immortality at his soon appearing. Fear God not man.

The desire for something more in our spiritual lives and existence is a shared experience among all of humanity. This desire is often difficult to identify and articulate. Expressing this desire in a Christian context can be even more challenging, especially since many Christian belief systems have concluded and teach there is nothing more to what already exists.

This spiritual doubt coupled with spiritual desire for something more is conveyed in the 1980's song, "I Still Haven't Found What I'm Looking For." Proclaimed to be a gospel song by its songwriters, the band U2, it is a poignant anthem that expresses the ache deep within for something more in life even after having experienced both the world and Christianity. The answer to the song's quest for what hasn't been found is the perfection and immortality only Christ can bring. Even when you receive the salvation of Jesus Christ, you will still groan in this earthly tabernacle (body) waiting for the adoption, to wit, the redemption of the body, yearning for completion of love and fulfillment.

The whole earth groans and travails for the manifestation of the sons of God, when their mortal bodies will put on immortality.[4.2] Ahead of every believer is a promised change that will complete the Christian experience and establish the city of God, a new heaven and earth. Only the city descending down from above will establish the satisfaction of the age-old search for complete love and the longing of our heart, ending the tragedy and heartache of life, and wiping the tears of sorrow forever from our eyes.

In the meantime, revivals and renewals provide one of the ways for an encounter with and for a deeper experience of the Holy Spirit. Experiencing more intimacy with Jesus in an outpouring (or move) of the Holy Spirit brings relief to God's thirsty and travailing creation. The deep desire of Christians to experience the fullness of Christ is one reason they hunger and pray for revival and a more intimate connection with Jesus. Even people who have not experienced the power of Christ are attracted to revivals and the possibility of an encounter with him. There, they often find what their hearts have always searched for—and they are never again the same.

One reason so many people miss out on the experience of a revival is that inevitably, critics rise up to discredit them. Often criticizing from a position of religious authority, they make people afraid to participate in or associate with spiritual renewals and revival. Why allow these antagonists to create fear in you and steal what is yours? Spiritual authority comes from God. Anyone opposing the work of the Holy Spirit is an unqualified authority no matter how esteemed or religious they appear to be.

Many people are unable to recognize Christ's work at a revival because it is hidden from them. This blinding may be a test by God to see if they are being offended by unfamiliar behavior or phenomena, are allowing pride to get in the way, or are rejecting the revival because of their belief system. But God has chosen the foolish things of this world to confound the wise. Don't let yourself be confounded. Be a little child hungry for Jesus.

Pray for the persecutors of revival and those blinded or with hardened hearts. Even though the critics, the offended, and assumed authorities show up to invalidate or diminish a move gathering notoriety, often times these very people get touched by the Holy Spirit. They sometimes, without planning to, participate in some of the more controversial elements, like falling down and laying on the floor while being touched by the Holy Spirit. Later, they admit: "It was the best experience of my life."

Discernment—a gift from the Holy Spirit operating in your life—will enable you to avoid deception and to recognize and avoid fanaticism, which as history records regarding past outpouring, can be expected to develop during revivals. Validate with Scripture, pray, and ask God to show you the truth regarding what critics are saying. Seek the Lord's guidance for anything you are not sure about. Ask him how you may participate in the revival or outpouring. He will always show you if you will ask and listen. The greater challenge today is to be blessed to participate in revival. Finding, experiencing, and participating in an outpouring of the Holy Spirit, is a rare blessing in a dry and barren time.

Being ready to recognize and participate in a revival goes hand-in-hand with your readiness for the return of Jesus. As wonderful as outpouring and revivals are, nothing compares to the magnificence of Christ's soon return.

Glory characterizes this return of Jesus within his people, a power and atmosphere that will transcend and elevate any previous experience God's people have had. It will be a holy manifestation of the authority, splendor and presence of the Lord, Jesus Christ, establishing a new heaven and earth. This glory will be revealed in you if you are prepared for his return.

The suffering of your present life, significant as it is or has been, is not worthy to be compared to the glory that will be revealed in you.[5.3] Allowing the Holy Spirit to change you into his image advances you in stages of glory until he presents unto himself a glorious church and bride, holy and without blemish. He will change your lowly, mortal body and fashion it to be like his glorious body when he comes to be glorified in his saints (people who believe).[1.11] Now is the time to allow Jesus's spirit to wholeheartedly own your life so you will not be ashamed at the time of his appearing.

The hope of all humanity and the pressing desire for his glory is Christ in you. He ignites the hearts of his believers with faith for this eternal change. Even though we do not know exactly how we will be or look, we know we will be like him, seeing him as he is when he appears to be admired in all of his believers. Settle for nothing less.

SUMMARY POINTS

- The return of Jesus is in his people.
- Jesus's return will change his worshipers to be like him.
- This book teaches that the return of Jesus is nothing physical or political; it is spiritual.
- Glory incomprehensible will be revealed in you at his return.
- The return of Jesus will change the mortality of his people to immortality and redeem the natural body.
- Jesus appearing in you is the event that could be called the rapture.
- Whether you believe in a literal rapture or not, it doesn't change the necessity of you being prepared. You still must be ready for the return of Jesus.
- Revivals and renewals are a concentrated outpouring of the Holy Spirit that refreshes Christians and converts unbelievers as they wait for Christ's return.
- Seasoned Christians find increased hope and joy in anticipating the return of Jesus within his people.

PART II

IMMORTALITY WHEN JESUS RETURNS

CHAPTER 4

Eternal Life Is Imminent

Immortality is an approaching reality—not a plausible, remote possibility. Scripturally, immortality and eternal life is fully substantiated without ambiguity.[5] The apostle Paul wrote to the Corinthians that if there is no resurrection or immortality of the dead, then Christ has not risen. And if Christ has not risen, then his preaching and their faith are in vain. If Christ hasn't risen, Paul would be a false witness and all believers would still be in their sins.[5.8]

More than a concept inspiring hope, the future delivery of eternal life, immortality, and the redemption of the body are essential elements of God's redemptive plan for humanity. Jesus modeled what is to come when he rose from the dead. He became the first of many brethren—those who through Christ are the children of God.[2.2]

Your mortal body will be changed to an immortal one when Jesus returns.[1.6, 1.11] It is not yet clear what you will be like when this happens, but it is clear you will be like him when he comes to be admired within his saints.[1.18] The failure to be prepared and receive this change into immortality upon the appearance of Jesus is catastrophic beyond measurement. Submit all of your heart, mind, and soul to the Spirit of the Lord Jesus Christ now and allow him to fully occupy the throne of your heart. Determine to be found ready, worshipping the Lord in spirit and truth, when he comes to be admired in all who believe.

Throughout history, people repeatedly ask, "Where is the promise of his return?"[7.27] The memory of and resulting sobriety from past incidents of God's judgment falling on a rebellious society are soon forgotten. Even though these judgments are documented in ancient biblical writing, they fade from memory and are regarded by newer generations as tales of old.[8.44]

Life in modern civilization, unfolding history, and the perceived future, tragic as they are, appear unchanging. There seems to be no indication of the prophetically declared, pending, and unprecedented event of the return of Jesus. Warning us from Scripture, the apostle Peter wrote that people "deliberately forget that long ago by God's word the heavens existed and the earth was formed out of water and by water. By these waters also the world of that time was deluged and destroyed. By the same word the present heavens and earth are reserved for fire, being kept for the day of judgment and destruction of ungodly men."[8.137] The promise of Jesus's return is being kept for the day of judgment, and it will come as unexpected as a thief in the night.[8.104, 8.105]

Do you have the assurance from the Holy Spirit that your salvation and relationship with Jesus is where it needs to be for you to qualify for and put on immortality at his return? Keep in mind the event itself (Jesus's return) will not prepare you. Many Christians trust in a version of the "rapture," a belief discussed in chapters three and six, to instantly deliver them from the world's (and often their own) troubles. They count on this rapture event as the means of entry into heaven regardless of their lives lacking devotion to Christ.

There is no reprieve to lives of impurity and rebellion to Christ when time expires. Only the blood and power of Jesus can provide salvation from sin and bring eternal life. It is precarious to believe conceptually you are saved without a true inward conversion and surrender to Christ. Relying on the rapture will not cover for your lack of consecration to him. Please do not risk your right to the immortality that all children of God are entitled to by ignoring a lack of devotion to Christ.

The Old Testament Law and prophecies flow in a central and consistent stream of foretelling a future day of everlasting peace and glory established by the fullness of the kingdom of God. Jesus enabled this kingdom to be realized and available for all who would believe in him when he laid down his life to ransom us from sin and rose from the dead. Since this atonement, his Spirit has been working to gather his children into one spiritual body for the completion of God's plan for mankind.

Completion of this plan and transitioning into everlasting life is imminent. The heartbeat of God's creation, traversing humanity's history, groans for the change that provides entrance into the eternal kingdom of God. The first Christians had a burning hope for the new heaven and earth and a faith charged by the promise and knowledge from God of the soon arrival of immortality. Your hope is the same. Jesus established the availability of salvation and eternal life by offering himself on the cross. He made available the world's most precious and sacred gift by applying his atoning blood to any and all who would believe.

The expectation of the return of Jesus and the change of his people into immortality, into his image—is now—not generations into the future. It will come as unexpectedly as when Jesus first appeared. Christ first appeared in Bethlehem, born to a virgin 2,000 years ago. That unexpected arrival began the most dramatic shift in the history of mankind's existence and relationship to God ever known. Unnoticed then by all but a few on the world's stage the appearance again of Jesus (this time in judgment) is going unrecognized but is at the door of the world. You must prepare without delay.

Preparation is done inwardly through allowing Jesus to rule your heart and submitting your will to his Holy Spirit. Many have a sense of the end of the world and, through fear and intrigue, pursue a variety of theories and practices. Reacting in the flesh to try and be ready by survival preparation, setting dates, quitting your job, and joining a religious or political sect do not prepare you. Doing the will of God and actively pursuing a personal relationship with him is what makes you ready. Reading books about the rapture, end-time prophesies, economic guesses, Armageddon, or who the Antichrist is will not make you ready. A love relationship with Jesus and the act of submitting to his will are what make you ready. God is our helper. He will never leave us or forsake us.

Jesus is the power performing the change to immortality and the redemption of the body upon his return within his saints. Everlasting destruction and separation from the presence of God occurs at his return for anyone who does not have the Spirit of Jesus living within their heart.[7.19] For those who know him, he will wipe away all the tears and banish sickness, sorrow, and death.[27.12] Make it your prayer that you, your family, your friends, and every possible person will be ready to receive the reward of God—eternal life when Jesus returns.

The triumphs, failures, and history of God's people under the Old Testament and dispensation of the Law are a type and a shadow of the Christian's overcoming walk today, in Christ's dispensation.

In the Old Testament, Moses led a subservient people from Egyptian captivity into a desert freedom entirely dependent upon the Lord God for sustenance. As said earlier, faith in God was essential for maintaining the courage to press forward to the destination of promise, a land flowing with milk and honey of settled peace and prosperity. During the journey, a mobile house of worship, a tabernacle, was constructed after the pattern given to Moses on the mountain. It was a sanctuary that was a copy of what is in heaven.[21.8]

This centralization and focus of fidelity and worship of God in a sanctuary established a greater call to faithfulness in serving the Lord while on the desert journey. Yet, not all of God's people remained true. Many disregarded his supernatural provisions. They waivered in trusting God's protection and promise and perished far short of their given inheritance. Others succumbed to the allurements of the flesh and the seduction of decadent forbidden gods. A generation faltered in courage to enter in and vanquish the inhabitants, thus sentencing themselves to a continuation of wilderness wandering.

In the midst of this infidelity, a remnant refused to acquiesce from the promises of God. They kept alive the memories of his miraculous deliverance from impossible circumstances. Tested men of the hour arose to fight the opposition. Joshua and Caleb trusted and feared God more than the reputed giants occupying the land. They led the twelve tribes into Canaan to engage the enemy, obtain their reward, and possess their inheritance.

So it is for us today and throughout this dispensation we live in. Only a remnant will end up saved and only a portion of those professing to be Christians will enter into God's reward: "Though the number of the children of Israel be as the sand of the sea, a remnant shall be saved: for he will finish the work and cut it short in righteousness."[10.4]

Faith to enter into God's promised inheritance culminated with the occupation and settlement of Jerusalem and the building of the first temple, a permanent replacement for the mobile tabernacle. Upon its completion three thousand years ago, the presence of God came into the new house of worship with power and glory as King Solomon dedicated the newly completed temple.

The pinnacle of the journey of God's ancient people (the Israelites) to their promised land reached its peak at the dedication of the permanent, new, original temple. So powerful was the resulting glory that the appointed priests fell to the ground and the people praised God in a mighty chorus of voices and awestruck hearts. This glory-filled temple shadowed the coming immortality in our own dispensation.

In this New Testament period, the completion of the modern temple (God's sons and daughters) will occur when the mortal body (temporary temple) puts on the final redeemed, immortal body (permanent temple). This immortal, redeemed body will be a dwelling place for the Spirit of God forever.

The return of Jesus completes this metaphorical journey (the spiritual fulfillment of the Old Testament patterns) of Christians in the New Testament period. Suddenly, as of old, the Lord will again come to his temple—you and me and all of his people—in power and in a significantly greater experience of glory.[1.1] Christ will fully occupy his people, the completed temple of God, redeemed by his blood, and transform us into immortality.

It is impossible to overemphasize the magnificence of the realization of God's plan within his people. You will taste of the worlds to come from your experience in walking with Jesus, but your eyes and your ears are unable to fully comprehend the splendor of the glory that will be revealed in us when Christ returns.[1.16] Call upon the Lord with a pure heart. Lift up holy hands unto him—none other shall enter into his reward. Choose life and the reward of living forever in the eternal presence and glory of the God of all creation. Prepare now and be ready.

Patience and continuing in obedience to the Holy Spirit are your protection as you seek the glory, honor, and immortality of eternal life. Suffering endured as a result of your past and present circumstances are not worthy to be compared with the glory that will be revealed in you upon the redemption of your body.[1.4]

Your perishable part must become imperishable and your mortal part must put on immortality and, then, death will be swallowed up in victory. Jesus Christ abolished death and brought life and immortality to light through the gospel.

In a moment—in the twinkling of an eye—you will be changed and your current body will put on the likeness of his immortal body.[1.6] As discussed on page 27, this is the change that can be called "the rapture." This change occurs when we are caught up to meet the Lord in the air.[1.14] An immortal, spiritual transformation will occur in which your physical body and soul are given their eternal tabernacle, resurrected into perfection by the sovereign timing of God and impartation of your redeemer, Jesus Christ. In this condition, you will inherit your place in the new heaven and earth, wherein dwells righteousness;[7.24] you will judge the world and angels (1 Corinthians 6:3); and you will dwell forevermore in the kingdom of the Lord, a new heaven and earth, in your heavenly place where the shining sun is superseded by the light of the Lamb, Jesus Christ.[12.16]

The righteous judgment of God will render to each person according to their deeds. Eternal life to those who by patience in doing good seek glory, honor, and immortality; but to those who are self-seeking and do not obey the truth but obey unrighteousness, they will receive indignation and wrath.[5.2]

Yet a little while and the wicked will be no more.[8.114] The Holy One of Israel will gather his children into the green pastures of abundance, and the tree of life will heal all nations. When that which is perfect shall come, then that which is in part shall fade away. Your heavenly city and blessed hope will be received when Christ returns and you are made immortal, being changed to be like him into immortality. This is a transformation the whole earth groans and travails for. It is an epic event the prophets of old foresaw and spoke prophetically of. It is a hope the apostles wrote of encouragingly with bold assurance.

Nothing compares to the presence of the glory of God. Over time, this glory is being realized within you and will culminate with the return of Jesus and his being glorified within his people. Pray for the faith to overcome and reaffirm your determination now to be found ready.

SUMMARY POINTS

» Immortality will be realized by God's people upon the return of Jesus.

» The dedication of the ancient temple three thousand years ago is symbolic of the perfection of God's holy temple that will occur when Christ fully occupies his people and transforms us into immortality.

» The righteous receive eternal life and the unsaved everlasting punishment.

» The redemption of the body and putting on of immortality is an essential promise for God's people upon the return of Jesus. This could be called the rapture.

» The current heaven and earth will be dissolved and a new heaven and earth established.

» Courageously assert your right to immortality. Press into God in faith and righteousness and patiently continue in his gospel, pursuing glory and honor and eternal life.

» Determine and prepare to be numbered in the glorious church Christ is presenting to himself not having spot or wrinkle but being holy and without blemish.

» Overcome the unbelief and distractions of the world that deny the blessing of immortal life. Establish the hope of God's promise and redemption of the body deep within your heart and make it an essential component of your life.

» Disregard erroneous rhetoric regarding the end times and keep your eyes on Jesus so you are found ready and watching, fruitful in his vineyard.

» Endure to the end. Overcome. Have the faith. Be ready and watching for Jesus. Let the promise of Christ in you—the hope of glory and the reward of everlasting life, immortality, and the redemption of your body—increase in you daily as you diligently watch, prepared for the return of Jesus.

CHAPTER 5

Characteristics of His Return

The return of Jesus and the end of all things are revealed throughout the Old and New Testament through a diversity of reoccurring themes. By becoming familiar with them, you will deepen your own insight and be able to more effectively evaluate teaching, weigh writing, and converse with others about the subject. An awareness of these verses will also help establish and develop your understanding of what to expect and be prepared for when Jesus returns.

Twelve of these themes or characteristics in the Bible relating to Christ's return are summarized below. Superscripts enable you to find the location of the verses in the topical reference section, Part V. Reading these verses collectively, topic by topic will increase your overall understanding. You can pursue even further clarification using study tools to review the original words and language of each Scriptural translation.

THE DAY OF[8,a]

Several Scriptures refer to "a day." They include:

- » The day of the Lord
- » The day of the Lord's wrath
- » The day of the Lord's anger
- » The day cometh that shall burn as an oven
- » The Son of Man in his day
- » The day of our Lord Jesus Christ
- » The day of the Lord Jesus
- » The day of Jesus Christ
- » The day of Christ
- » The day of God

Pray over these verses as you consider them in relation to the day of the return of Jesus:

It is the day of judgment and you must be prepared to face it.[8.2]

Cruel both with wrath and fierce anger it will lay the land desolate and destroy sinners out of it. The world will be punished for its evil and the wicked for their iniquity. The heavens will be shaken and the earth removed from its place in the day of his fierce anger and the wrath of the Lord of hosts.[8.1]

The great and terrible day of the Lord will be a day of wrath, a day of trouble and distress, a day of wasteness and desolation, a day of darkness and gloominess, a day of clouds and thick darkness.[8.5]

Seek righteousness and meekness that you may be hid in the day of the Lord's anger.[8.6]

Characteristics of His Return 49

A day comes that will burn like an oven and all the proud and all that do wickedly shall be stubble and the day that is coming will burn them up.[8.7]

The Son of Man in his day will be as the lightning that flashes out of one part under heaven and shines to the other part under heaven.[8.8]

Your confidence is in Jesus who, when you allow him to perform the good work in you and keep you sincere and without offense, will keep you until the day of Jesus Christ.[8.12]

The day of the Lord will come as a thief in the night and the heavens will pass away with a great noise and the elements will melt with fervent heat. Your hope is to be found ready, looking for the coming of the day of God when the heavens being on fire will be dissolved and the elements will melt with fervent heat.[8.16]

HIS COMING[8-b]

A common biblical expression used when referring to the return of Jesus is the "coming of the Lord" (or of the Son of Man, etc.). Jesus speaks of his "coming" in the gospels of Matthew, Mark, and Luke to describe his return. It is also used in Malachi (in the Old Testament) and in the letters by the apostles Paul, Peter, James, and John in the New Testament.

The Lord whom you seek will suddenly come to his temple . . . but who may abide the day of his coming?[8.18]

Malachi declares God will send Elijah the prophet before the coming of the great and dreadful day of the Lord.[8.19]

The coming of the Son of Man and the resulting judgment will be as unexpected as the daily concourse of the society in Noah's time just before the time the ark was sealed and the flood came and took them all away.[8.23]

Jesus is coming; from his throne of glory he will separate the sheep from the goats and bring the sheep from his right hand into the inheritance of the kingdom prepared from the foundation of the world.[8.26]

Patience is required until the coming of the Lord. It is drawing close as the fruit of the earth from the early and latter rain bears forth and is gathered.[8.43]

From the beginning of creation, things may seem the same, "Where is this coming he promised?" But just as one old society perished in the ancient flood, the heavens and the earth are kept in store, reserved unto fire against the day of judgment and perdition of ungodly men.[8.44]

WITH GLORY[8-c]

Experiencing the glory of God is one of humanity's greatest desires and is a profound hunger within the heart. The baptism of the Holy Spirit, the presence of God in revivals, and outpouring of his spirit on his people are glimpses of the glory of God. None of our current experiences of glory can be compared to the glory that will be revealed at Jesus's return. This is a marvelous hope and foundational desire of the Christian experience.

Jesus, the Son of Man, is coming in his own and his Father's glory and power. Being fashioned into the likeness of his glorious body is an indescribable hope you have as one of God's children.[8.58]

Revealed in you will be this glory when he comes to be admired in his people, changing your vile body to be fashioned like his glorious body.[8.58]

Watch and be prepared for this blessed hope and the glorious appearing of our Savior, Jesus Christ.[8.60]

Rejoice because as you participate in his suffering, you may be glad and have exceeding joy when his glory is revealed.[8.61]

REVEALED[8-d]

Christians are watching for the revealing of a beautiful gift currently not visible. Glory will be realized when the Lord Jesus is revealed from heaven with his mighty angels.

> You will be a partaker of the glory that will be revealed.[8.70]

WITH HIS ANGELS[8.e]

Angels have a role in the return of Jesus. They will be sent forth by Jesus to sever the wicked from among the just, to gather out of his kingdom all things that offend, to gather his elect from the four winds and the uttermost part of the earth to the uttermost part of heaven.

> He is coming in the glory of his Father with the holy angels.[8.74]

IN THE CLOUDS OF HEAVEN[8.f]

He is coming in and with the clouds of heaven.

GATHER[8.g]

Jesus is coming to gather his own, those described as sheep, the remnant of Israel and as wheat—his elect, the children of God scattered abroad. All things will be gathered in the fullness of time in Christ, both in heaven and in earth.

LIKE A THIEF IN THE NIGHT[8.h]

Watch for you do not know at what hour Jesus will come. Be diligent that your heart is not corrupted with worldly indulgences and the cares of this life so that you won't be caught by surprise.

> You must be ready for it will be in a time you do not expect.[8.98]

> It is coming as a snare to all who dwell on the face of the earth.[8.103]

> You are not in darkness that it should overtake you as a thief. You are of the children of light and the children of the day; therefore, watch and be sober.[8.103]

A DAY OF THE TRUMPET[8.i]

At the last trump, the trumpet shall sound and the dead will be raised incorruptible and we will be changed. This corruptible must put on incorruption and this mortal must put on immortality. [8.110] The final call and trump of God brings immortality. You cannot miss this; you must be prepared because there is no second chance or second trump. The Spirit of God pleads with all mankind to receive the gift of salvation his Son made possible through his sacrifice on the cross, not willing any should perish, before it is too late and the last trumpet sounds.

> The Lord will descend from heaven with a shout with the voice of the archangel, and with the trump of God.[8.111]

> He will send his angels with a great sound of a trumpet and they shall gather together his elect from the four winds, from one end of heaven to the other.[8.112]

SEVERING THE WICKED FROM AMONG THE JUST[8.j]

Speculation concerning who is being removed from the earth at the return of Jesus is clarified in the most sobering of warnings.

> The upright and perfect will remain in the land but the wicked will be cut off from the earth and the transgressors rooted out of it.[8.113]
>
> Evil doers will be cut off, but those that wait upon the Lord will inherit the earth.[8.114]
>
> For a little while and the wicked will not be, but the meek will inherit the earth.[8.114]
>
> He will destroy the sinners out of the land.[8.116]
>
> Jesus is sending his angels to gather out of his kingdom all things that offend and them which do iniquity. He will cast them into a furnace of fire. This is at the end of the world when the angels will come forth and sever the wicked from among the just.[8.120-1]

EVERY KNEE WILL BOW[8.k]

> Every knee will bow to the Lord and every tongue will confess to God that Jesus Christ is Lord.[8.125]

FIRE[8.l]

The return of Jesus is a day of vengeance for those who ignore or do not obey him. The impending judgment and fire is clearly defined and so foreboding that Christians should be fearless in warning others to repent before it is too late. Since everything will be destroyed in the ways described below, you are to live a holy and godly life. Prepare with all of your heart and soul and be ready. Allow Jesus and his Holy Spirit to rule your heart and your worship.

Chaff (or those not ready for the return of Jesus) will be gathered and burned with unquenchable fire.[8.129]

The same day that Lot went out of Sodom, it rained fire and brimstone from heaven and destroyed them all. Even thus shall it be in the day when the Son of man is revealed.[8.133]

If you are ready, you will not be hurt when the Lord Jesus is revealed from heaven with his mighty angels in flaming fire, taking vengeance on them that know not God and that obey not the gospel of our Lord Jesus Christ.[8.134]

The day of the Lord will come as a thief in the night and the heavens will pass away with a great noise and the elements will melt with fervent heat; the earth also and the works that are therein shall be burned up.[8.136]

The heavens and the earth, which are now by the same word are kept in store reserved unto fire against the day of judgment and perdition of ungodly men.[8.137]

CHAPTER 6

MISINTERPRETING THE REVELATION

Humanity has an inward sense that ahead of all mankind awaits a final judgment. References and suppositions relating to the end times can exploit this awareness and the accompanying fear. People want to know what to expect and how to avoid it. There is a common, esoteric appeal among Christians and non-Christians that creates a desire for theories and predictions. Consequently, an environment of fascination exists ready to be intrigued by the latest discovery or recurrence of end-time teaching, or as it is often called, prophetic teaching.

The commentary you will find from me in this chapter is from my belief that the book of Revelation is to be interpreted spiritually. This is not a precedent. In the Christian classic *The Journal of George Fox* (1624-1691), Fox frequently refers to the spiritual foes of Christ in the Revelation and identifies present conditions during his time as related to the Revelation. He does this in many of his other writings as did other authors of his time who were involved in the Quaker movement originated by Fox.

The book of Revelation with its descriptive vision of "things which must shortly come to pass" has been used as a central reference source of end-time interpretations, which are developed to supply the demand for explanations.

Personally, I have never been satisfied with the majority of teachings, sermons, charts, books, motion pictures, and television programs offering a variety of interpretations of the book of Revelation. I found that most seem fictitious, sensational, and earthly and of a different spirit than found in Jesus or the Scripture. The theories did not bring me peace or an inner witness from the Lord. Only in the comfort of Christ and his Holy Spirit did I find peace.

Many people are confused and must set aside a substantial amount of the end-time information they are acquainted with in order to hear what the Holy Spirit will teach them. "There must be more" is the cry from the heart of sincere seekers and Christians. Satisfaction for the heart's desire in the end times is to know that Jesus is coming back to be admired in all of his people and we will put on immortality.[1.15] Our hope of glory is Christ in us![1.12] Listen to what the Shepherd of your soul has to say regarding the end times; his sheep know his voice.

Approaching interpretation of the book of Revelation from a basis of the natural mind or religious tradition, and not from the same Holy Spirit as the original author was in, can result in misinterpretation. The flesh has an appetite for end-time teaching, especially messages with esoteric or insider knowledge.

The reality is that readiness for the return of Jesus is not dependent on the level to which you study or memorize these various end-time prophesy teachings. All the learning and expertise of theories, predictions, calculations, and prophesy will do nothing to prepare you for the return of Jesus if your heart is not repentant and born anew by his atonement. The message of the end times is the acceptance of the gospel of Jesus Christ, being filled with his Spirit, and living your life in devotion to him.

End-time teaching often creates or nurtures fear. Correct interpretation of Scripture, on the other hand, can enhance a proper fear of God and his judgments and bring conviction, but it doesn't incite a fear of pending events or disrupt the fruit of the Spirit. Christians are not called into a spirit of fear and you can choose not to participate in the anxiety that is often evoked by misconstrued prophesy concepts. Instead, fear the Lord and surrender to his voice so you are ready now and for the future. Press into holiness and a love relationship with Jesus Christ, walking in obedience to his Holy Spirit, and allow him to teach you in the Spirit the meaning of these Scriptures.

If you are a child of God, peace beyond understanding can be present within your heart as you wait for the return of Jesus. Knowing what is coming upon the earth and all people, you do not have to fear; instead, you can be ready and have confidence, living holy and godly lives. This is the theme of this book and concurs with the same instruction from Peter: "The day of the Lord will come like a thief. The heavens will disappear with a roar; the elements will be destroyed by fire, and the earth and everything in it will be laid bare. Since everything will be destroyed in this way, what kind of people ought you to be? You ought to live holy and godly lives (emphasis added).[8.105]

The most direct teaching in the Bible regarding the end of all things comes from Jesus and the apostles. Letters the apostles wrote to Christian communities comprise many of the New Testament books and provide modern Christians with less symbolic, more readily understood teaching regarding the end times and how you are to conduct yourself. This handbook for preparing for the return of Jesus does not emphasize the book of Revelation but treats it as a sum of the whole in understanding what Scripture has to say about his return.

The Revelation to the apostle John is the last book in the Bible and the only writing in the New Testament devoted to detailing a vision, revelation, and prophesy. Along with the book of Daniel, Revelation is one of the most often cited books in the Bible regarding teaching about the end times.

The book was written after Jesus appeared to the apostle John and instructed him to write what he saw in a book and send it to the seven churches in Asia. John then received prophetic visions of descriptive metaphor and revelations of dramatic sequences.

The book is a spiritual metaphor of truth and prophetic narrative of coming events. At the end, John is instructed to "seal not the saying of the prophesy of this book: for the time is at hand" (Revelation 22:10). The time was "at hand" even 2,000 years ago, yet readers often assume that the Revelation speaks of events and circumstances exclusive to their current geography, present time, or immediate future. Based on this assumption, they often literalize it within the scope of a subjective worldview and bias.

In addition to being misunderstood by many Christians, this book has been the subject of a long-running history of theories. However, interpretations of the vision the apostle John experienced while he was "in the Spirit" and documented while he was in exile on the island of Patmos is available to you through prayer and waiting on the Lord for understanding. This must be approached carefully and in an attitude to receive what the Lord would reveal to you. At the same time, avoid conjecture and the insistence to know more than the Spirit is showing you.

Do not assume what other teachers have put forth is accurate. This includes verifying and concluding for yourself the accuracy of this author's teaching. Search the Scriptures for yourself, pray for direction, weigh teaching, and allow God, through the same Holy Spirit the authors of the Scripture were in, to establish the truth for you. Though difficult to comprehend and tempting to form conjecture, the last book of the Bible is not sealed to Christians from understanding.

Several topics from the book of Revelation are commonly expounded on in end-time subject matter and, therefore, experience considerable disagreement. The resulting fruit of presumption and misinterpretation can show itself diversely in fear, pride, hunger for natural knowledge, diversion from spiritual pursuits, and allegiances to teaching and teachers.

Outlined below are seven of these common themes that endure variations of disagreement. They are presented and include my approach to interpretation to help you evaluate different teachings on the subject, develop your own interpretation, maintain rest in Jesus's peace, and sharpen your discernment. Pray, ask, and allow the Holy Spirit to teach you and decide for yourself as you consider the following themes related to the end-times:

THE RAPTURE

This term discussed in chapters three and four, refers to an end-time teaching or belief adhered to by many Christians to describe an event at the return of Jesus where all true believers are taken (or disappear) from earth to be with Jesus.

While the word "rapture" is not used in the majority of Bible translations, the Scripture most often quoted relating to the rapture is 1 Thessalonians 4:17, which says that those who are saved by Jesus will be "caught up to meet the Lord in the air, and there shall they be forever."[1.14]

This belief has many variations usually pertaining to the timing of the rapture. It is often debated if it will happen before, during, or after another end-time event you may have heard of: "the great tribulation." This is a time of woes and torments received by humanity, as described primarily in Revelation but also throughout Scripture, including the Gospels of Matthew, Mark, and Luke.

Many of the current rapture teachings include a variety of disagreements concerning timing; therefore, it's important to be ready because we don't know the timing. Believing that Christians can be caught up and changed during the rapture—even if they are not spiritually ready as Jesus commands all of us to be—can lead to a false sense of security: "So you also must be ready because the Son of Man will come at an hour when you do not expect him."[6.6]

This book declares that the return of Jesus will occur within his believers who are spiritually ready, those born again by his spirit, changing them to be like him.[2.6] As said before, this change could be called "a rapture," but it refers to the event in which Christ's own receive immortality and experience the redemption of their bodies. This is a fulfillment and completion of God's plan for mankind. While Jesus's own appear with him in glory, those who are not ready will perish, suffering the vengeance of eternal fire.[1.15]

TIMING

There are many differences of opinion regarding timing of events in the book of Revelation. Many involve predictions of dates (or ranges of dates) in the immediate past and future of the predictor. Most known predictions in the past 2,000 years have come and passed unfulfilled. During this writing, for example, well-known Christian teachers have set dates for the end of the world only to see their prediction fail to happen.

In addition to the timing of the rapture, people speculate about the time frame of the tribulation. Often, this period of destruction and woe is considered a literal, concentrated period of time and is often assumed to be at the door of the current generation.

The sequence of end-time events and the timing of the tribulation and the rapture is a topic of debate in prophesy theories. I believe looking to the future for the entirety of symbolic events to happen is a common mistake. As John recorded, "Seal not the saying of the prophesy of this book: for the time is at hand" (Revelation 22:10). My understanding is that the overall timeline of Revelation's events has actually been unfolding since Jesus Christ appeared on earth and bore the sins of mankind over two thousand years ago.

SPIRITUAL ANTAGONISTS

As the heading suggests, I interpret the Beast, the whore, the mother of harlots, Mystery Babylon, the False Prophet, the Dragon, and the Antichrist (a word not used in Revelation) to be allegorical of the Devil and spiritual foes of Jesus Christ and his people.

The whore, or mother of harlots, is the representation of the spirit that compels, rules, and conducts the religious practice of mankind in his and her fallen, unregenerate nature. This spirit persecutes people who have the Spirit and nature of Christ ruling their hearts, even as Cain persecuted and attacked Abel for his acceptable sacrifice.

The Beast represents the spirit of the world deceiving and driving humanity down the broad road of destruction that is void of Christ. These entities are spiritual forces. They are metaphorically described. They influence humans, but I don't believe they are past, present, or future human beings. These spiritual foes of Christ and his people have been and still are active opposing and fighting against Jesus and the plan of God. Even though they have been defeated by Jesus, they still operate in the spiritual realm influencing the fallen nature. They are being overcome by Christians and will ultimately be cast into the lake of fire by Jesus and his angels.

THE MARK OF THE BEAST

Spiritually interpreted, the mark of the Beast is mental and willful allegiance to the spirit that controls the fallen nature of humanity. I don't believe it is a literal name or number stamped or tattooed onto people's right hand or forehead. I feel it is more subtle and deceiving than that.

Believing the mark to be literal can create a significant amount of speculating and esoteric interest among end-time prophesy genres and can distract people from the already active spiritual warfare raging over mankind's souls. Taken literally, the mark would be a literal stamp of the name of the beast or the number of his name 666 on the right hand or forehead (Revelation 13:16-18). It seems most people would take exception to a form of 666 somehow forced onto them, including non-Christians.

Because I don't believe the mark of the Beast is literal, some may worry that, by teaching the mark is only spiritual, readers will be unprepared to resist the commonly taught literal interpretation. So let me dispel any such worry: if you are forced by any person, institution, cult, or government to have the number 666, or any form of it, marked, stamped, tattooed, printed, or implanted in any way on your hand or forehead—absolutely refuse no matter what it costs, including your life.

As I have said, I believe the mark of the beast is a spiritual condition in which a person submits or defaults to and worships the spiritual system and religions of the fallen nature of man (including carnal Christian systems). An atheist, though he denies the existence of God, is also in this condition as is someone who claims to be a Christian but is not filled with the Spirit of Christ. Mankind, in this condition, rejects Christ from genuinely ruling the throne of the heart. It denies his offered salvation and allows the beast to guide their life.

As a Christian, you don't have to fear spiritual, religious, or political systems. If you have a disagreement, you can protest in a lawful manner. These systems may persecute Christians and or operate under the influence of the spirit of the beast and amplify our need for wisdom to maintain obedience to Christ.

Jesus also never feared, taught, or purposely antagonized political governments. In his day, the Romans were considered foreign subjugators of Israel, once a sovereign nation of his ancestors. Yet when questioned whether it was right to pay taxes to Caesar, Jesus said, "Render unto Caesar what is Caesar's." He did not, however, compromise his allegiance to God. His speaking and standing for truth cost him his life through religious persecution and a governmental-approved execution.

THE ANTICHRIST

The common teaching about one final antichrist provokes a fear of a single human captivating the world. However, there were already many antichrists in the days of the apostles: "This is the last hour; and as you have heard that the antichrist is coming, even now many antichrists have come. This is how we know it is the last hour" (1 John 2:18, NIV). I do not believe there is coming one, single person who will be "the Antichrist." Nor do I believe in a literal temple of God where such a man would sit, but rather in a spiritual one. God no longer dwells in temples made with hands, people are his temple.

End-time discussions speculate about one person on the world stage to be the Antichrist. Every generation proposes its own candidates, but the book of Revelation does not use the word "Antichrist." It does speak, however, about the Beast and the False Prophet.

These references to antagonists in Revelation, I believe, are to spiritual entities, foes, and their activities imposed upon humanity and Christians. Discerning these antichrist spirits and guarding against them fortifies you against being deceived by any individual or system.

Again, some will criticize that this teaching makes you unprepared to stand against a one-world leader who forces you to take the mark of the beast. Therefore, I again advise the following: if anything close to a world dictator requires you to take some form of the mark of the beast on your forehead or hand, absolutely refuse, even if it costs you your life.

More relevant to today is the choice you must make regarding accepting politically-correct indoctrinations that ask you to reject or compromise biblical morality. Let Christ establish your moral fortitude and refuse to compromise your holiness or deny that Jesus Christ is Lord and King of your heart and soul, no matter the cost.

THE PHYSICAL RETURN OF JESUS

Many Christians interpret Scripture to mean that Jesus will return to rule on earth physically, essentially similar to his first appearance but with his resurrected body.

The message of this book, however, is that the return of Jesus will occur within his people; it is an event in which he will change them to be like him. This dispensation-fulfilling occurrence is a spiritual, miraculous, physically transforming event. How Jesus will, in fact, physically appear at that time remains to be revealed. It's also not yet apparent exactly what we will be like after undergoing this transformation.[1.19] The important message emphasized herein is that Jesus will change his people to be like him, enabling them to put on immortality when he is "admired" in all of those who believe.[8.59] You must be ready.

THE ONE THOUSAND YEAR REIGN WITH CHRIST

Described in the book of Revelation in chapter twenty, this period is used to support a wide scope of literal and spiritual interpretations, commonly called the "millennium." This time period commences with the binding of the Devil in the bottomless pit for a thousand years and the souls of those who did not worship the beast but were beheaded for the witness of Jesus, will live again and reign with Christ for a thousand years.

Ask the Holy Spirit to develop your understanding regarding this one thousand year time period. While you wait, pray and search the Scriptures for your own understanding, keep in mind that your primary concern is your spiritual relationship with Jesus Christ today. Being in a condition of redemption through Christ prepares you for the return of Jesus, his rule, and his kingdom now as well as after his return.

SUMMARY POINTS

» Speculating and literalizing the prophetic, symbolic, and spiritual composition of the Revelation continues to produce a supply of misinterpretation.

» End-time fascination can create fear and confusion, which is not of God. Christians especially must set aside a carnal desire for more "prophetic" teaching and learn to hear and be taught by the Scriptures and Holy Spirit.

» End-time prophesy topics can take on an esoteric appeal to the flesh and are not what prepare you for the return of Jesus.

» Anxiety over future events should lead a person to prioritize a closer and more trusting relationship with Jesus, not an attempt to control and figure everything out.

» Many people must reconsider current concepts and allow the Scriptures and Holy Spirit to validate and teach them.

» The potential problem to be aware of with rapture teaching is a tendency for Christians to trust in an outward event while inwardly remaining unprepared to meet the Lord.

» Those who have a relationship and trust in Jesus can remain at peace during turbulent and decadent times by the grace of his Spirit.

» If the Mark of the Beast is a literal mark, Christians must refuse it.

» The message of the end times is the message of salvation in no other name than in the name of Jesus. It is also a message of being ready for his return.

The glory of this latter house shall be greater than of the former, saith the Lord of hosts: and in this place will I give peace, saith the Lord of hosts (Haggai 2: 9, KJV).

For here have we no permanent city, but we are looking for the one which is to come (Hebrews 13:14, AMP).

CHAPTER 7

GLORY OF THE LATTER HOUSE

The temple King Solomon completed (see chapter four) represented the culmination of centuries of struggle and advancement toward the promises God's people fought to inherit. In this permanent house of worship, located in Jerusalem, God favored his people with the presence of his glory. Israel's wilderness journeys were now distant memories in this era of triumphant achievement.

During the opening ceremony of the new temple, King Solomon admonished the children of God to be vigilant, faithful, obedient, worship only the true and living God—to turn from idols. He declared that rebelling against God would bring the judgment of the Lord, the demise of God's blessing, and forfeiture of the security and protection of the city and land.

Tragically, approximately three hundred and sixty three years later, sin would reverse the attainments. Sovereign Israel divided into two kingdoms when King Solomon died. In approximately 605 BC, Israel's continuous rebellion against God's commandments and unheeded warnings from his prophets began a series of deportations of the remaining kingdom culminating in the judgment of the southern kingdom of Judah and Jerusalem. The permanent glorious house built by Solomon was leveled to the ground by Babylonian conquerors in approximately 586-7 BC. Judah's remaining occupants were deported under the yoke of Babylonian captivity.

Now in a distant land, the Israelites grieved the calamities of losing the blessing they had received from God. In particular, the remnant of Israel must have been tormented knowing that their rebellion and disobedience had caused the forfeitures of freedom and the good and glorious things the great God had given them in the past. A once free people of the Lord now suffered the plight of the vanquished. The memory of the great temple and the glory of God manifested was vivid in the hearts and minds of the original deportees.

What is your Babylonian captivity? How is your personal rebellion against God causing you to dwell in the midst of captors far from the land of your promise and freedom? Do you grieve the former house of your first love dimmed by deportation from the presence of his Spirit? Are the fleeting ways of this world a valueless substitute filling the intense void and longing in your heart? Has the sun set on your quest for freedom? Has your peace been forfeited with no faith to reclaim?

Your remainder of hope bent low from the plow of life's grief, sin, and wearisome trials is fertile ground for God to move and show his glory. Look up from your despair into the face of Jesus. He who ransoms your soul from death and who alone redeems you and sets your feet upon the land of the redeemed promises to move on your behalf. Child, he has not forsaken you; he extends his hand of mercy to lead you into the land of salvation through Jesus Christ. Reach out your hand, grasp his, and tell him, "Lord, I am willing." Then you will find and experience that whom the Son sets free is free indeed.

After approximately fifty years of captivity in Babylon, a company of Jews led by Zerubbabel embarked to Jerusalem to rebuild the temple of God. Included in this company were those born in captivity and a remnant of people who had experienced the glory of the former temple. When the foundation was laid during reconstruction, the old men who had seen firsthand the former glory of the "first house" wept in sorrow when they saw the diminished grandeur of the reconstructed temple (Haggai 2:3).

Seasoned Christians today may weep in sorrow when they compare their current experience with those of old memories of God's glory in their lives, but they have a promise of a more glorious house ahead. The glory of the latter house is declared to be greater than that of the former. The latter house shall be a house of prayer, a spiritual church, a people filled with the fullness of Emanuel, Christ with us. Remember the power and glory that fell in the midst of God's people at the apex of the experience of ancient Israel, the dedication of the great temple. And so will it be for us—God's people, at the apex of our experience—the return of Jesus. And the glory of this latter house, Christ in you, will be greater than that of any former and will establish the fullness of the kingdom of God forever.

Humanity is programmed to desire and long for an eternal kingdom that is a city of peace and safety. Jesus declared that "the Kingdom of God is within you" as he preached the good news of the kingdom of God on earth.[11.30] The apostle Paul also spoke of the "heavenly kingdom" and the writer of Hebrews of the desire for a heavenly country where God has prepared a city.[12.9] Peter understood the coming of a new heaven and a new earth.[7.24] The apostle John saw, in the Spirit, this heavenly city, the New Jerusalem, descending from above.[12.14] Abraham of old went forth by faith, seeking and waiting for the city whose builder and maker is God.[12.8]

Today, the remnant people of Christ are the temple in the new covenant. Waiting upon God in the love of Christ, we groan and travail for the restoration of all things spoken of by the mouths of the holy prophets. You will not be disappointed; the Lord is returning, and the glory of this latter house will be greater than that of the former. The Lord, your redeemer, whom you seek, shall suddenly come to his temple.[8.97] You must be ready.

Do not despair or be dismayed by your natural circumstances. Disregard Babylon's yoke, this world's hold, life's burdens, and the futile worships of the fallen nature. God will come. Be encouraged and do not give up hope. Marvel not at the clamoring world's hysteria and rejection of the light of Jesus Christ. Rise above the immoral atmosphere prevailing upon humanity, attempting to revile the purest of Christ's own people. Shake off the faithlessness and the persecution from lukewarm Christians who have a form of godliness but deny the power and reality of the experience of Christ. Be courageous and the banner of love over you will prevail. Yield a clean temple, in daily sacrifice wholly unto the Lord, hearts believing and without guile. You will see the fire fall. Jesus is coming. You must be ready.

SUMMARY POINTS

- » Hope for a city whose builder and maker is God and coming immortality help establish your thoughts and provide comfort through the tribulations of life.
- » Christians look for a coming, new spiritual city.
- » The latter house, the one to come, is greater in glory than the former one—the experience God's people have known to date.
- » No matter the extent of your captivity, God will still move and deliver you bringing you into the freedom of his son and kingdom.
- » The glory that fell at Israel's zenith, the dedication of the temple in Jerusalem, will not be as great as the glory that will come to the temple of God—his people, at the return of Jesus.

PART III

ONLY JESUS...

CHAPTER 8

SATISFIES YOUR HEART'S DESIRE FOR LOVE

Deciding if Jesus is your God and if you will serve him must be done while you have the opportunity, before your time on earth is over. Indifference will cost you eternity. The world was made by Jesus and yet the majority of humanity does not recognize him.[19.12] Compared to the vast number of people who have lived on earth throughout history, in the end only a remnant will choose Christ and serve him in Spirit and in truth and enter into the reward of eternal and immortal life.[10.4]

Why is the world so angry, antagonistic, and upset with Jesus? Why is the mainstream media relentless in defaming, slandering, and ridiculing authentic Christianity, demanding the world do the same? The answer is the enemy of your soul, the spirit of the Beast and the Antichrist, the enemy of Jesus and of your salvation in him.

This enemy is the voice of the false prophet presenting darkness for light and calling light darkness. You can overcome this enemy and eternal destruction by resisting the way of the world. Christ's power in heaven and on earth is available to defend you and enable your victory in Jesus Christ.

Mankind has set the calendar based on time elapsed since Jesus appeared on earth yet relentlessly works to eliminate the truth and witness of Jesus Christ from the earth he created. In the end, this deception will fail and every knee will bow at the name of Jesus.[8.125] You must overcome now in your time and serve Jesus and allow him to rule your heart and save your soul.

Time is short and many voices clamor for your affection. Only the truth can save you and make you ready for the return of Jesus. He is the way, the truth, and the life; no man, woman, or child will come unto God without him.[14.14] He is bigger than all the philosophies and is over all religions that profess him in name yet deny him in power. He is King now and forever and is the Prince of Peace and God with us. Jesus Christ alone is the savior and alone provides eternal life to humanity.

Without Jesus, humanity in the end perishes and each person at the end of their days will be told by him to depart to the place prepared for the Devil and his angels for he never knew them.[9.15] Don't let this be your destiny; serve God now and receive genuine salvation through Jesus Christ, the Savior of all mankind.

Before he became a Christian, the apostle Paul persecuted believers in Jesus, sending Christians to prison and having them stoned. Highly educated and self-described as a Pharisee of Pharisees, he applied an extraordinary zeal to persecuting the emerging belief in the Messiah. The book of Acts chronicles his conversion to Christianity. On the road to Damascus, he met God and cried out, "Who are you Lord?" Paul heard the Christ say, "I am Jesus, whom you are persecuting" (Acts 9:5). Decades of ignorance and hostility changed in the face of an encounter with God and Paul went on to become a leading proponent of Christianity.

You also, can experience Jesus—and when it happens, you will never again be the same. "If any man thirst let him come unto Jesus the savior of all mankind and he will never thirst again."[14.7] Taste and see that the Lord is good. Surrender your will to him instead of to your rebellious heart's lovers and masters. Only then will you find and experience what your heart has searched for all your years.

Experiencing the love of Jesus is the essence of your life. It is a mutual exchange between you and him, bringing your soul into peace, joy, and contentment. Jesus reveals himself and relates to you through his spirit of love. This love is superior to the love you experience in the natural realm. The love Jesus fills you with releases within you the ability to fully receive love and to love others. It heals you of a broken heart and wounded soul. It delivers you from the power of death, broken relationships, and a cold or distant perception of God. The love of Jesus is a free gift to all who receive it. Deep inner thirsts and the cry in your heart for relationship with God are satisfied. You were created for a love relationship with Jesus; once you have it, you are finally free.

Religions that require certain performances or rituals oftentimes lead people to believe that they must *earn* God's love through their own works or actions or submission to systems and people. Even while achieving acclaim for performing religious duties, the heart can remain closed off to God because it is still in its fallen nature. The unfulfilled longing for intimacy with Jesus can continue unsatisfied because of false beliefs, distorted conceptions of God, guilt, and shame over the perception of worthiness to receive God's love.

When rebellion is in the heart, it is unwilling to surrender to the love of Jesus because it wants the natural will to remain in control. The Devil, the thief, lies to your heart regarding all that will be lost if your soul surrenders to Jesus. He is the one that declares you shameful and unworthy of God's love. But God loved you too much to leave you in your fallen and lost condition, separated from his love. In the fullness of time, he unfolded his plan to bring men and women back to a restored love relationship with him. His plan shows the great sacrificial measure of his love and his affection through the completely free gift of salvation that he offers.

God's only Son, Jesus, is God's great gift of love. When you receive Jesus, you enter into the river of God's love and nothing can separate you from this love.[38.13] Search your heart now, while it is tender, and surrender it at the feet of Jesus. Allow for his will to be your will and for your heart to be changed and filled with his love. Choose life and let God's love in. Set your fears and feelings of unworthiness aside and receive your heart's desire at this moment and forever.

This love relationship with God is your choice. Jesus invites you into the peace and rest of his tangible love. It is a two-way reciprocation as the precious oil of Christ's love flowing into your heart prompts your own love and adoration to flow back to Jesus and your loving Father. In the course of this exchange, the childlike nature of your heart receives and gives pure love carried by the Holy Spirit. He helps you feel safe, worthy, and vulnerable; so you are able to release love unto him. Your prayer life is an exchange of love with Jesus.

In God's love, you are free from any unhealthy attachments to people, dependency on religious systems, and authorities for your relationship with Jesus. You require no human mediator to please in order to gain access to Jesus. In this condition, pure love flows freely and you genuinely love one another, both friends and the unsaved.

His love leads you from the prisons of guilt and shame into the innocence and joy of a trusting child within the land of the redeemed. Jesus, the Son of God, Creator of all things, calls you with his love into relationship for all eternity. Jesus is the Spirit and essence of all life, and all who would live forever must be changed into his likeness by allowing his love and Spirit to change and live within their heart. Experiencing the love of Jesus is a process as you overcome obstacles in the way.

Hindrances to a pure exchange of his love include sin, distraction, unbelief, and emotional wounds. Part IV offers instructions for receiving healing and freedom from these love blockages so that your relationship with Jesus can grow daily.

They will help you learn how to live a life prepared for the return of the Lord.

Experiencing the love of Jesus is every person's great desire. The Savior is close and wants to satisfy the longing in your thirsty soul for his affection with the love that he pours out like living water

Living in a love relationship with Jesus is the foundation for preparing for his return. This love relationship weathers the storms of life, enables victory over temptation, and causes ministry to flow through you. It brings rest from the disappointments of life and the burden of the fallen nature inherited from Adam's loss in the Garden of Eden. It satisfies your deepest desire.

Let your heart listen to and participate in the flow of Jesus's love. This establishes a holy, pure, correct, and healthy version of a Father and child relationship in which you feel safe, secure, and completely trusting. This connection with Jesus supports you through life's most difficult trials. It keeps your head above the waves of the world's noise, confusion, disappointments, and tragedies. This love gives you joy and peace when everything around you appears hopeless. It isn't a manufactured component of your will. It's a gift you learn to trust in and depend on. You will find that it never fails.

Unconditional forgiveness through Jesus is a manifestation of God's love. Jesus's love teaches that you can come to him despite your broken, sinful life and receive healing on the merit of his great gift to you. You are not required to earn this salvation, you only need to submit to it and receive it.[14.20] The process of purifying your heart (cleansing you from the things separating you from God) is a function of his love. God forgives you for everything when you plead Jesus Christ as the one who pardons and ransoms you from sin and your fallen will and nature. The gift of Jesus's salvation only requires a heart yielded to and willing to receive it.

Taste and see God's love for yourself. His Son, Jesus, earned it for you; you couldn't do it. He loves you because he made you, and he isn't willing that anyone would be lost. Forgiveness is his gift to your weary soul. His love is his gift through Jesus. He hasn't rejected you; he has called you. He sent his only Son to redeem you and find you, shepherd you and bring you back into a love relationship with him. He is relentlessly after the lost soul. The blood of Jesus does this for you; it is the most sacred and spiritually powerful gift known to man.

Your lifelong search and desire is a longing for love. Even in the best of human loving relationships, you are still not completely satisfied within your heart without Jesus. You are created to be in loving relationship with God through his Son. Until you receive and experience this love relationship, your heart is restless and unfulfilled.

Jesus teaches that you can enter his love relationship by taking his yoke, a form of connecting that allows you, to join with him by being harnessed to his will. In this connection, yoked by Christ's love, you learn more about him. You see that he is gentle and humble in heart and will provide rest for your soul.[15.1] He won't hurt you or take advantage of your vulnerable, exposed, and frightened heart. His yoke isn't harsh or sharp but is comfortable, gracious, and pleasant. His burden (the tasks and acts of service you do for him in love) are light and easy to bear.

He extends the invitation to all, every man, woman, and child who is weary, heavy laden, and overburdened, to come to him and find rest and refreshment for their soul. This is the love, the yoke from Jesus, that satisfies the heart's core desire for union with God.

When you experience Christ's love, when you become acquainted with it and pursue it, his love will flow out from you to a lost world. Your love relationship with Jesus makes you a conduit of his love to others. His light shines through you in your words, actions, and behavior. Jesus's love releases compassion in you for others. His love is like a river that fills you and then flows out from you as you minister to people. Being filled and releasing this love to those within your sphere of relationships and to the lost world you encounter helps to maintain a fresh flow of the river of God's love in your life.

Instead of containing the flow of love and growing stagnant, you release it with the leading of the Holy Spirit, and this release causes you to be refilled. As the love flows, you become a branch of the living vine, Jesus Christ; your light shines with the gospel of Jesus and his glorious love.

Jesus's love is different from earthly love. His love comes from God and is felt by you through his Holy Spirit. It is a supernatural love that is above the common experience of affection people have for their children or family. That love is a wonderful gift, but as good as it is, it cannot give you eternal life. The love Jesus paid the price to establish is the love that changes your heart, allows his Spirit to live within you, and saves your soul.

Religion cannot replace the need for Jesus's love. Even though men and women who have not submitted their hearts and wills to God can be religious they have a professed Christianity that is void of a loving relationship with Jesus. No worldly religions, philosophies, or love-deficient Christian organization can achieve the condition that heals the alienated heart within. All people must have an individual encounter with Christ in which they surrender to him in order to be saved.

Performing good works, studies, rituals, and ministry won't substitute for Jesus's love. These religious performances can bring a false sense of serving God. The fallen nature (the flesh or carnal mind) can be very involved with spiritual activities but never take on the yoke of Jesus or submit to his will. Such a condition will wear a person out, but the yoke of Jesus (the condition of being harnessed to Jesus's love) is easy and light and brings rest. Martha served and was troubled, but Mary sat at the Lord's feet and rested in his love.¹⁵·³ This was the better thing.

To be saved is to yield to the love of Christ, the Creator of all things, and to allow his Spirit to displace the spirit of the fallen nature and fallen world that is seated within your heart. The fallen nature is the spiritual legacy we inherit from the first and fallen man, Adam. To choose life is to be conformed into Jesus's likeness, beginning with the salvation he purchased for you on the cross and continuing in a relationship of love.

Open your heart to the pure flow of the Father's love into your soul. Surrender your trust to Jesus. Your love is precious to him. Give freely your heart; let Jesus fashion it, breathing into it healing and teaching you his trustworthiness and fidelity. You were created by him to live in his love, in the innocence of a completely trusting child, and the holiness of his transforming Spirit. He commands you to love him with all your strength and all your soul and all your might.²⁵·³ This is life.

Maintain connection with the love of Jesus every day. This love seeks you out and is continuously present, reminding you to keep constant communion with Jesus. Keeping this open flow of Jesus's love and connection with him is partially accomplished through unceasing prayer.³⁴·¹⁰

It's your spiritual right and the good will of the Father for you to be in a continuous love communion with him through his Son, Jesus. You must be vigilant and guard against the temptations and carelessness that interfere with your connection with the Lord. Worldly cares, pleasures, sin, and disobedience alienate you from the love of Jesus'a spirit of repentance and obedience keeps you in it.

Many times during Jesus's earthly ministry he withdrew to be alone with the Father. His actions serve as an example for you. Taking time to soak in the river of Christ's love is essential. Let prayer that is activated by the Holy Spirit and filled with his fruit be the core of your reciprocal love exchange with Jesus.

Live your life flowing in communion with Jesus's love. Your life is a testimony to your Lord. His yoke of love upon you is the basis for how you live. Seek first the kingdom of God through continuous connection with Jesus and your circumstances and the necessities of life will be taken care of.[41.6] Your life decisions regarding family, work, relationships, and ministry all flow from a spiritual union of love with Jesus that brings discernment to your choices and actions. This connection of love with Jesus brings hope to a lost and dying world, establishes the kingdom of God on earth, and makes you ready for the return of Jesus.

SUMMARY POINTS

- » God loves you and desires a relationship with you.
- » He loves you so dearly he doesn't want you to perish. He wants you to believe in him, but he won't force his love onto you.
- » He will go to great lengths to find those who are lost and bring them into a loving relationship with him.
- » Love for Jesus softens your heart and makes you more like him.
- » It is through Jesus and his Spirit of love that all things are restored.
- » Your deepest desire and longing is to be in communion with the love of Jesus.
- » Living in Jesus's love sets you free and empowers you to fulfill your destiny on earth and prepares you for the return of Jesus.

CHAPTER 9

RECONCILES YOU TO GOD

The history of humanity is a saga of man's endeavor to re-establish relationship with God. Since the fall of Adam in the Garden of Eden, mankind's heart has been alienated from God. This condition created a universal longing for a religion, or method, that would reconcile mankind back with the God of all creation.

The prophets of the Old Testament searched diligently to understand when God would bring salvation through Christ to the heart's need for grace.[18.56] In the fullness of time, God sent Jesus who alone sets free those who would believe in him from separation from God, bondage to sin, and the nature of the fallen man—the first Adam.[14.30]

Because rebellion and disobedience is the core of fallen humanity's alienated condition from God, the will of mankind fights against the free gift of reconciliation through Jesus. It seeks to obtain this gift without having to give up its own fallen nature. For this reason, the fallen nature (the flesh or the carnal mind) practices religions or philosophies without the presence of the Spirit of Christ in an attempt to fulfill its desire for spiritual connection. God's great plan for reconciliation with man is accomplished only through being born again through the blood of Jesus; all other religious experiences—no matter how spiritual or noble—are unable to provide salvation and eternal life with God.

God created you, loves you, and wants you to receive the gift his son bought for you. He inaugurated his loving plan for reunion with himself when his son Jesus, provided the sacrificial atonement (covering your sin) with his blood on the cross. Applying Jesus's blood sincerely and spiritually to your heart is the experience that reconciles you back to God. The blood of Jesus is the only acceptable atonement to God for your sins. No other religion or philosophy can do this.

Reconciliation to God must be experienced inwardly. This salvation is powerful and changes your heart when you allow Jesus and his Holy Spirit power living within you to change you from your fallen nature into the nature of the redeemed in him. It is a miraculous change when the fallen nature of your heart is transformed by the saving power of the blood of Jesus. It's like an internal earthquake; the old ground is broken up and the living presence of Jesus Christ is established. It is emotionally transforming; everyone who is born again has a very real inward change. Fruits of the Spirit—love, joy, and peace—accompany it.

Reconciliation to God through Jesus grants you the gift of salvation and eternal life. As said many times, God isn't willing that anyone should perish and not receive this gift.[4.6] The way to receive it isn't complicated or difficult to achieve. God has placed a witness in everyone that a Savior is near, Jesus, whose Spirit can transform and save your soul.

When you are reconciled to God through Jesus, you are born again and saved from the wrath of eternal separation from God, which is hell. You are brought into eternal fellowship with God through the Lord Jesus Christ and his Spirit. You have assurance when you die or when Jesus returns, whichever happens first, that you have the promise of eternal life.

Throughout history, most people have refused the gift of salvation in Jesus Christ. Because men and women's deeds or actions in the condition of the fallen nature are rebellious, mankind resists God's plan to change them back into a condition where they can have reconciled fellowship with him. Fallen humanity is influenced by the Devil through the carnal nature, causing them to harden their resistance toward God's salvation. The fallen will urges man to resist the belief that Jesus is the Savior of the entire world. This stubbornness—and resulting guilt—causes animosity toward Jesus and those who have him living in their hearts.

An example of the animosity of religious individuals against a follower of Jesus (and their inability to recognize spiritual truth and understand the gospel of Christ even in the presence of the power of the Holy Spirit) is found in Acts 7:55. Stephen, an early Christian leader and a "man full of faith and of the Holy Spirit" preached Jesus to the religious court using the Old Testament to admonish them. Upon confronting the religious leaders for resisting the Holy Spirit, Stephen sees a vision of God and Jesus. He describes to the audience what he is seeing; but due to their unbelief and stubborn resistance, the religious zealots dragged Stephen out of the city and stone him to death.

As evidenced by this unbelieving crowd, the fallen nature—the flesh—fights against the Holy Spirit and hates the light of Jesus. It rejects the salvation and reconciliation that being born again through Jesus establishes. Instead, it chooses darkness and the fallen will of man. The pleasures of the world, a mind too sophisticated, religions that allow the carnal nature to rule, and a heart filled with rebellion and unbelief all deny that Jesus alone transforms the heart and reconciles your soul to God.

The Devil works to blind men and women to the saving power of Jesus Christ. He persecutes the genuine witness that Jesus is the Savior. He ridicules the belief in and saving exclusivity of Jesus and offers endless arguments, deceptions, diversions, and counterfeit portrayals of Jesus to prevent God's creation from accepting the true Spirit of Jesus. He will not prevail because Jesus defeated him on the cross. The time is coming when every knee will bow and every tongue will confess that Jesus is Lord.[8.124] Confess it now, before time expires and the great and dreadful day of the Lord comes.[8.19]

Religious people are not immune from the Devil's deception. They may acknowledge Jesus as Savior but resist his Spirit from transforming their own fallen heart. The Devil devours the unsuspecting soul in this condition. If a man is religious but not transformed from his fallen nature, he is still lost. It doesn't matter how many spiritual words he uses or what kind of Bible he reads. Unless he is born again through the power of Jesus and filled with his Spirit, he is not reconciled to God—he is not saved.

Jesus's appearance in his people through the Holy Spirit ignites controversy. It disrupts and conquers the religious kingdom of the Devil. World religions void of the tangible inward experience of the atonement and reconciliation of man to God through Jesus are prison houses for the souls of the lost. If a Christian religion allows for the carnal will of man to exercise itself contrary to the Holy Spirit, then it has strayed from or never originally had fidelity to Jesus Christ.

Acknowledging Jesus, speaking of him, and professing him, cannot save someone if it is done in the carnal nature. Acknowledging Jesus is Lord with a transformation of the fallen heart saves us. Allow the refining fire of the Holy Spirit to search and purge the hidden dross of the old man or woman within you that professes—but does not possess—the Spirit of Christ.

Your reconciliation to God can only occur through Jesus. This is when Jesus's blood transforms your heart and his Holy Spirit takes residence within you, ruling upon the throne of your heart. From this condition, you receive eternal life and grow in maturity in Christ. This reconciliation with God, through Christ, is the essential foundation to make your heart ready for the return of Jesus.

Are you living in the reconciliation of Christ? If not, now is the time to change. In the midst of the surrounding darkness of the fallen condition, mercy transmits to your fainting heart the key to victory. It is a gift delivered neither by earthly might nor power but by his Spirit. Sustaining grace and the power to overcome the flesh is the most precious thing known to fallen, lost, and desperate humanity. It is the blood of the Lamb, the shed blood of Jesus Christ applied to the altar of your heart, immersing you in its cleansing grace that empowers you to obtain eternal life. This grace will overcome the Devil, his Beast, the False Prophet, and the Mother of Harlots. Give glory to God for Jesus and his precious saving blood.

Your heart's longing and desire for spirituality and relation with God is fulfilled when you allow the Holy Spirit to remove your will and surrender it to the will of God. Receiving the gift of Christ's sacrifice for you on the cross and the Holy Spirit into your heart reconciles you through Jesus back to God for all eternity. In this redemption you have eternal life.

If you have not done so already, confess to the Lord you are a sinner. Ask him to apply the blood he shed on the cross to your heart and reconcile you to God. Surrender your will for his.

When people speak of being "born again," they are referring to the transformation that happens when the blood of Jesus changes a person from their fallen nature to being Christ-filled. You are changed when you receive the blood of Jesus and allow it to be applied to your fallen nature, sins, and separation from God. You are born anew, receiving a new nature founded upon Jesus and submitted to his Holy Spirit. This transformation from your old self to a person reconciled to God through Jesus is what is meant by being born again. You must be born again to be reconciled to God and see his kingdom.[16.4]

Reconciliation to God is the good news of the gospel and occurs when a person has surrendered to the will of God, is forgiven through the atonement of the blood of Jesus, and is maturing in obedience to Jesus through his Holy Spirit. This is a prerequisite for preparing for the return of Jesus.

With all diligence, allow Jesus to be Lord of your life. It is the everlasting gospel of good news to all mankind.

SUMMARY POINTS

» God speaks universally and in every human heart that only Jesus can reconcile you back to himself.

» No other person or savior can provide the Holy Spirit, the essence of Jesus.

» The Spirit of Jesus Christ and his atoning blood alone saves.

» Other religions cannot reconcile the heart and soul back to God.

» When the blood of Jesus changes your heart, it is a surrender of your will to the mercy of God. This is accomplished by his grace alone—not by good works, ceremony, or ritual.

» Jesus's death on the cross and his blood applied to your fallen heart and nature is the only way God in his mercy reconciles you back to himself.

» Salvation through Jesus is a free gift given to all who accept it into their heart and who follow his spirit.

» To experience the blood of Jesus canceling your sins and reconciling you to God is the greatest experience you can have.

» The gift of God is eternal life.

CHAPTER 10

Ransoms You from Sin

God speaks to your heart by convicting and making you consciously aware of sin. This is the beginning of hearing the voice of the Lord and learning to obey it.

Sin alienates you from God who desires fellowship and relationship with you through his Son and the Holy Spirit. When you sin, you defile his creation and grieve his Holy Spirit. Jesus sent his Holy Spirit to convict you and teach you to have victory over sin. Examples of his conviction include feeling of disobeying your conscience, remorse over your actions, an attitude of sorrow toward God and a feeling of guilt for your sins.

If you allow the fallen nature to rule your will, you do things contrary to the conviction of the Holy Spirit. Sin can then harden your heart, dull your conscience, and quench the voice of conviction. This causes you to be powerless against sin you become a servant to harmful behaviors. Once you begin to ignore conviction, confusion can set in and the ways of the world start to seem acceptable.

Over time you will develop and mature in your ability to hear the convicting voice of God, which is an important part of preparing for his return. Accepting the conviction of the Holy

Spirit and obeying him by stopping and avoiding sin in your life is the beginning of the process of being led by the Spirit.

Be careful to remain sensitive to the Holy Spirit who speaks to you when you are grieving him in action or thought. In other words make it a point not to willfully ignore his gentle voice and thus start to extinguish it. It is important to stay tender in the Holy Spirit and not grow legalistic or harsh in judging yourself or others.

Jesus came to free you from the bondage of sin. Only he can deliver you from the consequences of the fallen nature. By offering himself as a living sacrifice on the cross, he once and for all established the atonement for all humanity to be reconciled back to God. Jesus freed you from the sting of eternal death, and he gives you this gift of salvation with no requirement for earning it. It is a gift that must be accepted and applied to your heart and soul in order to be realized. Though it is offered without price, you must surrender your will to his will.

You can know the will of God because you are living in the era of the New Testament. This is a dispensation of time in which God declared that his will and commandments would be written upon your heart and within your mind instead of on outward tablets.[17,20] It is a time when he would teach you inwardly by his Spirit that Jesus is Lord. The beginning of his speaking to you and making you aware of his universal law is through conviction of your conscience and the awareness of being in separation from him.

He created you to desire connection with Him; but as you grow older, this inward conviction can become calloused. Every day, you face spiritual decision points that determine your direction in moving you closer or further away from a relationship with Jesus. Trouble, loss, and trials in your life, though difficult, can cause you to again sensitize to the inward convictions.

His mercy to save you reaches into your heart to make you aware that you are alienating him and that you need him. If you listen to the convicting light within you and seek to obey it, you will discover that the light is Jesus Christ. This Holy Spirit of Jesus teaches you not to sin but to grow and mature into his likeness.

You are ransomed from sin by the blood of Jesus applied to your heart. Jesus Christ offered himself up to God the Father as a sacrifice on the cross to make atonement (pay the price) once and for all eternity for the sin of all humanity. When you allow the supernatural blood of Jesus to cleanse you of your sins and save your soul, you receive the free gift of God, the good news of the gospel. You receive eternal life.

There is a fight over where you will spend eternity. The world's standards and religions are in conflict with the Lord's. They allow for sins, beliefs, and conduct that the Holy Spirit convicts against. They present and encourage you to idolize religious organizations and personalities in the world while subordinating the conviction of the Lord in favor of the rule of the idol.

There comes a point when you must choose whom you will follow. Will you choose the world's way with its own morality and fallen religions or God's way with his instruction through the Spirit and Scriptures? It's up to you to determine to follow God's way and be willing to pay the price in crucifying the flesh to do so because the promises of God are for the overcomer.

Not obeying the conviction of the Lord makes you vulnerable to sin. After awhile, the conviction is desensitized and you enter into confusion, bondage, and bias toward sin. Things that grieve the Holy Spirit and defile the person become normative. It is far more serious than people realize when you willfully deny the conviction of the Holy Spirit. Disobeying the Lord and remaining separated from the salvation of Jesus places you in jeopardy of hell.

Confusion and the inability to discern truth in everyday conduct can be the result of resisting the conviction of the Holy Spirit. The same erosion or lack of discernment is often applied in religious practice. When a person operating in the fallen nature gets into Christian leadership, the religious organization he or she leads can end up supporting sinful conduct (sexual immorality, adultery, abortion) instead of speaking the truth in love with moral integrity.

These leaders and organizations sometimes promotes endless arguments attempting to exonerate sin, especially sexual immorality. Often the arguments come from a compromise with the Devil's ways, which seem more attractive than God's ways. Cultural pressure and indoctrination also erode the ability to stand for truth, clearing the way for moral confusion and passive acceptance of error.

Dogmatism can also hinder the Holy Spirit's work in helping you overcome sin. Legalistic teachings use religious language to attack sin but without the love of the Holy Spirit. Rules for diet, attire, courtship, submission, what women are allowed to do in the church, etc. can create dogma that may not be relevant to the culture or leading of the Holy Spirit. Inventing man-made rules as your conviction rather than yielding to the Holy Spirit's conviction can result in a judgmental spirit and bondage to man.

Yielding to and obeying the conviction of the Holy Spirit by turning from sin is necessary to grow in Christ. The Lord wants you to be obedient to his inner voice and to maintain righteousness unto him. The Lord is also patient with you because he knows you are human and weak, yet he may discipline you in different ways to keep you from straying if, for example, you become lazy or rebellious. His forgiving grace, though, is not a license to keep sinning willfully.

In order to be fully alert to the return of Jesus, diligently endeavor to obey the Holy Spirit when he convicts your heart of sin. Listen carefully and don't allow fanaticism or legalistic rules, such as what you should eat and wear to substitute for or attach to the Lord's conviction. Being humble and sensible in your daily walk helps guard against this. It frees you to enjoy the blessings of the Lord. Moderation allows you to enjoy Gods provision and keeps you from getting excessively attached to them or even idolizing them.

The more you mature in obeying the Holy Spirit and resisting sin, the greater your sensitivity to Jesus becomes. In order to be found watching, you must be receptive to the nature of Jesus and able to discern his still small voice. Guard your heart and keep it ready for the blessed appearance of your Lord.

The Spirit of God pleads with us to change our ways and receive the free gift of salvation through Jesus. When we die, we face judgment from the Lamb of God, Jesus, who is the only advocate that allows us passage into eternal life. A life of rebelling against and rejecting God's Holy Spirit and his Son, Jesus Christ, forfeits eternal life.

If you are not sure of your status, pause right now and surrender your heart to Jesus. Ask him directly to apply his atoning blood to your heart for the forgiveness of your sins. Listen to his voice and sincerely obey him. He won't let you down.

Living in forgiveness through the atoning blood of Jesus frees you from your sins and makes glad your soul. Happy is the one whose sins have been forgiven. It is a wonderful thing to lay your sins at the feet of Jesus and allow his blood to cleanse you. When the Devil accuses you of being worthless to God, declare the blood of Jesus in defense. Jesus came to destroy the work of the Devil and reconcile man back to God. When the Son of God sets you free from sin, you are free indeed. The Devil is destroyed in your life. Don't let him back in.

Guilt, shame, and condemnation are washed away in the blood of the Lamb. Let your heart rest in this great atonement. Feel the freedom it brings. Know the joy of a heart ransomed by the blood of Jesus and a life ready for his return.

SUMMARY POINTS

» The Scriptures reveal that God's will is to resist sin.
» You become aware when you grieve the Holy Spirit through sin.
» Your first hearing of his voice is often through the awareness or conviction of sin.
» Your awareness of sin should convict you and lead you to the atoning power of the blood of Jesus.
» If you repeatedly ignore his convicting voice within you, you can become hardened to sin.
» Sin comes in many forms and causes varying levels of conviction.
» Sin separates you from fellowship with God through his Holy Spirit.
» The mercy of God forgives you of your sins when you sincerely ask for forgiveness and repent.
» The gift of Jesus—unearned by you or anything you could do—is the profound expression of God's love for you.
» You cannot work around sin; you must surrender to Christ's sacrifice for you.
» Happy is the one whose sins have been forgiven.
» To be pardoned from your sins by the atonement of the blood of Jesus applied inwardly to your heart is the dynamic good news of the gospel message.
» How marvelous it is be reconciled to God without earning it, but rather, by receiving the good gift of his Son.
» Jesus ransoms (releases) you from your sins and gives you eternal life.

CHAPTER 11

LIVES WITHIN YOUR HEART

Jesus desires intimate, heart-to-heart communion with you. It is a relationship you can feel and experience. Your companion, the Shepherd of your soul, seeks connection with you in the purity of his love. This is a two-way exchange of love. By the washing of his blood, your heart has access to the heavenly fellowship and exchange of love the merciful God desires. This is where the kingdom of God is found.

The first great commandment is "thou shalt love the Lord thy God with all thy heart and all thy soul."[25.2,3] In submission and reception to the love of God, you will find the relationship that is the desire of your eternal soul. You establish the heavenly nourishment to your soul, the communion of the child of God with the heavenly Father—a two-way exchange of the divine love that is Christ.

Many people, however, resist transformation of the inner soul by the blood of Christ. They go to great lengths to study religion and theology in order to feel justified while not having to crucify the flesh. This stubbornness by the unregenerate will of man to intellectualize the gospel creates a diversity of theological theories, debates, rituals, and creeds that are equally present in large organizations and informal home gatherings. Attached to these creeds and doctrines can be a variety of works, knowledge, religious and political ambitions, achievement, competing systems, and even criticism and persecution of the genuine expression of the Holy Spirit.

A pure experience with Jesus is unavailable if intellectualized cognitively yet not received experientially. You can understand and take the position of Jesus hopefully or mentally but if the old man (the fallen nature that is the flesh) is not transformed, you are not surrendered to the Holy Spirit.

Taking the yoke of Jesus upon you, being born again, filled with the Holy Spirit, and praying ceaselessly are all experiences in Jesus. Learning from the Scriptures by the Holy Spirit is also an experience. Your intellect is a gift in your walk with God. When you experience Jesus and submit to his will, he can use your mind and intellect to advance his kingdom.

The Father and the Son dine within your heart.[17.19] The result of salvation is the dwelling of the Father, Son, and Holy Spirit within you, in your heart and soul, where God desires relationship and intimacy with you in an exchange of holy love. You experience this love; it isn't something you have to observe from afar or intellectually. It is a wonderful experience when the Lord takes up his abode within you and drives out the illicit love of the world's idols.

Experiencing Jesus and his love is what heals your heart.[37.3] The love Jesus extends to you heals you of your pain and suffering.[18.7] Many emotional wounds and a broken heart seem beyond repair in the natural. But a love experience with Jesus heals you of the incurable broken heart.[18.26] It is a supernatural experience with a love and a peace that the intellect cannot fathom.

In Christ's day, the religious leaders (the Pharisees) were his opponents. Many of them seemed to disregard the heart's desire for love in favor of rules. The sick and broken of the time weren't moved by the rules. They remained miserable. It was the experience and touch of Jesus that set them free and healed them, physically and spiritually.

Salvation through the blood of Jesus is an experience that heals the old, miserable, spiritually sick, carnal man. It causes you to be born again into a renewed spiritual man or woman, filled with the Holy Spirit of Jesus. This experience comes in power and in signs and wonders.[36.33] The good news of the gospel is the message of experiencing and upholding Jesus Christ as your Spirit-filling, sin-healing Savior.

You experience your relationship with Jesus through his Holy Spirit who fills you and teaches you and leads you into truth.[31.6] As you grow in your relationship with Jesus, you learn how to obey and serve him, hear the voice of his Spirit, and worship him in his love. As a result, out of you flows fountains of living water—the ministry and fruit of the Holy Spirit.[18.32]

Personal, spiritual conditions that don't have the Spirit of Christ, regardless of expertise or knowledge of Jesus or the Bible, are also void of the salvation only Jesus can provide.[14.23] This is why head knowledge of Jesus cannot save your soul when you lack obedience to his Spirit. Jesus is after the sincere, believing heart that is open to and accepting of his Holy Spirit.

Intellectualizing spiritual truths can cause you to resist being born again. The flesh takes on many covers to avoid being crucified. You might find yourself substituting learning and religious study for experiencing the Spirit of Jesus. It can also creep in after an initial experience in the Lord and deceive you into pursuing knowledge outside of the Spirit of God. This knowledge of God can cause your flesh to swell up with pride and be detrimental to others and yourself. Knowledge and understanding are to be desired; but if it is acquired at the wrong time or without the guidance of the Holy Spirit, it can nurture arrogance or even unbelief.

Misapplied knowledge can make you very religious but keep you separated from a relationship with Christ. Some religions can quote Jesus and teach about Jesus yet at the same time criticize and oppose any appearance or experience of Jesus within a believer or church assembly. Other religions prioritize protecting the power and influence of the organization instead of promoting the experience of walking in the Holy Spirit. They will persecute anyone or any move of the Spirit that diminishes the prestige of the organization.

Independent critics surface to disclaim and slander moves of the Holy Spirit. They have a carnal, religious idea of what church or revival should look like, and they cannot stand any affront to their beliefs. It's important for you to pray to the Lord to lead you to Christian assemblies and churches that honor the Holy Spirit.

A religion without the Holy Spirit often persecutes the Spirit-filled, true believers because the fallen nature of man naturally persecutes the born-again condition—the Spirit-filled walk in Jesus and the gifts received from the Holy Spirit. This is the same persecuting spirit that caused Cain to slay his brother, Abel: Abel's sacrifice or religious practice was acceptable to God (symbolic of faith, in the acceptable blood atonement) while Cain's sacrifice (of the earth, the fallen will) was not.[17.21]

Today, this battle can evidence itself when the Holy Spirit is purposely quenched in meeting and ministry by the persecuting nature of the religious flesh. Their vocabulary may be religious and their harassment somewhat subtle, yet the end result grieves and quenches the presence of the Holy Spirit. For example, many religious leaders argue that the gifts of the Spirit (mainly healing and speaking in tongues) have ceased from being available to Christians. Others teach that revivals where the Holy Spirit is operating are either not genuine or they are works of the Devil.

Fight against the Devil who persecutes the experience and the Spirit of Jesus by cultivating an intellectual Christian religion void of the Holy Spirit and an endless array of non-Christian religions of idol and cult worship. These false religions cannot save us. Only by receiving and experiencing Christ's atonement are we saved. So, if we practice a religion but don't experience the inner transformation within our heart by the blood of Jesus, we are still lost and in the fallen condition. We remain subject to the god of this world—the Devil.

It's vital to not grieve the Holy Spirit. It hardens your heart and creates a religious profession that's void of the true Spirit of Christ and his gift of salvation. The result is walking dead men. If this is you, repent and ask Jesus to rekindle his life within you.

Jesus leads you into relationship with him. If you are a new Christian, be aware of your tender condition and your susceptibility to allowing people or religious practices to substitute for a direct relationship with God. Your own history of relationships can also interfere with you trusting the Lord in developing a direct relationship with him.

For instance, people who experience abandonment by their father may have difficulty trusting God, but the call from Jesus to everyone is to experience him and come into relationship with him and the Father and to labor fruitfully within his kingdom. Through him, you become a son or daughter of God. As you learn to trust Jesus and his Spirit, you grow and deepen in your relationship with him.

Over time, your relationship with Christ becomes seasoned. Just as God's people, the Israelites in the Old Testament, matured in their trust in the Lord and had faith to enter into the rest and promised reward; today, God's children grow in maturity and relationship with God as we journey toward our reward. The Christian experience is not static but one of advancement as we "grow into the fullness of the stature of Christ."[27.5]

As you advance in your relationship with Jesus, you will still experience trials from life's difficulties; but even in the midst of these trials, you have Jesus who comforts you and will never leave you. He also disciplines you as a father does a child, out of love for you and for your well being. Don't be discouraged in the midst of them because the result of trials and disciplining is a deeper trust and relationship with the Lord as you become more like him. Beautiful is the experience of a relationship with Jesus that grows more trusting and intimate over time. Stay close to Jesus and never lose the desire for the loving communion and relationship with Christ; it is a fountain of fresh daily water that nourishes your soul.

Knowing, experiencing, and obeying Jesus is the way of the prepared heart. Jesus paid the price that breaks every wall and inhibitor for you to have a direct relationship with him and the Father. They come into your heart and connect with you. Jesus wants a personal relationship and individual experience with you, and he gives you his Holy Spirit to facilitate the relationship. Your ongoing experience and relationship with Jesus is a primary condition of establishing your heart to be ready, watching for his appearing.

SUMMARY POINTS

- » Jesus declared that if you follow him, your yoke will become easy and your burden light.
- » Salvation in Jesus is a relationship with him, the Father, and the Holy Spirit. It is a communion enabled by Jesus's atonement and a continuation in obedience to the Holy Spirit.
- » Salvation is an experience in which you accept God's free offer of grace through Christ's sacrifice on the cross.

- Love of Christ is an experience. Intellectualizing it tends to feed the fallen nature of the flesh and does not facilitate the inward born-again experience.
- You obey Jesus by allowing his Holy Spirit to lead you and flow through you.
- Worldly religion exalts the fallen nature through head knowledge and achievement without the inner submission to the blood of Jesus.
- The religions in the fall, the unregenerate condition, persecute the Christ-filled religion as Cain persecuted Abel.
- Practicing and maturing in an inward relationship with Jesus prepares you to be ready for his return.

CHAPTER 12

FULFILLS SCRIPTURE AS SAVIOR

Jesus preached that "everything that is written by the prophets about the Son of Man will be fulfilled." As He fulfilled these prophetic writings, Jesus often declared it to those he was teaching. [18.27] His disciples, in turn, understood instances that were the fulfillment of these Scriptures.[18.31]

After Jesus's death and resurrection, the first apostles and converts preached the gospel, reasoning out of the Scriptures (at that time the Old Testament) that Jesus was the Christ.[18.44,46] It was by God's power and Holy Spirit that Jesus was revealed to be the Messiah. The same Holy Spirit opens the interpretation of the Scriptures to you.

The thirty-nine books in the Old Testament prophetically and symbolically declare the coming of Jesus.[18] These books reveal, through a variety of historical and prophetic writing styles, God's plan for sending a Messiah, Jesus, who would save all of humanity from their sins. The books also follow the history of the Israelites which is a metaphor of the church today. Their actual story symbolically reveals that God would one day rise up a Savior, a High Priest, who could make atonement for the sins of the people once and for all, ending all further sacrificial requirements.[27.7]

The Old Testament history and prophesies of the Israelites also metaphorically depict other spiritual truths, such as the Christian walk of faith, believing God's promises, overcoming obstacles, and God's plan for the restoration of all things.

The New Testament includes twenty-seven books and follows a central theme of salvation through Jesus.[18] It records the fulfillment of God's promise of a Savior and identifies the many instances in which Jesus fulfilled the Old Testament prophesies concerning himself. The New Testament authors drew from the psalms and the prophets to prove that Jesus was the Christ. The first Christians reasoned, debated, and preached in the Jewish temples that Jesus was the long-promised and anticipated Savior sent by God.

In his time, most of the people of Israel failed to recognize Jesus as the One who had been promised because they were looking for a natural (temporal) savior. They understood the Scriptures to point to a savior to deliver them from political subjection, and reestablish a nation under their control. They were looking for a political deliverance not a spiritual Messiah to ransom the souls of humanity and give eternal life.

Others were preoccupied with the cares, toils, and ambitions of life and were either too indifferent or distracted to realize the truth of what was happening right before their eyes. Few were prepared for a Messiah that ministered to the inward condition of the soul and healed the outward physical body while preaching the kingdom of God on earth.

When Jesus did not deliver their self-serving desires but, instead, challenged their selfishness with the good news of the gospel, he was persecuted, especially by the religious hierarchy, because he threatened their prestige and did not fit the expected concept of the promised Messiah. A lack of faith and tenderheartedness caused many to miss the Savior in his day.

Now, in your day, determine not to miss the promise of the present Messiah, Jesus. Don't be offended by him or remain unwilling to let go of your willful desire for your life. The Scripture says you can be born again and receive eternal life at his return. Living full of the Holy Spirit and in fellowship with the Lord prepares you for the fulfillment of his appearance. You need to be ready when Jesus comes again to fulfill Scripture and all things.[18.53] Allow the Holy Spirit to give you discernment and to guide you away from beliefs that are not in Spirit and in truth. Don't be ashamed of the gospel of Jesus Christ.[28.8] You must be willing to suffer indignities and be scorned in choosing to follow Jesus and his Holy Spirit.

Jesus declares that his sheep know his voice and will not follow another.[14.12] Follow the voice of the Good Shepherd so you can hear and understand the Scriptures and what the Spirit says to the churches regarding his return. You must be born again and filled with his Holy Spirit.

Take time to review the Bible passages in Part V concerning Jesus's fulfillment of Scriptures, which declare Jesus to be the fulfillment of the promised Savior of all mankind and provide essential guidance for being ready for his return.[18]

SUMMARY POINTS

» The Scriptures point to the singular truth of the everlasting gospel that Jesus Christ is Lord and Savior.

» The Old Testament was a preparatory period for the coming of Jesus who alone reconciles your soul to your God and Creator.

» The Prophets of old were given revelation regarding a future Messiah.

» The unrivaled epic event of all human history was God sending his only begotten Son as Savior of all mankind, as recorded in the Scriptures.

- » The Scriptures and all creation declare the glory of God and every heart has a witness that Jesus Christ is Lord.
- » The Scriptures, when interpreted by the Holy Spirit, avoid the fallen nature's endless arguments and debates. They can be reliably used to prove Jesus is the Messiah.
- » The New Testament authors used the Old Testament Scriptures to prove that Jesus was the Savior.
- » The Scriptures are our handbook for being ready for the return of our Savior, Jesus.

CHAPTER 13

CREATED THE HEAVENS AND THE EARTH

The secret to the mystery of creation is in Jesus Christ.[19.16] Your heavenly Father created the heavens and the earth by and through his Son, Jesus.[19.17] This wisdom has been hidden to the worldly man and woman whose world perception is through the natural senses and who ignores the enlightenment of the Spirit of God.[19.12] The Spirit of truth, the Holy Spirit, reveals mysteries to you and bears witness that creation stands as a product of the power and majesty of the life and light, Jesus Christ. God made the universe not by what is seen but by what is unseen[19.23]

The non-Christian world fails to see that Jesus is the image of the invisible God. A big part deny the Scriptural fact that God created the heavens and earth or consider that he did so through Jesus. They, instead, prefer to debate a variety of creation theories and religions.[19.17] One day, every knee will bow and every tongue will confess that Jesus Christ is Lord.[8.125]

Many people do understand that God is the creator but don't realize that he created all things through Jesus.[19.11] The firstborn over all creation, all things were created in heaven and on earth, visible and invisible, by Jesus and for Jesus. Through him all things were made, including you, and without him nothing was made that has been made. He was chosen before the creation of the world and created all things for himself. He is the exact image of the invisible God.[19.17]

Science does not conflict with the truth that God is the creator of the earth; he is also the creator of the natural laws and order that science organizes and measures.

For many, the debate over the age of the earth is a stumbling block to believing in God. But the age of the earth does not change your essential need for the blood of Jesus to be saved. Your need for Jesus is the same whether the earth is six thousand, six million, or six billion years old. Efforts to measure and determine the age of the earth do not conflict with faith in Christ.

It's true that scientists can discover and measure many things about the universe, but science cannot prove the absence of a higher creator who holds everything together. Science also can't prove the earth wasn't created by the power, wisdom, and understanding of God through Jesus Christ. It's only man's opinion, limited in scope, that concludes that there is no God or that everything evolved from nothing. The whole, observable universe reflects a created order. "He created the worlds and the reaches of space and the ages of time."[19.18]

Wisdom and understanding helps you avoid confusion from scientific theories and propaganda. Your heart is secure in the knowledge of his supreme power and in knowing that God is the creator of all things. Your personal relationship with Jesus will prevent you from being moved or shaken by scientific-sounding speculations and philosophies that deny there is a God or that the universe and mankind were created by him.

These theories often come from people swelled by their own intelligence or their anger and rebellion toward God. They put forth complex and scientific sounding articles and lectures with the intent to intimidate people and make them feel they are ignorant. Bold in their assertions, they make speculations to deny God as if they were law but, in reality, they are propaganda (or at best, guesses). As enlightened and smart as they try to sound, they are unable to recognize God has used the foolish things of this world to confound the wise. They, too, as we all must, will one day stand before the Lord to give an account of their time and actions on earth.

The world fails to comprehend how significant the exclusive salvation of Jesus is in whom God created all things and through whom God reconciled man to himself. You can see the truth, though, because of the enlightenment of the Holy Spirit who witnesses to the supremacy of Jesus. He is not only Savior but upholder and ruler of all things.

You can trust Jesus unequivocally knowing he was with God before the creation of the world, and through him God created the world and you.[19.11] The Holy Spirit gives you the gift of faith and "by faith we understand that the universe was formed at God's command, so that what is seen was not made out of what was visible."[19.23]

He knows who you are and he meets every need you have. He is the heir of all things—all things were created by him and for him—and he upholds the universe. Whether thrones, powers, rulers, or authorities, all things were created by him and for him.[19.17]

Your heart's desire and longing is to be in union with your Creator, and Jesus makes this possible. God was pleased to reconcile all things to himself through his Son and the blood he shed on the cross. He calls you and reconciles you to himself. You are his. He knew you before the foundation of the earth was laid.[19.15]

Resolve to always cling to and obey the One who died for you, reconciling you to the Father. Absolutely refuse to let anyone steal your inheritance and salvation in Jesus with vain arguments regarding creation that deny there is a God. Unequivocally commit your heart and will to the Creator of all things and serve him diligently, determined to never—under any circumstance—sell out your birthright in Jesus. Guard your heart so that you will be ready when he returns and establishes his new heaven and earth.[7.24]

Mankind is blessed by the love of such a great God. Our souls are blessed that Jesus has all of God's fullness dwelling within him and is the head of the body, the church, and that through himself, he reconciles us to God. You can wait in sober but joyful expectancy for the appearing again of this great Savior to establish you within his immortal kingdom forever.

SUMMARY POINTS

» God created the heavens and the earth through Jesus.

» Many unbelievers attempt to use scientific or esoteric sounding theories to deny that God is creator of the universe. This propaganda is designed to intimidate believers and those seeking truth.

» God made the earth and mankind by his power, wisdom, and understanding.

» Jesus rules heaven and earth and holds all things together.

» Jesus is the image of the invisible God.

» Jesus is the radiance of God's glory and the exact representation of his being.

» Jesus is before all things; he is the firstborn over all creation. All things were created for him; and in everything, he has supremacy.

» Christ is the head of the body, the church, and reconciles to God all who will believe in him through the blood he shed on the cross.

PART IV

How to Be Ready

CHAPTER 14

Protect God's Dwelling

You are the temple of God.[21] In the Old Testament, a constructed building was his temple; but in the New Testament dispensation we now live in, Jesus has taken up his abode within you—in your heart and soul. You are now the holy dwelling place for his Spirit, and you are responsible for keeping his temple pure.

The lust of the world tempts you to desecrate your body and mind, which are part of the temple of God. The Enemy constantly pressures, entices, troubles, and addicts you in an effort to violate the sacredness of your body and soul. Cultural and media messages try to manipulate and program your mind, encouraging you to accept and desire the misuse of God's temple. Defiling the temple of God in these ways breaks your spiritual fellowship with him.

You learn not to defile his temple by yielding to Jesus and the power of his Holy Spirit to help you remain pure. It is imperative to allow the Holy Spirit to assist you. You will receive spiritual rewards in the form of inward blessings of love, joy, and peace as a result of your obedience to guard and keep his temple holy. These blessings of well-being surpass the fleeting evasive pleasures of the world.

Chapter seven discussed how the Old Testament temple was a figure of Christ's relationship with Christians—his temple today. In this way, the Old Testament history of God's people is an outwardly symbolic metaphor of the inward spiritual journey of the Christian in the current New Testament time we are living in.

As the ancient children of Israel journeyed through the desert toward the Promised Land, God revealed to them a plan for building a tabernacle. In this mobile and temporary house, worship and sacrifices were performed, conducted by a designated priesthood.

Once established in the inherited land, the Israelites erected a permanent temple in Jerusalem. The apex of Israel's spiritual experience culminated at King Solomon's dedication of the new temple in Jerusalem when the glory of God fell on this house of worship, thoroughly overwhelming the priests and the people. All Israel rejoiced and enjoyed the marvelous blessing of the presence and favor of God manifested in power and glory within the temple.

This spiritual outpouring in God's temple symbolized Jesus's sacrificial atonement on the cross that established an inward spirit-filled relationship with believers. It also symbolized (potentially in your lifetime) the pending new move of God leading to immortality at the return of Jesus. In other words, the glory the Israelites experienced at the dedication of the permanent temple in Jerusalem reflected the completion and glory the children of God will experience at the return of Jesus because they are his temple now.

When Jesus shed his blood on the cross, he figuratively entered into the most sacred place of the temple once and for all—referred to as the Holiest of Holies. Upon entering, Jesus reconciled all mankind back to God. This ended the literal sacrifices and the designated priesthood. The tabernacle of God was now available to all men (including Gentiles, not just the Jewish people called Israel). No longer does the Father dwell in temples made with hands but now has come and dwells *within* men and women in their hearts and souls.[21.3]

The High Priest of this New Testament covenant is now Jesus Christ. Those who believe and receive Jesus as their Savior are born again through him and constitute a royal priesthood made up of all true believers.[27.7]

Regarding this salvation we have today, the prophets of the Old Testament searched and inquired as to who the Spirit of Christ within them was referring to. It was revealed to them that it wasn't for their time period but for those in the time to come—this time—the dispensation of the New Testament.[18.56]

All people are the temple of God and all human life is sacred. You must choose if you will allow Jesus to have his rightful occupation. If you surrender to him, Jesus becomes your High Priest who enters the Holiest of Holies of his sacred tabernacle in you; he will rule upon the throne of your heart and cast down all former ruling and contrary idols, including the kings of self-will and lust.

With reverence, fear, and trembling, you have a sacred obligation to keep your life and body holy. Allowing your fallen will to rule your heart desecrates the temple of God. Resisting the Holy Spirit, remaining in your fallen will, and continuing carnal religious practices result in sin, disobedience, and desecration of the temple of God. If you have not the Spirit of God, you are not one of his.[21.2]

Defilement comes from within, through the unregenerate nature that is contrary to the Holy Spirit.[23.3] Carelessness, compromise, and assertion of the old nature can cause you to disregard the gentle voice of the Holy Spirit and dethrone Christ from being the ruler of your heart.

The fallen will exalts itself in sinful and prideful ways, but it also emerges in more subtle religious expressions, such as performing Christian practices in the nature of the old Adam, unregenerate by Jesus Christ. Flesh-pleasing rituals, recitations of repeated sayings, and pursuing prideful, political ambitions within the church are examples. Sin and compromise are given expression through your actions and pride. In many cases, it takes accurate spiritual discernment to identify the disguised areas of your fallen nature—those places in which the carnal man is operating.

When the fallen will asserts itself against the genuine Holy Spirit, born-again experience (regardless of Christian rituals, ceremonies, or words), Christ is put to death afresh.[21.10] The temple of the Holy Spirit is defiled by the sins of lust, carnal assertion, and rebellion. These things cause the sacredness of the human creation to be demeaned. Pursuing the lusts of the flesh violates your connection with the High Priest and King of your heart, Jesus Christ.

Polluting the temple of God incurs consequences.[21.3] We are accountable for this disobedience and end up with unwanted results, reaping what we sow. Repentance (turning away from the sin) and asking for forgiveness are necessary when you are guilty.

Historically and biblically stated, the heart of mankind continues to grow worse and worse. It is imperative to do the opposite: be obedient to the Holy Spirit and keep your heart pure and ready. Jesus Christ, your High Priest, enables you to keep his temple holy. Trust him and allow him to help you do this. The Spirit is willing but the flesh is weak. When you make Jesus your High Priest, Bishop, and Shepherd of your soul, he gives you the Comforter, the Holy Spirit, to empower you to maintain his holy temple.

The Holy Spirit convicts you of the impurities within your heart when your thoughts, actions, and words grieve him and defile his temple. Through this conviction, the Holy Spirit teaches you to be sensitive to his leading and helps guide you away from temptation and sinful conduct, including religious pride. Any time your conduct puts a strain on the close communion you need with Jesus, you will feel remorse, but the yoke of Jesus (symbolic of our harnessed attachment to Christ) and his burden is easy, light, and not hard to bear.

Contrary to the world's practice, you are able to keep the temple of God holy through the Spirit of Jesus Christ. Bountiful rewards of blessing the world is unable to fathom are yours, including rest for your soul, when you are adorned with the yoke of Christ.

We are called—commanded—to keep the temple of God holy, to pursue and allow the fullness of the stature of Christ to grow up within us. Keeping your temple pure helps you prepare for the return of Jesus.

SUMMARY POINTS

» In the Old Testament, God instructed his people to first build a mobile tabernacle and later a permanent temple, consecrated to him.

» Today, in the New Testament of Jesus Christ, your body, heart, and soul are the temple of God, and his Holy Spirit dwells within you.

» All human life is sacred; each person's soul was created to be a temple for the Holy Spirit.

» Jesus Christ is the King and High Priest who sits upon the throne of your heart.

» You defile the temple of God and fail to keep it holy when you operate in the fallen nature. That defilement is also known as the will of the old Adam who is not regenerated by the blood of Jesus,

» Society and culture promote dishonor to the living temple of God. Many Christians are careless in resisting these pressures.

» Outward rituals and allegiance to various denominations, rules, and doctrines do not maintain a holy temple. Infilling of and obedience to Christ in your heart is what maintains this holiness.

» Christ instituted the royal priesthood of all believers; resist the temptation and pride of the flesh to exalt yourself in religious title or non-Christ-ordained authority over others.

» The Holy Spirit convicts you and enables you to resist temptation and keep the temple holy.

» God honors and blesses the individual who keeps his temple pure.

» Keeping the temple holy to God is essential to having your heart ready for the return of Jesus.

CHAPTER 15

Keep Your Heart Holy

Holiness is a requisite of readiness for the return of Jesus. The pure in heart shall see God, who dwells on earth in his holy temple—his sacred creation, man and woman. Presenting yourself as a living sacrifice (by staying holy) unto God keeps you ready for when Christ returns.

Defilement of God's temple, (your body) erodes your preparedness for Jesus's return within you and jeopardizes your eternity in God's presence.[21.3] Therefore, forgiving others who sin against you, staying pure in heart and mind, and living in love through obedience to the Holy Spirit keep you alert and ready for the return of Jesus.

The antagonist to holiness—sin—abounds in a variety of categories. Religion cannot exonerate sin. The cause and effect of impurity, unforgiveness, and disobedience lodge in the heart, mind, and emotions. Religion, in general, has a history of falling short of providing the soul's remedy for mankind's sin-prone, trial-weary existence. Relief only comes from repentance, change, and the power of Christ. Distractions from holiness, addictions, and the world's pleasures are fleeting and will always come up short in the end.

The way of holiness is the way of peace and of communion with the Lord. Growing into the fullness of the stature of Christ into his image is a journey of righteousness, forgiveness, and obedience.[8.56] The objective of holiness is for you to be found watching, oil burning in your lamp, and your heart in undivided devotion to the Lord Jesus Christ. Being free from the idols that hold you captive and putting lust and addictions beneath your feet are your Christian privilege through the power of the Holy Spirit.

To experience freedom, you must discontinue secret sins and disobedience in your life. Examine again your relationship with Jesus. Is it strong enough to deliver you from sin? You may consider yourself a Christian, but is your heart *fully* surrendered to him? Will it be able to prove its exclusivity in devotion to Christ alone or do multiple allegiances exist? Are you accommodating any secret accords with immorality? Do you resist the Holy Spirit and consider it your right to refuse to extend forgiveness? Have you allowed Jesus to heal your broken heart and bind it up from its wounds? Now is the time to repent and change your ways, pursuing righteousness fully committed to living for Christ.

Surrender to the Holy Spirit and apply the wisdom and correction given to you by the godly people he puts in your life. Contrary to the message of the world, there *is* a spiritual place of safety you can maintain, a hidden place of holiness and a condition free from lust and immorality.

Politically-correct terminology and media indoctrination cannot force you from your place of righteousness in God. It cannot change one component of the law of God that is written upon the hearts of all men and women. The New Testament standards of God do not change. He is holy and you must be holy.

The enemy of your soul attempts to change society's natural conscience and the laws of righteousness that God places within every man, woman, and child. In the end, though, mankind's attempt to justify sin will still not change the laws of God. Don't be fooled—God does not condone sin, no matter what the culture or media promotes. If you believe God does condone sin, you could be lulled into a lukewarm condition that puts you in jeopardy of forfeiting eternal life for your soul. The majority of television programs and movies care nothing about your soul.

Fear God and keep his commandments; do not fear man and his propaganda that idolizes sin and worships the creature over the Creator. God's sheep know his voice. Listen to the Good Shepherd who speaks to your heart and choose life. Enter into the abundant pastures of peace and relationship with your Creator.

Jesus taught that those who would see God are the pure in heart.[23.1] Worship the Lord your God with all of your heart, with all of your soul, and with all of your mind. The Lord of your life is the Lord of your body, and he has called you into a walk of holiness. Offer yourself up as a living sacrifice; be holy and pleasing to God because of your love for God not because you are striving to be legally compliant. You were bought with a price by Christ, and you are not your own—you are Christ's and your body is his.

Diligently make sure you are a faithful guardian and steward of Christ's purchased possession, which is you! Guarding and keeping your heart holy makes you ready to see God. Defilement separates you from him and ultimately incurs judgment just as the ancient Israelites experienced.

Specific laws governing conduct and worship had been delivered to the Israelites by God and continuously emphasized by the prophets when neglected. God's people were consistently warned in the Old Testament to repent of sinful, rebellious ways.

Infidelity (or as the Bible describes it, "whoring" after other gods) brought the twelve tribes of Israel into chastisement and judgment by God. Their rebellion, disobedience, sensuality, and their worship of false gods was likened to an adulterous woman; it ultimately brought final judgment upon the people God had chosen to call his own.

Time after time, God patiently warned his people to repent and change their ways. He required a holy people who followed and honored his statutes and commandments allowing them to enjoy the reward of a fruitful, plentiful, and peaceful life.

Contrary to the belief of those who thought recompense would not happen, many continued in their sinful ways unwilling to repent and return to God and his statutes. Therefore, judgment fell on the kingdoms of Israel and Judah in their appointed times. Fallen from their former sovereignty, the surviving people of God lived in bondage to foreign captors.

Endless is the mercy of God; and in his chosen time, he revealed a greater plan through the appearance of Jesus, who is the Savior of the entire world. In this new era or dispensation of God's relationship to his sacred creation, which we live in, God no longer governs by outward laws but now writes his laws and commandments upon the fleshly table of the heart and mind of mankind.[17,20] This inward witness and teaching of Christ establishes a spiritual priesthood made up of all believers.

Remember, as a believer and priest unto him, you are the temple of God. Prior to Christ, strict ordinances required fidelity and holiness unto the Lord through obedience to the law and rituals outlined in the law. Today, under the current dispensation, God's people are commanded to keep the law of God written upon their hearts and minds by his Holy Spirit and to be holy even as he is holy.

God does not require anyone to bow to the altar of uncleanness and defilement. He is a God that lifts up his people unto holiness and purity and the resulting peace. The God of salvation never enslaves his people to lust and decadence; instead he frees his sacred creation to joy and contentment through his son Jesus. Our God is above any rival. He puts down all contrary authority, wickedness, and twisting of the truth and has established Jesus Christ as King now and forever.

This King, the Lord Jesus, is opposed by mainstream culture and media which promote morals contrary to the morals God has written upon the hearts of humanity. Their perversion and decadence will not lead you into a liberated freedom of consciousness. On the contrary, debauchery is a violent master imposing slavery upon the indulger and demanding forfeiture of a relationship with God and eternal life with him. You must overcome the world system that worships the beast and ennobles immorality. Judgment is at the door of this sinful and adulterous generation.

Imagine the shock and anguish experienced by Noah's contemporaries or the residents of Sodom and Gomorrah when the time to repent ended and the judgment of God commenced.[6.10] Judgment and the end of favor is the most terrifying condition a person can experience. Be determined not to let this happen to you. Overcome by following Jesus now before your time to do so expires.

Following Jesus requires authentic holiness which emerges from the heart. It begins as an inward character trait and produces external fruits of the Spirit. It is your normal every-day requirement to offer up yourself—body, soul, and mind—as a living sacrifice unto God. Holiness is a requisite because God is holy. Your unfolding Christian experience is maturing and transforming you into the image of Christ, the image of God. A holy life continuously develops within you as you grow in Jesus.

People often mistakenly believe that the holiness God requires comes from external performance or conduct. Another common misconception is believing that holiness is a result of following established rules and legal requirements according to different belief systems. This incorrectly leads people to believe that they can achieve holiness based on the things they do, regardless of their heart's motive. But inside your heart is where the battle for holiness is fought and won because that is where the motive for sinful actions that defile a person originate.[23.3] The Holy Spirit who lives within you will guide you into the righteousness and holiness that is acceptable to God, which is relational and feasible—not legalistic.

Prayer helps you to identify subtle impurities. During prayer, the Holy Spirit may teach or convict your conscience of correction needed in areas of behavior and conduct contrary to Christian living but not formally identified in the Bible.

Allow the Holy Spirit during times of prayer to instruct you to recognize sins. Many are obvious, including sexual misconduct, cheating, adultery, drunkenness, lying, and others which are specifically identified in the Scriptures and by the Holy Spirit. Others are more subtle to discern, such as abortion.

Prayer will help you take time to hear the voice of the Lord and discern the more subtle sin in your life that is grieving the Holy Spirit. Some prayer can be during a longer quiet time of waiting on the Lord. You can also pray briefly throughout the day regarding unfolding situations in order to receive help and discernment from the Holy Spirit regarding how you should respond.

Defilement can arise in other ways such as when the Enemy sows pride and superior behavior in the heart. This kind of sin develops from trusting in religious performance, achievement, and acts of righteousness. It often comes from following rules that a certain person or sect consider necessary to be holy.

The rules may actually be virtuous and of practical moral benefit, but the wrong motivation of the heart and pride is what can defile you. Self-righteousness and pride can result in diminished love and compassion for others and especially anyone outside of the religious belief system.

This is one reason why Jesus called out the religious leaders of his time and likened them to painted white graves who were camouflaging their true hearts' condition inside, which were full of dead men's bones.

Holiness can be difficult to cultivate when Christians, especially religious leaders, preach against sinful activities while they themselves are engaging in them. Immature believers and seekers are hurt by their hypocrisy and these scandals weaken their faith. You must understand that your walk is between you and God. Whether or not others—including Christian leaders—yield to temptation, your sinful behavior is never justified.

Cultural pressures constantly exert influence—and the media attempts to program your identity and life compass. Predetermine to not automatically accept common opinion of what society and the media portray as normal behavior and politically correct beliefs. Reject the indoctrination of the world and resulting eternal shipwreck and allow the Holy Spirit to be your teacher and keep you in the safety of a holy and pure life.

A wide variety of temptations constantly tests your character and challenges the sincerity of your Christian integrity. How you act when you are not in public can provide insight to the condition of your heart. Be aware that relationships and family life are directly affected by your conduct and the holiness in your life. Business, careers, and earning your livelihood can exert pressure on you to lower your values. Your conduct and level of holiness in how you handle these pressures are a window to your heart and directly affect your business relationships and family life.

It's not a sin to be tempted; it's how you choose to react that can be sinful. Every temptation includes a way of escape. The longer you consider the temptation, flirt with the idea of engaging in it, and even begin to participate in it, the harder it is to escape the temptation. Flee from temptation and idolatry! Choose to run from it by following the escape.[22.8]

You can't do it on your own—the Holy Spirit helps you. He provides a deliverance from lusts and addictions. He is the one who convicts your heart when you are doing, contemplating, thinking, or saying things you shouldn't. Look to and trust the Holy Spirit to deliver you and he will.

Jesus promised to never leave you or forsake you, and he backs it up with his presence and action. If you have unrepentant sin in your life, take the time right now to pray and repent before God and ask his forgiveness.

Temptations come to everyone and will affect you in different degrees. Developing defenses and predetermining what you will do when they happen will help you be ready to overcome them. Pray for the awareness to keep yourself from impurity in the many different settings you encounter. Pray also that you don't willfully resist the Holy Spirit's conviction when he is warning you.

So many people are unprepared for the return of Jesus because they don't have the awareness, spiritual weapons, and tools to overcome their temptations. But we have the most powerful weapon of all—access to the Holy Spirit. For example, when you are tempted to commit a sin, addiction, lust, pride, idolatry, etc., stop your thoughts on the sin and direct yourself to Jesus and his Holy Spirit. Turn away from the temptation; take yourself away if need be. Pray to and wait on Jesus to extend his power. Purposefully redirect your thoughts and wait on the Spirit. The Lord will break in and help you defeat the temptation, extending his comfort and peace.

Allowing the Holy Spirit to help you in the midst of temptations is a key weapon in maintaining a holy life unto the Lord. Christianity is active; the kingdom of God must be taken. You must overcome and enter into it by faith using the spiritual weapons and tools God gives you, including prayer and the promise that there will always be a way of escape.

The choice to keep your heart and mind pure is up to you. Holiness is pursued by establishing your heart in scriptural truths and Christian integrity. Let sensitivity to the Holy Spirit and a carefulness to not offend him govern your thoughts, words, and activities.

Determine to have a spirit of love in all of your relationships and in your witness to truth. Allow the Holy Spirit to temper your actions. For example, instead of rebuking someone for their offense against you, the Spirit may lead you to show them acceptance and kindness. Sometimes, you might feel it's best to avoid a situation but, instead, the Holy Spirit could lead you to confront it. Learn to not fight his prompting.

Defiling the temple of God is avoided by constantly being on guard and responsive to the prompting and checks of the Holy Spirit. As you learn to seek his guidance, you will become more sensitive to the words you speak and you will choose to avoid activities that grieve the Spirit.

Your awareness of the consequences of ungodliness increases as you mature in Christ and continue living prepared for his return. In contrast, sin strains and often breaks communion (spiritual connection) with God. Like storm clouds blocking the sun, unholiness hinders the flow of God's Spirit and protective covering. Physical, emotional, and relational wounding can result when you defile God's living temple and do not maintain the holy and righteous stewardship of it.

Yielding to temptation and lust permits sin to gain a foothold in your life and can ultimately make you a slave to that sin or lust. This makes flowing in the fullness of love difficult. It can cause you to diminish and lose the fruit of the Holy Spirit and potentially take on confusion, dependency, bitterness, complaining, sadness, fear, anxiety, and addictive behaviors.

Fruits of holiness are yours to reap now in this life as a result of obediently preparing for the return of Jesus. Experiencing the fruits of the Spirit, such as love, joy, and peace is one of the Lord's greatest rewards for righteous living.

Being holy does not bring you unhappiness, a boring life, or a lack of pleasure. Non-Christians may view holiness as strict rules that take the joy out of living and look upon you with ridicule, but the reality is that you have something wonderful that they are unable to comprehend or experience.

Growth in holiness results in God trusting you with more of his kingdom work and revelation. Increasing your level of communion and connection with Jesus allows you to experience the expansion of the flow of the grace and love of Jesus Christ in your life. You will be increased with grace to minister to others, and your own relationships will be strengthened. Power and the favor of the Lord will be strongly on you for ministry. Love will flow freely in your relationships and your connection with Christ. Your compassion and sensitivity toward others increases along with the freedom to give and receive love unconditionally and minister as a peacemaker. Holiness prepares you to see the Lord and be ready for his return.

SUMMARY POINTS

» Holiness is a conduct and condition resulting from a relationship with Jesus and from obeying his Holy Spirit in resisting sin.

» Without holiness, you will not see the Lord.

» Holiness is an attribute of God, and he requires you to be holy even as he is holy.

» You must choose to be holy.

» The ability to be authentically holy is given by your helper, the Holy Spirit.

» The Holy Spirit convicts you of sin, leads you to repentance and helps you resist temptation.

» Assistance to break the chains of addictions, unforgiveness, and unrighteous living comes from God and his Holy Spirit.

» Characteristics of the fruit of holiness include love, joy, and peace.

Keep Your Heart Holy

» Empowerment to stay pure and resist defiling temptations is provided by the Holy Spirit.

» Holiness is a condition of reverence and consecration to Christ.

» The rate at which you mature in the Lord and deepen your spiritual connection with him is directly related to the level of holiness in your life.

» Inward spiritual blessings are evidenced by a close sense of the Father's love, joy, and peace independent of your outward trials.

» Promotion and trust with revelation for ministry are given and increased when your life is holy and pleasing to the Lord.

» Holiness allows you to experience and participate in the establishment of the kingdom of God.

» Freedom to grow into the fullness of the stature of Christ (Ephesians 4:13) is a process of holiness in your life.

» Pre-establishing integrity in your heart and avoiding harmful things that grieve the Holy Spirit protect you.

» Sexual purity and chaste conduct help maintain holiness.

» Straining your relationship with the Lord is one of the consequences of immorality and can place your salvation in jeopardy.

» Genuine love flows unrestricted into and out of you when you lead a holy life.

» Holy-Spirit-inspired holiness sets you free from bondage to sin and prepares you for the return of Jesus.

CHAPTER 16

MAINTAIN SEXUAL PURITY

God's will is for you to abstain from sexual immorality.[23.22] As a Christian, you will face a variety of temptations. It is not a sin to be tempted; it is when you give in to the temptation that it becomes sin. Maintaining sexual purity is an essential attribute of what it means to be a Christian and to be ready for the return of Jesus.

The Internet, the increasing acceptance of sexual content in the media, and the world's indoctrination of immorality amplify the assault on the mind from every direction. An increasing atmosphere of licentiousness requires additional fortitude in not compromising with this spirit of sensuality, which leads people into sexual immorality in thought and in deed. You must, by the power of God, be fortified and increase in resistance to the pervasive flood of immorality. When the enemy comes in like a flood, the Spirit of God rises up superior to deliver his people.

Promiscuity as a way of life does not lead to lasting happiness and contentment but ultimately leads to the soul's destruction. Inward peace eludes the life lived in compromise with lust and sexual immorality. Allowing lust to prevail in your life can make you a slave to it. Lust then becomes a master imposing its demands.

If you continue in immorality, it can become embedded in your heart eventually ruling your life and controlling your thoughts. Once immorality is entrenched, it becomes difficult to see the truth and to have the determination and perseverance to break free. The conviction and power of God is required to overcome. Choose to turn from compromise and its unfulfilling promises and live a life of purity unto God. The comfort of the Holy Spirit will be a constant presence for you when you maintain a chaste and pure heart.

God created sex as an exclusive intimacy reserved for the marriage covenant. Sex outside of marriage dishonors God's temple and distorts your fellowship with him through the Holy Spirit. The body is for the Lord and not for sexual immorality.[23.10]

The Bible offers considerable instruction regarding sexual purity and morality. Many of these related verses are listed in Reference 23 in Part V. Take the time to study them frequently as you reflect on this chapter. It can't be overemphasized how important it is to be acutely aware of the Bible's perspective on moral purity. This is possible by being thoroughly acquainted with the relevant Scriptures.

Not all topics of morality are specifically covered in the Bible, but sexual morality is clearly addressed. Some of the Bible's authors even record examples of previous society's sexual sin and the consequences for not repenting.[23.32] They advise Christians to not believe clever and biased interpretations condoning participation in sex outside of a marriage covenant no matter what the excuse, argument, or cultural norm.[23.19]

They advise this because keeping yourself sexually pure serves and worships God. Scripture teaches that sex is an intimacy reserved for the covenant of marriage, which is between one man and one woman. God created us male and female, establishing his natural laws of marriage and the joining together of his creation. It is the consummation of two becoming one in a marriage of fidelity before God and man. The Lord calls us to lead a chaste and holy life and does not leave ambiguous the results of moral disobedience.

The Bible teaches that the sexually immoral will not inherit eternal life and will end up in the lake of fire unless they repent.[23.33] There is an acceptable and honorable way for men and women to have a relationship of physical intimacy. It is within the context God has established—marriage.

There is also a way for men and woman to be free from dishonorable relationships and conduct. Mercifully, the Lord provides an escape for those ensnared in the secret sin, addiction, and slavery of sexual immorality. Obeying the conviction of the Holy Spirit, repenting, and practicing genuine recovery from sexual immorality leads to the return of a spiritual connection with the Lord. When you are sexually pure, you maintain a close spiritual connection with Jesus.

Your conscience speaks to you regarding sexual morality. Jesus is the Light of the World who has lit the heart of every person and this light shines inwardly upon your conscience. His inward witness is grieved when your original innocence is violated, either by choice or against your will. Because of this presence and natural awareness of the inward laws of God, every man and woman is without excuse for not being obedient to the Spirit of God.

Our moral conscience competes with the fallen nature—the old Adam, the world and its temptations. The world's standard of morality asserts itself in defiance to the natural laws of God. The fallen flesh, not content to indulge in secret sin, seeks to establish sin and decadence to be esteemed in society while vilifying the voice of righteousness.

Extensive indoctrination through media, educational institutions and organizations attempt to reprogram the natural laws of morality that are in the human heart. Don't be discouraged by what you see going on around you, God counters society's increasing opposition to God-inspired morality with the witnesses and voices he raises up in the land and with the laws he has written upon every person's heart. In the end, righteousness will prevail and every knee will bow to Jesus.

Hearing the Lord through your conscience and obeying him in the correction and direction he provides are the first steps in being led by the Holy Spirit and hearing the voice of the Lord. The Comforter has come, and he convicts the world of sin. Jesus told his disciples he would not leave them alone but that he would send the Holy Spirit to help and teach them.[41.10] The Comforter, helper, and teacher is the Holy Spirit.

Not obeying the leading of the Holy Spirit on your conscience to repent of sexual sin incurs consequences, which according to biblical authors, can end up with eternal separation from God. Sexual immorality places eternal life in jeopardy and those who continue and don't repent of it won't inherit eternal life.[23.9] Search the Scriptures objectively and you can't draw another conclusion. You can only believe or not believe the Scripture. Anyone who teaches contrary, making excuses for immorality, will be held to the Scriptures and the witness of the Holy Spirit on their day of accountability.

God has not rewritten his statutes to accommodate society's view on morality. Society in varying degrees of tolerance may accept that sex outside of marriage is permissible. The world may continue to grow increasingly morally promiscuous, but God's view on the subject remains the same.

God didn't change to excuse the people of Sodom and Gomorrah. In fact, Peter teaches that the fate of the inhabitants of Sodom and Gomorrah is an example of the consequences that sexual immorality can bring for us today.[23.30] Jude likens their indulgence in gross immorality as an exhibit of perpetual punishment and warning of undergoing the punishment of eternal fire.[23.32]

Common sense reveals that certain sins have a more devastating impact on your spiritual life and the lives of others. The Bible says most sin is outside of the body, but when committing sexual immorality, you sin even against your own body.[23.12] Sexual immorality breaks your fellowship and growth in Christ, violates yourself, defrauds others, places your salvation in jeopardy, and leaves your heart unprepared for the coming of Christ.

Falling into sin and having your heart hardened usually doesn't happen overnight. Just like your growth in spiritual maturity, it is a gradual process. The longer the impurity is continued, the harder it becomes to be set free and return to your place in the Holy Spirit.

When men and women's hearts become calloused to the Holy Spirit, they can give up their principles. Conviction departs, lust is not guarded against, and the inner witness, conscience, and conviction God has placed in them are quenched. If you willfully commit fornication, ignoring the warning of the Holy Spirit, then your mind can become corrupt and you can jeopardize your redemption in Christ.

In this condition, many people continue to be religious. They hide immorality from their outward appearance, but inside they are defiled and the rule of Jesus, the Holy Spirit, is violated.

If your heart is ruled by fornication, then Christ is not enthroned upon your heart; your will is not submitted to him. You can lose his Spirit and risk becoming none of his.

Most people don't set out to establish a life compass of immorality. A dearth of role models creates an absence of teaching by example. The few examples of righteousness that do exist in the land can be drowned out by the clamoring voices of the flesh's allurements. Corruption of the innocence of a person's childlike nature can occur willfully and unwillfully. Defrauding one another sexually occurs when sexual relations designed for the sanctity of marriage are illicitly conducted outside of marriage.

Cultural values and family standards often don't teach a chaste and moral way. Media sensuality relentlessly presses its promiscuity onto the public, ingraining into people's minds a worldview of morality that is contrary to God's standards.

Those who have unmet needs in the areas of love and acceptance can be vulnerable to sexual misconduct as well. A variety of unhealed wounds of the heart and soul seek pain relief by engaging in sexually addictive behaviors. They experience a false intimacy with illicit media and relationships.

If you feel any of these conditions relate to you, don't despair. God is a God of pardon and forgiveness. He calls you out from sin and wants to give you another chance to turn toward him and walk in righteousness. Repent, ask his forgiveness, and live your life for him.

The indoctrination of immorality by media and culture especially targets young people who are more susceptible to propaganda and are in the process of defining their principles. If this is you, keep your eyes and integrity on Jesus and his plan for your life. He will never let you down.

Know, too, that those who corrupt young people are warned in the Bible of the severity of the consequences in the judgment to come. Jesus said it would be better for them "to have a great milestone fastened around [their] neck and to be sunk in the depth of the sea than to offend one of these little ones.[22.25]

God is not willing that anyone should perish eternally, so he sent his Son to save whoever would believe in him. But he also calls people to repent—be truly sorry and change their ways. The Holy Spirit will convict people of their sexual immorality. In response, it's our duty to not make excuses for the acceptance of sexual sin within the Christian lifestyle and community.

Sexual immorality is so contrary to God's way for us that the apostle Paul instructed the church at Corinth not to associate with anyone who calls himself a brother but is sexually immoral.[23.8] How much more, then, must you avoid a Christian organization or group that twists the original meaning of Scriptures and words in an attempt to elevate immorality to a righteous persecuted status? They may label anyone willing to speak the truth against unrighteousness hateful and a bigot. Don't let their corruption change what you know to be true.

Why would you forfeit your eternal life by accepting a teaching that seems heroic to practice sexual immorality? Their politically-correct argument condoning immorality will dissolve to terror in the day they answer to God for how they represented him during this life.

For example, some teachers use unrelated Scriptures and unsustainable, scriptural interpretations to condone sex outside of the marriage covenant. They did this in the days of the apostle Paul, too, but he advised the Christian community located in Ephesus to not be persuaded to believe that practitioners of sexual immorality will not receive the wrath of God. He warned the Ephesian church to let no one deceive them with vain or empty words claiming that the sexually immoral would still have an inheritance in the kingdom of God.[23.19] That warning is still true today.

There are many positions regarding the issue of sexual morality for Christians. Some try to mitigate the law of God upon the hearts of men and women. They become outspoken, activists seeking acceptance for sexual immorality, many even within a Christian context. Seeking to be validated as Christians and reverse the guilt from themselves, they blame the Christian voice of morality for judging them. Different Scriptures are used to support a variety of immoral beliefs, no matter how obscure the Scripture.

This confusion of interpretation can be avoided and an accurate understanding gained by listening to the same Spirit that inspired the men who originally wrote the Scriptures. When you reflect on the Scriptures and allow your teacher, the Holy Spirit, to instruct you, he leads you to be holy and to remain sexually pure. This means marriage is the only acceptable relationship for a sexual union. A committed but unmarried relationship does not qualify. Scriptural interpretations that allow for sex outside of the marriage covenant are like the vain and empty words Paul warns the Ephesians to be on guard against.[23.19]

Do not be among those who refuse the instruction of the Lord and seek exoneration for their sin. Genuine Christians who take a stand for righteousness may seem judgmental, but God requires his people to not compromise with sin, no matter how craftily it's packaged, and to speak the truth in love.

Some of the hottest battles and tests that Christians fighting to remain ready for the return of Jesus will face, now, and in the future, pertain to not accepting the moral indoctrination of the world and the pressure of political correctness and compromised Christianity.

If the culture and media make you feel guilty because of your God-given conscience and the Holy Spirit's conviction that sexual immorality is wrong, then make sure your principles are clearly defined. You will be pressured into accepting worldly views unless you trust God over man. God is bigger than the media's sexual indoctrination. His grace and favor rest upon the upright in heart.

As Christians, you are called to love your neighbor but never to lay aside the breastplate of righteousness. Lift up the banner of the holy and righteous God; he is worthy to be served in righteousness. Do not fear the voices that would replace dark for light and light for dark. God is ever with you, and the victory is the Lord's.

Will you accept the charade and propaganda refashioning sin and immorality into the norm making abstinence and purity derogatory? What principle will you determine in your heart? Can you reject indoctrination and believe in the morality God decrees? Your life in Christ depends upon it.

The body is for the Lord and the Lord for the body; it is not for sexual immorality.[23.10] Lust entices men and women to unlawfully and blasphemously use God's sacred gifts in harmful and desecrating ways. Lust is a spirit and a lord that demands subservience. It is a god that has power to enslave men and women in lifestyles of sexual immorality.

Sexual impurity alienates you from Jesus. It allows for the entrance of confusion and opens the heart's door to becoming subservient to lust. When this happens, the heart becomes more and more alienated from the Spirit of God. If immorality is continued and not repented of, you become disconnected from spiritual communion with Jesus and grieve and dishonor the Holy Spirit. God commands you to worship him alone in a chaste and holy life. You cannot serve God and the world, which contains the lord of lust, at the same time.

Lust says there is no deliverance for the addiction, but the Spirit of the Lord Jesus Christ says he is able to conquer and set the captive free. Prove this for yourself by repenting of the sexual sin in your life and allowing the Spirit of Jesus to set you free. The power of the Holy Spirit is wonderfully demonstrated in defeating the power of lust, requiring only a willing and trusting individual desirous to be set free. Close fellowship with Jesus through his Holy Spirit is the essential breath you breathe in living the spiritual life free from defilement.

You may be feeling conviction right now and the need to repent. If your thoughts or deeds have been indulging in immorality, make the decision to repent—ask for forgiveness and allow the Holy Spirit to help you turn away and walk free in purity. God is faithful to forgive us if we are faithful to repent and ask for forgiveness. There is no sexual sin God cannot forgive you of and cleanse you from if your heart is willing.

God wants you to come back to him. Do not say, "Maybe he'll accept someone else but not me." He has not given up on you and he wants you to change and turn to him. People who repent and seek God for change receive his power to grow stronger to resist the temptation and find enduring wholeness and purity. The power of God must be allowed to purify you of all secret sin and immorality within your life. He will set you free, help you resist temptations, and put your feet upon the path of holiness.

Freedom, healing, forgiveness, and cleansing from sexual sin is available through God's mercy. Listen to the conviction within you that lets you know you are grieving God and his statutes. Next, yield to this voice convicting you of sin and allow repentance to emerge within your heart. The blood of Jesus Christ cleanses you from all sin if you sincerely ask God to allow it to cleanse you. Be obedient to change when you feel the prompting of the Holy Spirit. Honestly turn from any sexual immorality in your life. Sincerely desire to change by the power of Christ. Though the degree of your addiction to lust might seem overwhelming and unconquerable, in Christ Jesus all things are possible.

If you are currently struggling with moral defilement, repent, and ask the Lord to forgive you and cleanse you from any sexual immorality and from defiling his temple. You can do this right this moment. Don't be like those who don't want to repent and let go of sin; this is a precarious position. Do not let it be yours. Turn from and break off the sinful conduct, people, places, and things related to temptation, immorality, and sexual brokenness.

After repenting and praying to be free, pray for the Lord to bring inner healing to your life. Ideally, in a Christian church, leaders can recommend Christian counselors experienced in counseling people who desire to be free of sexual sin. Pray for God to bring his faithful counselors into your life. If you are afflicted, consider joining a recovery group or attending a seminar with a solid Christian foundation that takes a scriptural and loving approach to recovery, strengthening the heart to be pure.

Prayer from Holy Spirit-filled counselors facilitates the ability of the Holy Spirit, the power of God, to bring healing to wounds and sexual brokenness from the past. This allows for a deep cleansing of lingering residues of hurt, shame, and disobedience that hinder spiritual growth, the ability to fully connect in relationships, and your freedom to fulfill God's purpose for your life.

Break the chains of bondage from memories, promiscuousness, perversion, and abuse by choosing to allow the love, power, and purity of the Holy Spirit to break off sin and bring restoration and healing. Freedom from the past and power to live pure in the present and future is available and is a reality in Jesus Christ.

Claim this freedom for yourself. Everyone has the opportunity to be forgiven, delivered from shame, and be set free to forgive their abusers and themselves. You can live a new life in Christ. We serve a merciful God who delights in saving the lost and healing the broken hearted.

To remain free, make walking in purity your priority. It is possible to return to a condition of spiritual chastity. Continue in the victory by listening to the conviction of the Holy Spirit upon your conscience and choosing purity. Choose to flee fornication and say, "no" to temptation in the power and grace of God. The Lord can return you to a child-like nature that walks in innocence and contains a mind dwelling on whatsoever is lovely and pure.

In this nature of innocence, you will understand and observe in your conduct that sex is reserved for the sacred covenant between married people. Marriage should be honored by all and the marriage bed kept pure because God will judge all the sexually immoral.[23,26] The Holy Spirit gives you the power to maintain purity while unmarried and the power for married Christians to maintain purity within marriage.

God's people, both unmarried and married, must practice self-control, and a life of purity in submission to the Holy Spirit. If you are a married Christian, your bed should be undefiled. If you are an unmarried Christian, surrender your body and will to the Lord. He will help empower you to purity so you can present yourself a chaste and pure bride or groom to the Christian husband or wife he gives you.

God provides this power because he is the one who created sexuality and the human reproductive system and the rules of appropriate conduct. Since you were originally created to be holy (before the fall of man), allow Jesus to change you into his stature and return you to that condition of holiness. The completion of that change will occur at his return, but your conduct until then needs to be performed in the right moral context to please him and to ensure you are ready.

The kingdom of God on earth is an emerging reality, and you are a citizen of a heavenly realm. This fellowship of blessing and communion with the Lord Jesus Christ is your daily bread. Jealously guard against any immoral intrusions that try to rob you of this life.

Resist temptation, repent, and wait on God to forgive and cleanse you when you have sinned or allowed lust to enter your life. Walking in purity enables the fruit and gifts of the Holy Spirit to flow freely in your life. Accept nothing less than this fruit and prioritize his love, joy, and peace to be a desired place you continually walk in.

Maintaining purity requires more than following religious rules. The evil things coming out of your heart are what defile you—"evil thoughts, murders, adulteries, sexual immorality."[23.33] Simply following a list of rules without predetermining in your heart to remain pure will not be enough. While rules have a good intention, without the Holy Spirit's guidance, they can end up ineffective at a crucial moment, or they can create rebellion against the rules. This backlash is a result of legislating morality without seeking to bring the heart into obedience to the Holy Spirit. Honor God and your body through choosing purity and abstaining from sex outside of marriage.

Your thought life is where the battle in your heart is won. The tempter, the Devil, tries to convince you that it is natural to sin sexually and that it's not something you can avoid. Lacking a life of sexual purity—including a clean thought life—and the chaste conduct of your body disconnects you from the Holy Spirit and eventually your authentic Christian life. As long as the enemy has access to your mind, he has access to your heart.

Allowing for unclean thoughts to persist and choosing to allow them to develop defiles you and corrupts your mind. This is the lust in the heart of a man that Jesus equated to committing adultery in the heart.[23.2]

The war is over your heart. Does your will enthrone Jesus Christ, the Son of God, or the devil, the god of this world and fallen man? Who do you allow to rule the throne of your heart? Discontinue any thoughts or activities that grieve the Holy Spirit within you. Choose life. Choose Jesus. He will help you, pick you up when you fall, forgive you, and give rest to your weary soul.

Abstinence before marriage, fidelity, and righteousness within marriage, avoidance of sensuous elements, and modesty in conduct are important components of a pure life. Applying discretion to everything you do is essential. How you conduct yourself, how you dress, the relations you have with the opposite sex, and your media choices should be individual decisions tempered by the leading of the Holy Spirit and your particular susceptibility to temptation.

Idle time can lead to temptation, too, so fill it with wholesome activity. What you choose to look at and think about needs to be determined with a moral perspective and the conviction of the Holy Spirit. Prayer and aligning yourself with godly counsel and community will help you establish the appropriate boundaries. The key is to allow the Holy Spirit to rule your heart and give you the ability to practice these things. Deep in your heart, hidden from observation, do not make an accord with sin.

One revealing test of the depth of your faith is your ability to reject the media's promotion of sex outside of marriage. Do not be bridled by secret sin in your own life. You need fortitude of mind and independent character to think for yourself and allow the voice of the Holy Spirit to contradict the world's message. Remember, we must fight for our inheritance and be overcomers. You must be confident in your faith in order to endure the ridicule, slander, persecution, and legal challenges of taking a stand for sexual purity.

Victory is yours when you learn to allow the Holy Spirit to help keep your thought life clean. Do as the apostle Paul advises: keep your mind on "whatsoever things are pure, whatsoever things are lovely, if there be any virtue, think on these things."[23.20] Joyous, at peace, and happy is your experience when you walk this way. Trust the Holy Spirit to give you victory over lust even if it seems impossible. God faithfully gives you his Spirit to help you live a fruitful life whether married, unmarried, widowed, or divorced. He never leaves or forsakes you.

Temptations, many of which appear when least expected, require pre-established integrity and boundaries in order to escape. The Holy Spirit is a gentle voice that warns you of the impending spiritual consequences. Sometimes the warnings of the Holy Spirit are dynamic, urgent, and immediate. Either way, it is a dangerous spiritual condition to ignore the voice of the Holy Spirit and quench the conviction.

Learn to flee temptations in thought and in actual situation just as Joseph fled the advances of Pharaoh's wife (Genesis 39:12). Resisting temptation often means distancing yourself from it. You will know by experience, by the Scripture, and by hearing the voice of the Holy Spirit the consequences of entertaining and giving in to the temptation.

Maintain healthy friendships and community and work on getting healing from emotional brokenness so you don't fall prey to enticement in your areas of weakness. Walk carefully and avoid the situations that are temptations to you. Have a godly and healthy awareness of sexuality, reserving sex for marriage. See people as God sees them, looking at their hearts. Value and respect others, determining not to defraud anyone sexually.

There is strength in knowing that the Holy Spirit always gives you the ability to overcome temptation and to remain pure.[22.8] It's not within your own power to maintain the purity that Jesus desires for you to walk in because the heart of man is essentially prone to wickedness. Without the power of the Holy Spirit, people encounter temptations that seemingly cannot be resisted. For example, the Devil tries to gain a foothold in your life by taking advantage of weaknesses like loneliness and addiction. Resisting during these times of vulnerability may seem impossible.

When temptations like these arise, remember what to do: take your eyes and thoughts off of the temptation and turn to and wait on the Lord. When the Holy Spirit breaks in and rescues you, the temptation flees. This prayerful weapon of resistance is a key to a pure thought life, which is the foundation for walking in sexual purity. Remember, it's not a sin to be tempted; it is a sin to yield to the temptation, to not stop the development of the thought, and to commit the deed.

You will never be tempted beyond what you are capable of withstanding.[22.8] The Lord always provides a way of escape. However, your own free will can easily be tempted away from the way of escape. The further away you are allured, the narrower the door of escape becomes. It, then, becomes increasingly harder to resist or escape and may result in a degree of spiritual, emotional, and physical consequences.

Fleeing fornication includes fleeing situations, thoughts, and environments. It is imperative, then, to search your heart and see if you believe the Scriptures and the witness of the Holy Spirit regarding sexual immorality. Once you have the principle of purity established within your heart, you can diligently look to the Holy Spirit to deliver you from temptation. Maintain a constant vigilance to not grow slothful or complacent in guarding your purity.

Remember that no matter what level of Christian maturity you have obtained, you are susceptible to the temptation of sexual immorality when you least expect it. You need the Holy Spirit for discernment and to warn you of potential compromising situations. The heart that is ready for the return of the Lord is the one that trusts and waits upon the Holy Spirit to deliver it from temptation. Put on the breastplate of righteousness and make your stand for righteousness.

To summarize, God desires you to be sexually pure. When you are faithful to confess your sins, God is faithful to forgive you. Repenting of sexual immorality is the first step toward purity. Trust that God is strong enough to give you what you need to be free of lust and servitude to sexual sin.

The next step is stopping and avoiding the former lusts and sin. At the same time, seek godly mentors and counselors who will help you make wise choices and pray for you. Christian recovery programs can equip you with tools that will help you stay pure.

Finally, inner healing reaches down to the roots of your wounds and sins and brings you into a deep cleansing by the blood of Jesus. It is the blood of Jesus that saves, heals, and delivers you. Don't regard it lightly or turn from its cleansing and redeeming power. Call upon it to refute the allure of lust and provide cleansing to a repentant heart.

A repentant heart and purity unto the Lord is the way of peace. When a man or woman walks in sexual purity before the Lord, their ways are pleasing unto him. The Lord honors the sacrifice of a heart entrusted to him and kept pure for his glory. He desires this because he is holy and his spiritual blessing pours out upon the upright in heart. Godly love, joy, and peace from the heavenly Father, which the sexually pure enjoy, are something the immoral world is not acquainted with. The Lord delights in the pure and innocent heart, and he bountifully extends his favor upon those hearts. Regardless of outward temptations and trials, the pure in heart enjoy the ever-present peace and joy of the Lord.

Blessed be the name of the Lord; and holy is the Lord our God for he has redeemed us with the precious blood of his dear Son and caused us to be called his very own sons and daughters. The glory that awaits those who have been cleansed and walk free is not seen or fathomed, but we know that the pure in heart shall see God.

Thank you, Jesus, for this great gift of salvation and freedom, our pearl without price. Let your Spirit and love rule upon the thrones of our hearts so that we are ready to see you when you appear.

SUMMARY POINTS

- » It is God's will for you to be sexually pure.
- » The Holy Spirit empowers you to maintain sexual purity.
- » Love flows freely through the morally pure person.
- » The sexually impure will lose their salvation if unrepentant.
- » Unhealed relational wounds can cause sexual misconduct.

- » Prioritize God's will for you over society's cultural and media indoctrination.
- » Sexual immorality brings you into slavery to the god of lust.
- » Jesus will forgive and restore the sexually immoral who sincerely repent.
- » It's not a sin to be tempted. The Holy Spirit rises and defeats the temptation and addiction independent of your own strength.
- » Pursuing purity allows you to return to and maintain a spirit of chasteness.
- » The fruit of peace and joy and the blessing of the Lord are with the sexually pure.
- » Sex is a sacred use of the body that is to be reserved for the sacred covenant of marriage between a man and a woman.
- » Repent, receive healing, and practice purity in making your heart ready for the return of Jesus.
- » Become versed in the Scriptures in Reference 23 of Part V, and return to them frequently for instruction.

CHAPTER 17

Forgive Everyone Always

The heart adorned with the sweet fragrance of forgiveness is the heart free to grow into the fullness of the stature of Christ. The yoke of the Savior resplendent in forgiveness provides rest to the weary soul of the oppressed.

Choose life. Choose to forgive and receive the mercy poured out by the Holy Spirit. He empowers you to forgive those who sin against you and to reconcile with brothers and sisters. Experience for yourself that the arm of the Lord will sustain you, forgive you, and reward you as you forgive all of your enemies and those who have wronged you.

Feel how bitterness, revenge, debt, and anger are dissolved from their claims against your body and heart as you bless those who have treated you wrongly.[24.5] Extending forgiveness allows you to make your home in the joyous dwelling of the redeemed surrounded with the magnificent presence of the Lord.

Choosing not to forgive makes you unprepared for the return of Jesus. Bitterness and the absence of joy are the fruit of an unforgiving heart. But your brokenness is healed and sins are forgiven as you forgive those who have sinned against you. The Holy Spirit will protect you from harm's way, help you establish protective boundaries, and provide you with healing and the heart to forgive others.

There is a spirit of reconciliation that God can provide. By his mercy, a power to love and forgive can be gifted to you, enabling a compassion and spirit of forgiveness that breaks the yoke of the sins and violations committed against you. You can learn to discern the timing and presence of this gift by listening to the Holy Spirit. He creates within you a conviction, compassion, and a sense of urgency over the situation. This signals that his power is available and that now is the time to forgive and/or ask for forgiveness.

It is vitally important to use this powerful gift because if you don't forgive your brothers and sisters on earth, your Father in heaven will not forgive you.[24.2] The spirit of reconciliation is a gift from the Lord. Applying it brings healing and the experience of a fountain of peace that increases with no end.

Forgiveness sometimes comes in stages as the Holy Spirit continues to work and heal your heart. Be careful not to restrict the full work of forgiving or that you choose to allow elements of bitterness to remain. For instance, have you said in your heart that you forgive someone but secretly look for God's judgment and punishment to come upon him or her?

Jesus said to bless those who despitefully treat us. Speak in love to those who mistreat you, and pray for them. Offer your cheek and your back, yet inform the transgressor in truth of any impropriety against you.

Forgiveness relinquishes the right to get even and it reprieves the debtor from owing you an apology. It dissolves a spirit of revenge and pardons the violator. It puts God in control of convicting the violator to make restitution and to repent. When you sincerely forgive, you are set free. This allows you to complete your healing from trauma, wounds, and offenses you have endured. You are free to go on and flourish, bearing fruit for the glory of God.

Mending offenses between people is part of the Christian walk. Jesus's great work is to reconcile you to God, and he asks you to reconcile with your neighbor. He wants you to be free of roots of bitterness and unforgiveness that clog the flow of his love and make you sick in spirit and in body. Human nature demands retribution, but Jesus teaches us to love and do good to our enemies.

Courageously open in abundance the flow of God's blessing by receiving his mercy to reconcile with those you are at enmity with. Start with forgiving your close family and friends. Forgive and release yourself and those who have hurt or wronged you. Take hold of the mercy of Christ and allow the Holy Spirit to move and direct you in his anointing of reconciliation. Dwell in Christ's love and praise him for pouring out his blessing of being able to forgive and experience reconciliation. Become like the lamb and let the true Shepherd lead your heart into pastures of love where mercy to forgive and reconcile grow in abundance.

Blessed are the peacemakers for they will be called the sons of God (Matthew 5:9). The favor of God rains down on your soul in a sweet presence of peace speaking "well done" to your obedient heart for moving in his anointing of forgiveness and reconciliation. He will put the will and courage in your heart if you let his Spirit break up the hardened places. Be alert to follow his promptings, for he sets and opens the time and moments. Then, in obedience, take the action to extend forgiveness and move to reconcile in sincerity.

Ask those you have offended to forgive you. In mercy go forth to minister in love and set right that which was captive by enmity. The Lord will be your strength and courage; you need not fear what man can further do to you. His love, in the power of forgiveness ordered by his Spirit, will accomplish its purpose and not come back void. All things must bow to his love.

Watch for indications of the Lord's moving to empower you to forgive and or to reconcile with people. You may be convicted by prompting of the Holy Spirit, words and testimonies from other, and things you read. Conviction begins to loosen the hard soil of your heart and sows compassion, love, and the desire to mend situations. The bitterness, anger, desire for revenge, and feelings of entitlement after being wronged give way to forgiveness and helps you to realize your own brokenness and contribution to the strained relationship.

When you follow the Spirit's prompting, fear of man will be surpassed by the urgency of obedience to move in the Lord's timing. You are able to forgive those who have sinned against you without demanding retribution. The beautiful peace of reconciliation is released as you go to your brother or sister in the humility of Jesus and give with no demands to receive forgiveness. Bars of impenetrable iron suddenly break and captive hearts are set free. Mothers, fathers, sons, daughters, friends, former spouses, colleagues, and enemies are reconciled. The love and peace of Jesus are over everyone when you sincerely desire blessing for those who have hurt you.

Reconciliation creates a new relationship by adding or restoring Christ's love and forgiveness to your relationship with another human being. Pray a sincere blessing unconditionally to everyone within the hurtful situation. Mothers and fathers, reconcile to children. Men and women, forgive former spouses. Sons and daughters, reconcile to parents. Friends, forgive friends. Let the power of the Lord be over all. Establishing appropriate boundaries through love and in integrity expose any continuing wrongs.

Boundaries remove you from harm's way and protect you from further physical and emotional harm. They allow you to admit and speak to the offender the truth about the offenses in love, when it is appropriate. Christian counselors and books can help you further understand and apply boundaries in your life.

When you ask for, receive, and extend forgiveness and reconciliation, your life will experience a new release for ministry, relationships, and fellowship with the Lord. In the Lord's kingdom, spiritual Zion, there is no enmity, no more pain or defrauding, wrong or violence. All bow and sit in his kingdom in the bond of everlasting peace.

Central to your life in Jesus and preparation for his return is forgiving all who have sinned against you and sincerely asking those you have hurt if they will forgive you. Jesus clearly teaches that we must forgive those who have sinned against us even as our Father in heaven has forgiven us; but if we choose not to forgive, our Father in heaven will not forgive us.[24.4]

Forgiveness doesn't require you to remain silent or accept further violation, abuse, or harmful conduct. Be aware of the Lord's timing for you to forgive and examine your motives for taking time to forgive. For instance, are you allowing time for forgiveness and healing? Or are you unwilling to let go and forgive? It's a common mistake to delay forgiveness because your will doesn't want to let go of the offense even though your heart is ready.

When you repent in godly sorrow for grieving the Holy Spirit with the offenses you have committed, the Lord will forgive you. Laying aside all enmity and bitterness, repenting of your contribution and freely forgiving others is necessary for you to receive his forgiveness and prepares you for the return of Jesus.

SUMMARY POINTS

» Forgiveness is a key component of your life in Christ.

» The power of God gives you grace to forgive when in the natural it seems impossible. It delivers you from the destructive effects of unforgiveness.

» Emotional and physical sicknesses can have roots in unforgiveness.

» Carrying unforgiveness is a burden to the soul.

- » The ability to minister and love fully is restricted by unforgiveness.
- » Relationships are greatly strained and broken by unforgiveness.
- » Your own forgiveness from God can be contingent on your forgiveness of others.
- » Forgiveness is not a denial of the hurt you feel or the transgression perpetrated against you.
- » Establishing appropriate boundaries protects you against further violations and offenses and makes it safe to forgive.
- » The Holy Spirit helps you genuinely forgive from the depths of your heart.
- » An anointing of power to forgive is available from Jesus. It uproots bitterness and delivers you from unforgiveness.
- » The redeemed children of God live with no enmity; their hearts are ready for the return of Jesus.

CHAPTER 18

Embrace Emotional Healing

Our lives on this fallen earth endure a barrage of sin, tragedy, and offenses that wound the heart and soul, affecting our identity and experience of love. Our own sins defile the temple of God and produce emotional consequences. These often hidden wounds and traumas can hinder fulfilled relationships with others and with God. In turn, this also slows or prevents growing in the stature of Christ. Peace with oneself can seem elusive, but Jesus is the remedy calling all who are weary and heavy laden to take his yoke upon them and find rest.[15.1]

In this imperfect world, emotional wounds can be inflicted from a variety of sources. People who are hurt and wounded themselves often perpetrate and hurt others. Your parents, for instance, may have done the best they could within their own imperfect conditions, but they still may have been unable to provide you with the entirety of love, acceptance, discipline, and self-esteem that you needed. Sometimes their parenting failures are much worse.

Traumas, abuses, and relational dysfunction can deeply wound your heart and distort the flow of love in your life. For example, trusted friends, authority figures, loved ones, and spiritual leaders can betray and violate your trust. But there is a friend you can trust unequivocally who will never leave you or forsake you—Jesus Christ. He will heal you and set you free.

When you are born again, you don't arrive at the destination but begin the journey of growing into the full stature of Christ. You make significant advancements on this path as you repent of sin and are healed from its consequences, from inner wounds, and from dysfunctional behavior.

Inward healing and the increase of godly emotional health continues the sanctification process (growing into the fullness of the stature of Christ). This increased emotional health guards against religious performance, projecting brokenness onto others, and camouflaging unhealed inner wounds. Emotional healing and health allows for advancement in preparing for the return of Jesus

Life's blows wound you, and you carry your sins as burdens of guilt and shame. But God's power redeems and turns ashes into beauty. You can sit at the feet of the Master and let your tears flow freely on him as the woman did at the home of Simon the Pharisee when Jesus had dinner there. Because of her sincere repentance, even this notorious sinner's transgressions were forgiven. She worshiped the Savior for the gift of setting her free with his eternal ransom, by pouring out the perfume and alabaster box of her heart onto him. She adored Jesus and loved much because, as Scripture declares, "He who is forgiven little, loves little."[24.6] You, too, can safely pour out the perfume of your heart upon a receptive Savior.

The most enduring and powerful inward healing comes from a direct encounter with the power of Jesus. His people, ministers, and counselors of righteousness also are facilitators in helping create an environment where the love and power of Christ can freely flow. In these setting of prayer and inner healing, you can be freed of traumatizing memories and bitterness and be empowered to forgive those who have offended you. The healing of these wounds frees you from harassing spirits because they have no foothold.

Like a physician's prescription can ward off disease, so can inner healing, prayer, and counseling in a Christian context provide medicine to your heart to help you walk in the light. The experience and knowledge exercised in counseling, primarily when applied from a foundation of a true Christian perspective, is profitable in bringing relief, growth, healing, and developing a greater fulfillment of your life's destiny.

Search for counselors and ministers that can help you in your Christian growth. As you search, pray for the Holy Spirit's faithful witness and gifts of discernment to allow you, Christ's child, to test, prove, embrace, or avoid ungodly counsel, including substituting religious characteristics for the fruit of the Spirit. Using religion to cover wounds can happen subtly, deep within your inner person, when you allow religion to substitute for the work of the Holy Spirit to bring healing and life.

As you tenderly come to the Lord for healing, religious idolatry can develop from relying on a form of godliness that denies God's power. For instance, maintaining strict rituals but refusing to forgive and be freed of bitterness can allow the fallen nature to grow back under the disguise of religious attributes. Be on guard against this religiosity creeping into your life. Love and Christ's leading help guard you against religious narrowness and dogma. It allows you to derive your Christian identity from a relationship with Jesus and the fruit it produces.

Some Christians criticize Christian counseling and therapy even though the goal is to remedy unhealthy behavior and emotional wounds. Often, these critics are people and religious systems in their own broken condition. They might be trying to protect themselves from the unpleasant task of crucifying the flesh, repenting, and dealing with their ungodly dysfunction.

Religious organizations can also oppose Christian therapy and counseling because of its similarities to psychology, which has non-Christian origins. In addition, they don't recognize the fruit and positive results of Christian counseling when guided by the Holy Spirit and Scriptures.

However, inner freedom is outward freedom. If the Son sets you free, you are free indeed. Jesus heals the brokenhearted and binds up their wounds. He does it for adults; and never forget, he especially does it for the little children.

Even so, it's surprising that counseling experiences providing so many people with emotional freedom and a closer relationship with Christ are criticized so negatively. This spirit of criticism can be compared to the indignation directed at Jesus for the healing he did on the Sabbath.

It is important for you, the child of God, to discern and identify godly emotional healing that promotes growth in Christ's love. The Holy Spirit helps you identify practices contrary to sound doctrine, so you can avoid them. Wise personal boundaries resulting from mature and healthy emotional healing and growth are your best allies for recognizing and keeping out contrary teaching, religiosity, and intrusions from the world.

Confiding in other Christians and receiving wise counsel is biblical and desirable but must be chosen wisely. Abuses such as gossip and unsound advice are the consequences of not choosing carefully who you confide and seek council from. The flesh of friends and counselors has its own motives. You must discern and guard from placing too much confidentiality in people who are immature, worldly, and potentially unwilling to work on their own emotional health. However, mature and godly people with counseling ministries and Christian professionals can be used by God in your life to assist you in being healed in heart and mind and becoming emotionally and relationally healthier.

Participation in small groups for recovery can be healing, too. Reflecting on your behavior in a small group setting can provide you with insight into your relational conduct in everyday life. For example, you might realize you are often angry and controlling while in the group setting. That reveals areas of healing that you need to work on.

While in the group, also be aware if you are able to maintain your own boundaries with unhealthy people, edify the group, overlook offenses, and seek the welfare of all. With an attitude and willingness to grow in the love of Christ, examining how you relate to others while you are participating in a small group settings can result in positive changes that establish more appropriate boundaries and enlarged compassion for others. Pay attention to your conduct while participating in small groups and ask the Lord to show you where you can make changes.

In addition to Christian therapy and small groups, godly music is a time-honored, safe way to experience emotional healing. Available in a variety of songs and styles, worship music gives glory to God through praise in song.

Engaging in live worship in the corporate setting of a church community can be very healing and restorative no matter what your emotional condition is. The signature of many revivals and church movements has been the fresh music honoring Jesus that helps people enter into the presence of the Holy Spirit and worship the Lord. Playing worship music in your home or other settings can help in much the same way and it creates a healthier atmosphere than listening to worldly media.

The Holy Spirit can also create remarkable windows for inner and emotional healing through revivals, which are periods of intense outpouring of the Holy Spirit. Rest assured, the shaking, rolling, quaking, shouting, falling down, speaking in tongues, and numerous other *"phenomena"* unique to revivals and renewals are effecting transformation of the inner man through significant mental, emotional, and spiritual healing.

Accelerated healing in this atmosphere can be unrivaled. Both modern revival participants and those from the past testify to the freedom experienced from the power of God during these meetings.

The outward manifestations people experience during an outpouring of the Holy Spirit can signify an internal plowing up of sin and wounds accompanied by healing and cleansing of hurts, shame, fear, and addictions. They can also simply be the result of a personal encounter of the Holy Spirit and genuine renewal of peace and love for God and others.

It may be difficult to distinguish between a genuine and self-imposed manifestation of the Holy Spirit. But through experience and discernment, you can recognize the genuine manifestations of the Holy Spirit even if you don't understand them. This includes discerning when someone is in the spirit while ministering or just acting like it.

Though the phenomena unique to revivals may seem strange or undignified, remember that the wisdom of God is foolishness to man. He confounds the wise and tests the hearts of all men and women.

Historically, and as seen throughout the narrative in the book of Acts, a mighty outpouring of the Holy Spirit usually is the catalyst for revivals. This power of God destroys the work of the Devil and brings people into salvation and healing through Jesus Christ.

Critics of revivals and the unusual manifestations that result from them have a hard time denying the fruit in the lives touched by the power of the Holy Spirit during these events. The fruits for example include salvation, repentance, physical and emotional healing, restored marriages, forgiveness, joy, closer connection with Jesus, and new zeal and energy for ministry. Yes, fanatics will show up, but the majority of people attending are average people who are thirsty for more of God, the kind you would want as your neighbors.

Since it's difficult to honestly criticize the people who attend revivals, the detractors (usually religious and claiming to be Christian) criticize the revival leaders and the manifestations of the Spirit in the people. The criticism traditionally focuses on specific incidents, quotes, or terminology, distorting and amplifying them into issues essentially insignificant in order to slander the revival. Neither revivals nor their leaders are perfect, but the Holy Spirit is perfect. Detractors are not to be feared no matter how religious they appear to be or how eloquently they speak.

You will know if a revival or a manifestation of the Spirit is not of God because the Holy Spirit will give you a witness. This can be the unique way God speaks to you regarding a situation that your natural eye cannot accurately discern. For instance you normally may never consider attending a revival, but the Holy Spirit brings it to your attention and compels you to go.

When it is not of God, the Holy Spirit will show you if the actions and teachings are of the flesh or the Devil. Fear God. Fear offending his Holy Spirit—not man. Enjoy all God has for his children, and allow the Son to set you free with his power.

Books have been written, and more are sure to come, that warn Christians about the undignified behavior at a revival meeting, (like laying on the floor or shaking). These authors try to remove the splinter from the eye of the revival while maintaining and promoting heavy logs of religiosity. The Holy Spirit will take care of error. God's people can tell what is real or not.

Why should someone getting healed physically and emotionally by the power of God and visibly shaking because of it be offensive to religious critics while the hysteria of a sporting event or rock concert are considered acceptable? Don't be on the criticizing end of something God is doing because you don't understand it or have no precedent for it. Love is the prevailing attribute.

Investigate for yourself Christian books and counselors addressing emotional and inner healing. These words of counsel can be beneficial to you even if you are emotionally healthy. It can help you recognize emotional barriers to your capacity to continue to develop in the fruit of the Holy Spirit. Take steps to address and overcome them.

Prayer can help you to be delivered and set free from bitterness, unhealed memories and unforgiveness. Avoid the conditions that lead to religious idolatry, fear of man, pride, and performance for acceptance. Root causes of addictions can be healed and holiness and purity can be further enabled through emotional healing. Cleaning up the inward plate is more important than the outward appearance and prepares you for the return of Jesus.

SUMMARY POINTS

- » Emotional scars and wounds are sometimes difficult to detect and can impede one's growth into the likeness of Christ.
- » Inner healing helps guard against substituting religious attributes to mask unhealed inner wounds and willful assertions that are contrary to God.
- » Your relationships become more respectful and genuine as you grow emotionally. You stop projecting your own anger and hurts onto others.
- » Your principles and personal integrity are realized more consistently as your emotional health increases.
- » Your personal boundaries and your respect of others' boundaries become healthier and appropriately maintained.
- » Healing of inner wounds brings deliverance from harassing spirits associated with them.
- » Christian therapy and counseling should provide a confidential accountability and a safe environment for healing.
- » Worship music often facilitates healing and intimacy in your relationship with Christ.
- » Revivals and renewals provide profound windows for powerful, emotional-healing encounters.

- » Emotional healing promotes your growth in Christian maturity and sanctification and helps sharpen your discernment.
- » Emotional healing promotes your ability to release forgiveness toward others and yourself and frees you from bitterness.
- » Emotional healing expands your capacity to extend love and receive love and helps you prepare you for the return of Jesus.

CHAPTER 19

Follow the Shepherd

Everyone who has confessed belief in Jesus Christ and received his Spirit within their heart is a member of his family. Jesus is the Shepherd of this diverse family made up of people from every race, culture, and locality.[27.4] The hierarchy structure places Jesus as the head and Shepherd with his believers as equal brothers and sisters to each other.

Different spiritual gifts and ministerial callings create positions of service within this body of believers. While still equal to one another, Christians respectfully submit to leaders who hold the authority of spiritual office, which is to serve not lord over the sheep. These leaders have spiritual gifts that help them fulfill their calling, but Jesus is always the head and leader of your life. When you allow a man or woman to interfere with or assume this role, you can fall into idolatry toward man and infidelity to Jesus. Spiritual abuse occurs when people, creeds, or organizations instead of Jesus and his Holy Spirit control your life religiously.

Your heart is safe when you completely trust in and surrender to the Shepherd of your soul while also giving and receiving love in fellowship with brothers and sisters in Christ.

A community of believers, such as a church, is healthy when its members have personal relationships with Jesus and are united in love for each other. They share experiences of his Spirit in worship, meeting, fellowship, and ministry to those in need. It isn't healthy when performance requirements, dictatorial submission to a leader, organization, denomination, or fear of man exist in the community.

Jesus is the leader of the family and the Shepherd who watches over his flock. It is comforting to know that someone has your best interest at heart—someone who will never fail you. He is a benefactor you can trust with your entire heart. Time and again, Jesus proves himself the faithful and good Shepherd of your soul. His desire is for you to grow up into the fullness of his likeness. Jesus knows you have the dependency that sheep do, and he can relate to all of your fears and pain and sorrow.[27.6] He brings emotional and spiritual rest to his flock. He helps you during life's difficulties and tragedies.

Jesus protects you, his sheep, from wolves and other dangers. He came and destroyed the works of the Devil, and he protects you from the Devil's attacks. The Shepherd keeps you safe from the roaring lion's assaults. Though you endure trials and the Devil seeks to destroy you, he can never break into your soul to defile and ravage you when Christ is your Shepherd. Jesus is your true Savior; he is not a hireling that would flee at the presence of danger. He is jealous for all of his sheep and will seek out the lost one to bring him or her back to the sheepfold.

Loved ones may have betrayed you, but Jesus is not like them. He can be trusted in every circumstance, even with your soul. He invites you to see that he is true. He will never leave you or forsake you, and nothing on earth can separate you from his love and oversight. Jesus understands that you might be afraid to trust him, especially if you have been hurt by a parent, loved one, or authority figure. The Holy Spirit heals you of these wounds and allows you to deepen your trust in Jesus. He gives you the courage to establish boundaries against the abusers and develop the heart to forgive. As your will is relinquished, you learn to trust in Jesus, the Shepherd, to lead you and keep you safe. Your trials mature you and deepen your confidence in Him.

Jesus establishes men and women with his heart to minister to and help shepherd his flock. The Holy Spirit calls forth these men and women in ministry capacities; the Bible refers to them as pastors, teachers, apostles, elders, and prophets.[27.5] These ministers may or may not be formally designated with these titles. The qualifier is the Holy Spirit, a good report, and seasoned obedience within the community of Christ.

In these capacities, men and women who have the heart of the true Shepherd can effectively lead, teach, council, and provide direction for individuals and church communities. These gifted members of the body are a blessing to the sheep. They are trustworthy and called by the good Shepherd; they are not hireling that will betray the flock. Hirelings are primarily motivated by worldly gain—monetary and status rewards, which are a sign they don't have a genuine calling or have possibly strayed from the truth.

The flock is a diverse community of equality containing a variety of gifts, callings, capacities, and authority. All have their place and are equal components of the many parts of the body of Christ. You are a part of the family and body of Christ—brothers, sisters, and friends—with no hierarchy that would bring control, subservience, and idolatry to the flock.[27.11]

Jesus's sheep, the body of believers, gather together for Church.[27.8] *Church* can refer to the church building, the church service, or the church members. Revival meetings can be a different kind of gathering than a church gathering because many people come who are not believers nor part of a community of Christians.

Often believers do come; and so, revival meetings can also be called *renewal* meetings in which seasoned Christians gather in a revival-like atmosphere for renewing, deepening, and refreshing of being filled with the Holy Spirit.

Christians need this fellowship of a church community of believers who assemble together for worship and ministry. The good Shepherd leads his flock, and the flock is healthy when it is together. It can be difficult, though, to find assemblies where the Holy Spirit shepherds the community and the sheep experience the love of the good Shepherd in their midst and in one another. You have to depend on your Shepherd to lead you and establish you into community. There are no perfect ones. Allow him to direct you to a church. It may differ from your preferences, but it will be where he wants you.

The Holy Spirit creates the bond of love in which the sheep fellowship and relate to one another. When you flow in the love of the Holy Spirit, you have a love and acceptance for one another. When you gossip or are divisive, you are checked within your conscience. Sometimes you don't feel worthy of your fellow Christians' love and so you hide from it behind works.

It can be awkward and frightening to love one another within a community because the possibility for pain exists. Praying for discernment and defining personal boundaries allow you to recognize emotionally unsafe people and decide the extent of closeness you want to develop. He will protect you from harmful people and systems and lead you elsewhere, if needed. You can have peace and grace to not be offended if you feel slighted or unrecognized within the flock because you know that the Shepherd always cares. He gives you a forgiving and tolerant heart.

This bond of love keeps no record of wrongs and is a wonderful thing to experience within a fellowship. It's a delicate balance for the elders and pastors to oversee this love and keep down domineering, backbiting, and elitism. Healthy leaders guard against and diminish the politics that creep in and quench the work of the Spirit.

Instead of seeking advancement or being critical of others, learn to sense areas the Holy Spirit would like you to serve and minister in. Don't be afraid or offended to minister in obscure and hidden ways. God can elevate you in due time. As long as you are in obedience, you will be contented and the flock will benefit. If you want to be first in God's kingdom, become a servant to all.

The natural inclination of the fallen nature of man is to idolize a person or belief system. The flesh tends to want someone else to be their spiritual mediator. This concedes a personal and spiritual power to potentially abusive spiritual leaders who are not led by the Holy Spirit. When this happens, the fallen nature can stay unchanged with an unsubmitted will to Jesus. But Jesus calls you to take his yoke and to follow him, the Shepherd.

Once you are able to discern the Shepherd's voice, you are able to submit to men and women ministers and leaders who are full of the Holy Spirit while always maintaining your allegiance to Jesus. Submitting to authority doesn't mean allowing yourself to be controlled, pressured financially, or intimidated. It means that you accept and support those who have been called by the Holy Spirit to exercise the office and ministry they are responsible for. If you have a disagreement or need to confront someone you can do it according to the policy of the particular assembly.

Unbelief says you cannot discern the Shepherd's voice for yourself. An unbelieving heart can be unwilling to submit to the changing power of the blood of Jesus and, therefore, it will not be able to hear the Holy Spirit.

Refusing to obey the Holy Spirit is refusing to follow the Shepherd Jesus. When you do not obey the inner leading of the Holy Spirit, you are refusing the guidance of your Shepherd and opening your ears to the hireling's directions. The carnal nature will follow a personality or a religious organization, but it will not submit to the Holy Spirit. This is why you must crucify the flesh, bringing your heart and soul into obedience to the Holy Spirit, to Jesus your Shepherd.

Isolation from the flock is unhealthy. Sheep are created to be in community, and when you follow a path that separates you from other Christians, you are susceptible to increased temptation. The Shepherd's voice leads you into love and fellowship with one another, not into isolation or exclusivity. Finding this community often is difficult, but the Shepherd will always sustain you.

Happy are the sheep who know and follow the Shepherd's voice. Hearing and obeying the voice of Jesus through his Holy Spirit brings contentment, rest, peace, and fulfillment to the believer. When you keep your eyes on him and obey his commands, which are easy to bear, you experience happiness.

Your allegiance to Jesus surpasses a commitment or a dependency upon a person. Jesus gives you the power to trust him above any person and makes you able to discern if you are letting someone or something become an idol and control you. Once you are hearing and obeying the Shepherd's voice, you are able to discern God's ministers from self-serving ones.

The ministers Jesus establishes help the sheep better hear and obey the one true Shepherd, Jesus. They teach and lead the sheep to hear and discern Jesus's voice for themselves.

Community within the flock of Jesus is the rightful heritage of the sheep. From the beginning of the New Testament until now, believers have gathered together for fellowship and worship. You receive love and refreshment in church gatherings and build up one another in love. The Spirit of the Lord is amplified and the experience of his presence shared among those gathered together in his name. Sheep are better off when they stay together.

Following and surrendering to your Shepherd, Jesus, prepares your heart for his return. With a surrendered heart, you will be able to listen to the prompting and guidance of his Holy Spirit. By hearing his voice and obeying it, your heart is sensitive to and ready for his appearance.

SUMMARY POINTS

» Jesus is the head of your religion and salvation; his people share equal status possessing different gifts, authority, and ministries.

» Jesus is your high priest, abolishing a hierarchy among men and women and establishing all of his saved children as spiritual priests.

» You have a personal relationship with Jesus, your Shepherd without man as mediator.

» You experience Jesus in the community of believers who are all one in him.

» You are members of the great Shepherd's flock led by Jesus, the Shepherd of your soul.

» You are to acknowledge genuine spiritual authority, pastors, and leaders.

» Your relationship with Jesus is direct through his Holy Spirit, not through someone else. His ministers only teach, shepherd, and direct you to experience Jesus in this way.

» Your relationships flow from a surrender and allegiance to Jesus and not from a dependency on man.

» God designed you to be in community with believers, but you must be on guard against isolation or elitism within the church body.

» Elitism and cliques within a church community grieve the Holy Spirit. Do not participate in them.

- » Finding authentic churches can be difficult, but Jesus will always be with you and minister to you even if a local flock is not available.

- » The presence and spirit of Christ's love is the bond of your fellowship in church communities not performance, rules, mandates, or rituals.

- » Members of Jesus's sheepfold prepare and maintain readiness for his return.

CHAPTER 20

OBEY GOD IN SPIRIT AND IN TRUTH

God, who is a Spirit, requires you to worship him in Spirit and in truth.[31.4] Jesus gives us his Holy Spirit, the Comforter, who leads us and guides us into this truth.[31.6] This gift from God, which Jesus made available to everyone, is the way Jesus leads us in his will and connects us with himself.

The characteristics of the Holy Spirit in your life are love, joy, peace, goodness, kindness, faithfulness, and patience.[32.12] Disobedience and rebellion are the bane of mankind's relation with the Lord. Lack of obedience disenfranchises your inheritance as a joint heir with Christ. Rebellion dulls your heart and mind, resulting in a state of slumber unprepared for the return of Jesus. But the Holy Spirit instructs you to obey Jesus and his commands and disciplines you when you are stubborn and disobedient. It's better to be obedient than experience the pain and troubles that develop from disobedience.

You learn to obey and be led by the Lord by learning to experience and follow this Counselor or Comforter. Ignoring the Holy Spirit or quenching his operation in your life results in growing hardened to his presence so that you continue to live in the fallen nature of the flesh and not in the will of God. It can also cause you to emphasize religious practices that don't save the soul but, instead, appeal to the flesh without convicting it toward repentance. This can make you a slave to people.

The Holy Spirit is a wonderful gift to a fallen humanity, much better than silver or gold.[31.1] When you listen to and obey the Holy Spirit, the Lord adorns your life with the fruit of the Holy Spirit and he equips you for service. The Holy Spirit teaches you and helps you understand God's ways and his Scriptures. "The wind blows wherever it pleases. You hear its sound, but you cannot tell where it comes from or where it is going. So it is with everyone born of the Spirit."[31.3] If you have never been filled with the Holy Spirit, ask Jesus right now to fill you with his Spirit.

When you receive his Spirit, you will be able to understand the Scriptures, receive teaching from others, and conduct your life through a relationship with the Spirit. The Holy Spirit also conducts a two-way exchange of Jesus's love and your love. In this way, Christianity is bidirectional—love coming from the Father to you and your love extending back to him. This bidirectional exchange of love is a process of obedience and reliance upon Jesus.

Christianity is distinguished by its reliance on the supernatural guidance of the Holy Spirit. While he was on this earth, Jesus devoted considerable instruction concerning the Holy Spirit. He taught how God's redeeming graciousness will not deny you the gift of his Spirit if you ask him.[31.1] The Holy Spirit is what changes you into the likeness of Jesus and works within you to transform the inner man to be like him. As you become like Christ, you evidence the fruit of the Holy Spirit and grow into the fullness of the stature of Christ. The Spirit and power of Jesus moves through the body of Christ, in ministry and gifting, which helps you grow into his image.

There's a war over your growth into this image. The fallen nature of humanity resists the Holy Spirit and the Holy Spirit fights against the fallen condition—the spirit of the flesh. For people who are born again by the blood of Jesus, his Spirit consistently works through them. Unfortunately many religious organizations start out sensitive to the working of the Holy Spirit, but over time their belief structures and religious systems sometimes develop contrary to the work of the Spirit, rendering him quenched and no longer welcome.

Your carnal mind and flesh resist and challenge your transformation into mature Christians in the likeness of Jesus. The hardened heart persecutes the Holy Spirit. This persecution not only comes from religious systems that have quenched the Holy Spirit but also from other sources that feel threatened by God's Spirit (which convicts) and from the Devil (who agitates and stirs things up).

The heart that relies on an outward religion doesn't usually understand when the Holy Spirit is moving, but God does not seek to please the mind of the natural man. He will often manifest in ways that are peculiar to the natural senses. The gift of praying in tongues is a good example. God often tests Christians with gifts such as tongues to see who will stand by the move of his Spirit and who will deny it or persecute it.

The Holy Spirit always lifts up Jesus as the Savior. A good test for discerning if the Holy Spirit is operating rather than an unholy spirit is to ask this: is salvation through the blood of Jesus declared as the only power capable of defeating the Devil's works and the only power to save people's souls? The answer must be that only Jesus can save you. There is no other way to salvation.[14.17]

A contrary spirit will allow for additional paths to redemption with God that do not include Jesus. The ongoing conflict fighting for the heart and allegiance of mankind is between philosophies that deny or add additional personalities and methods to displace or share the exclusive salvation of the Savior, Jesus Christ.

Jesus declared that the Holy Spirit would bring to remembrance the things he was speaking. Men under the anointing of the Holy Spirit wrote the Scriptures under the direction and inspiration of this Spirit. Without the Holy Spirit in you, many things would be hard to understand and you might practice things that seem correct but are contrary to Jesus's teaching. His Spirit teaches you the truth and provides peace and comfort as you grow in Christ.

As you mature into Christ's likeness through his Holy Spirit, you will develop a deeper relationship with him and with Spirit-filled Christians who help you not to stray. It is a process, often accompanied by many victories and many trials, but you will receive healing through the ministry of the Holy Spirit and his ministers. The Scripture tells us he heals the broken-hearted, and he will heal you because the Holy Spirit is actively helping you transform into the likeness and image of Christ.

As your relationship with him matures, you learn how to become more sensitive to the Spirit's leading, to obey him, and to resist temptation. While temptations and deceptions try to cause you to stray from following the Holy Spirit, the Spirit is faithful and gives you victory over temptation and error. He uses Scripture and his people to warn you and minister to you to stay on the correct path toward eternal life. By obeying, you will be aware and sensitive to the times when you grieve the Holy Spirit so that you can correct your path. Learning to obey keeps you safe in the Peace of Jesus.

The Holy Spirit, in addition to providing truth and discernment, bestows gifts that are to be exercised within the body of Christianity and outward to a lost world.[32.10] The apostle Paul's writing provide considerable instruction and teaching concerning these gifts.

Some Christian organizations deny or oppose the power and gifts of the Holy Spirit and are like those described by Paul as having a form of godliness but deny the power.[36.44] Don't fear critics of the gifts of the Holy Spirit and doctrines teaching that somehow the gifts are no longer valid. These teachings and people have no spiritual authority. Believe what the Scripture and the Holy Spirit teach. The Holy Spirit reveals if the flesh, fanaticisms, or the occult is trying to operate in the disguise of the gifts. The Lord is gentle and faithful to guide his people in this area.

God's people and ministers evidence the fruit and gifts of the Holy Spirit in their lives. It is by his Spirit that he calls men and women to spiritual offices and ministries. The entire body of Christ is called to be ministers and take their place and operate in their received gifts from the Holy Spirit. You are also called to be obedient to God in Spirit and in truth.[31.4]

Being ready for the return of Jesus is about you and your determination to overcome the obstacles and trials that stand in the way. It is about you doing the will of God and entering into the inheritance you are entitled to through Jesus. You are in control of your actions and behavior, and you determine your destiny. It is about you and your obedience to Christ. There is an eternal inheritance, and you are the heir. There is a place designated for you in the kingdom of heaven, and it will be given to you if you overcome and serve Christ with your life here on earth. You are a son or daughter of God; you are not an obscure outcast or a nameless member of an organization.

God made you to be the heir of all things. You must determine to not fear people who dictate how you must serve in religious toil, performance, and payment. Jesus paid the price for your inheritance. It's obtained without money or performance and it comes through being born again by his Spirit, cleansed by his blood. Choose to enter into the promised condition, a land of milk and honey that Christ makes available to you through his Spirit.

Our hearts desire more of Jesus and his Holy Spirit. God's people thirst for and adore his presence. We value, revere, and appreciate when he sends the rains of his Holy Spirit upon us. Pray for rain to pour out on this dry, thirsty, and desolate land. Remain obedient to Christ's Spirit. Desire and anticipate the appearing of Jesus to bring immortality. We don't know when he is coming, but we know the Holy Spirit teaches, fills, and prepares us to be ready for his appearance and return. The Son of Man will come in an hour when we do not expect him.[6.3] We must be found obedient and ready.

SUMMARY POINTS

- » The essence of Christian living is to be filled with and walk in obedience to the Holy Spirit.
- » You experience Jesus's love and have communion with him through his Holy Spirit.
- » The gift of the Holy Spirit distinguishes the gospel of Jesus Christ from every religion in existence.
- » The Holy Spirit teaches you and leads you into truth.
- » Persecution of the Holy Spirit is persecution of Jesus.
- » The gifts of the Holy Spirit don't make sense to those who trust in the fallen nature.
- » The Holy Spirit changes you into the nature of Jesus.
- » The Holy Spirit comforts you in all situations and leaves you with the fruit of love, joy, and peace.
- » Jesus baptizes you in the Holy Spirit. You may or may not exercise the gift of tongues when you are filled with the baptism of the Holy Spirit. Speaking in tongues is not a prerequisite; it is only one of the gifts of the Spirit.
- » Like clothing that eventually wears out, this present dispensation did away with rituals. The true worshipers now worship God in Spirit and in truth through the Spirit of his Son, Jesus.
- » Living your life in obedience to the Holy Spirit prepares you for the return of Jesus.

PART V

SCRIPTURE REFERENCES

Background to Scripture References

Yet] first [you must] understand this, that no prophecy of Scripture is [a matter] of any personal or private or special interpretation (loosening, solving). For no prophecy ever originated because some man willed it [to do so—it never came by human impulse], but men spoke from God who were borne along (moved and impelled) by the Holy Spirit
– 2 Peter 1:20-21, AMP

Unlike most other material, the Scriptures never become old or dated; instead, they continue to grow fresher with increased vitality over time. Multi-dimensional, the Scriptures will expand in meaning, insights, and instruction as you continue in your Christian walk and grow deeper in your experience with Jesus.

The depth and breadth of Scripture is understandable when you consider that over forty different authors wrote sixty-six books under the inspiration of the Holy Spirit. This constitutes an assembly of considerable and diverse material. The majority of the Old Testament was written within a period of approximately 1,500 years. Its books document the era from the creation of the world and Adam in the Garden (approx. 4,000 BC) up to the time of the prophet Malachi (approx. 500 BC).

The New Testament books were written by eyewitnesses (Jesus's apostles) and other Christians who documented the events prior to the birth of Jesus up to the period after his resurrection. It begins with the books of Matthew, Mark, Luke, and John, which provide four different accounts of Jesus's ministry and teaching. These four books are commonly referred to as the "Gospels."

The book after the Gospels is the Acts of the Apostles. The title, Acts, refers to the actions of the first Christians as they formed the beginnings of the church. One of the most notable Christians in this book is the apostle Paul, who initially was an enemy and fierce opponent of Christianity but was instantly converted to a follower of Christ by a dramatic and personal encounter with Jesus. This experience, detailed in the book of Acts, propels Paul to become a leading author of books and letters that comprise much of the New Testament.

As a whole, the New Testament is vitally important to us because it speaks about the time period that the world has been living under for the past 2,000 years. This period is referred to as the dispensation of grace and salvation in Jesus Christ. The Old Testament prophesies God's plan for this dispensation period. In this way, it is a metaphor, an example or a shadow that compares the events and worship of God's people under the Old Testament Law to the events and worship of God's adopted sons and daughters under the New Testament grace of Jesus Christ.

As you review the references in this text, allow specific passages to speak to you in your present condition and pray for the Holy Spirit to reveal the Bible as a whole and in the different sections and categories. A Bible school diploma is not required for you to understand Scripture. However, as you gain understanding, you must guard against the desire of the flesh to exalt itself in the knowledge and supposed divine insight/ revelation that you will be receiving. Instead of believing you are the prophet for the hour, become the servant of Christ ready to minister His truth and serve others in the power of the Holy Spirit. Humbly fulfill your calling and exercise the gifts that God has entrusted to you within the body of Christ and a lost world.

The Bible, when interpreted in the same Spirit as those who wrote it, is your manual. It is your scale to weigh all truth, all religions, and all conduct of your life. It prepares you to be ready for the return of Jesus.

The Bible versions used for this reference section include four different translations: King James (KJV), Amplified (AMP), New International Version (NIV) and New American Standard Bible (NASB).

For a richer understanding of the original authors and the Holy Spirit's intent, read these Scriptures in all four of these translations, as well as other versions. You can read various Bible translations using popular online Bible collections, such as BibleGateway.com or Biblos.com.

Table of References

Part I

The Return of Jesus

1. The Return of Jesus Is within His People 189
2. You Will Be Changed to Be Like Jesus 191
3. His Appearing and Return Is in You 192
4. Your Inheritance Is Received at the Return of Jesus 193

Part II

Immortality When Jesus Returns

5. Immortality and the Redemption of Your Body at the Return of Jesus 195
6. Humanity and the Majority of Christians Are Not Ready 196
7. The Time of Jesus's Return 198
8. Characteristics of the Return of Jesus 203
    a. The Day Of 203
    b. His Coming 205
    c. With Glory 209
    d. Is Revealed 211
    e. With His Angels 211
    f. Coming in the Clouds of Heaven 212
    g. Gather 213
    h. Like a Thief in the Night 214
    i. A Day of the Trumpet 216
    j. Severing the Wicked from the Just 217
    k. Every Knee Shall Bow 218
    l. Fire 218
9. Judgment Day 220
10. Only a Remnant Will Be Saved 223
11. The Kingdom of God 224
12. The City of God 229
13. The End: Matthew, Mark, and Luke Parallel Accounts 231

Part III

Only Jesus...

14. Only Jesus Can Save You 232
15. He Fulfills Your Heart's Desire for Love 238
16. He Ransoms You from Sin 241
17. He Lives within Your Heart 244
18. He Fulfills the Scriptures regarding the Savior 246
19. He Created the Heavens and the Earth 254

Part IV

How To Be Ready

20. Watch and Be Ready 257
21. You Are the Temple of God 257
22. Keep Your Heart Holy 259
23. Maintain Sexual Purity 262
24. Forgive Everyone Always 266
25. Let Love Be Your Only Motive 270
26. Embrace Emotional Healing 274
27. Follow the Shepherd as a Member of His Church 275
28. Fulfill Your Ministry 277
29. Recognize Christian Leadership 279
30. Esteem God's Authority Over Man's Authority 281
31. Worship and Obey God in Spirit and in Truth 283
32. Honor the Gifts and Fruit of the Holy Spirit 287
33. Crucify the Flesh and the Carnal Mind, and Walk in the Spirit 288
34. Pray Always 293
35. Utilize the Weapons and Armor of the Holy Spirit for Readiness 294
36. Believe in Miracles, Signs, and Wonders 295
37. Avoid Pride and Stay Humble 300
38. Expect Trials and Persecution 303
39. Overcome and Obtain Your Inheritance 305
40. Fear God, Not Man 307
41. Trust in the Lord and Surrender Everything to Him 309

PART I

THE RETURN OF JESUS

REFERENCE 1 — The Return of Jesus Is within His People

1.1 Behold, I will send my messenger, and he shall prepare the way before me: and the Lord, whom ye seek, shall suddenly come to his temple, even the messenger of the covenant, whom ye delight in: behold, he shall come, saith the Lord of hosts (Malachi 3:1, KJV).

1.2 Thee righteous will shine forth as the sun in the kingdom of their Father. He who has ears, let him hear (Matthew 13:43, NASB).

1.3 On that day you will realize that I am in my Father, and you are in me, and I am in you (John 14:20, NIV).

1.4 [But what of that?] For I consider that the sufferings of this present time (this present life) are not worth being compared with the glory that is about to be revealed to us and in us and for us and conferred on us! (Romans 8:18, AMP).

1.5 For whom he did foreknow, he also did predestinate to be conformed to the image of his Son, that he might be the firstborn among many brethren (Romans 8:29, KJV).

1.6 Take notice! I tell you a mystery a secret truth, an event decreed by the hidden purpose or counsel of God). We shall not all fall asleep [in death], but we shall all be changed (transformed) In a moment, in the twinkling of an eye, at the [sound of the] last trumpet call. For a trumpet will sound, and the dead [in Christ] will be raised imperishable (free and immune from decay), and we shall be changed (transformed). For this perishable [part of us] must put on the imperishable [nature], and this mortal [part of us, this nature that is capable of dying] must put on immortality (freedom from death) (1 Corinthians 15:51-53, AMP).

1.7 And we, who with unveiled faces all reflect the Lord's glory, are being transformed into his likeness with ever-increasing glory, which comes from the Lord, who is the Spirit (2 Corinthians 3:18, NIV).

1.8 For while we are in this tent, we groan and are burdened, because we do not wish to be unclothed but to be clothed with our heavenly dwelling, so that what is mortal may be swallowed up by life (2 Corinthians 5:4, NIV).

1.9 [He planned] for the maturity of the times and the climax of the ages to unify all things and head them up and consummate them in Christ, [both] things in heaven and things on the earth (Ephesians 1:10, AMP).

1.10 Until we all reach unity in the faith and in the knowledge of the Son of God and become mature, attaining to the whole measure of the fullness of Christ. Then we will no longer be infants, tossed back and forth by the waves, and blown here and there by every wind of teaching and by the cunning and craftiness of men in their deceitful scheming. Instead, speaking the truth in love, we will in all things grow up into him who is the Head, that is, Christ (Ephesians 4:13-15, NIV).

1.11 But our citizenship is in heaven. And we eagerly await a Savior from there, the Lord Jesus Christ, who, by the power that enables him to bring everything under his control, will transform our lowly bodies so that they will be like his glorious body (Philippians 3:20-21, NIV).

1.12 That is, the mystery which has been hidden from the past ages and generations, but has now been manifested to His saints, to whom God willed to make known what is the riches of the glory of this mystery among the Gentiles, which is Christ in you, the hope of glory (Colossians 1:26-27, NASB).

1.13 When Christ, Who is our life, appears, then you also will appear with Him in [the splendor of His] glory (Colossians 3:4, AMP).

1.14 For this we declare to you by the Lord's [own] word, that we who are alive and remain until the coming of the Lord shall in no way precede [into His presence] or have any advantage at all over those who have previously fallen asleep [in Him in death]. For the Lord Himself will descend from heaven with a loud cry of summons, with the shout of an archangel, and with the blast of the trumpet of God. And those who have departed this life in Christ will rise first. Then we, the living ones who remain [on the earth], shall simultaneously be caught up along with [the resurrected dead] in the clouds to meet the Lord in the air; and so always (through the eternity of the eternities) we shall be with the Lord! (1 Thessalonians 4:15-17, AMP).

1.15 And to [recompense] you who are so distressed and afflicted [by granting you] relief and rest along with us [your fellow sufferers] when the Lord Jesus is revealed from heaven with His mighty angels in a flame of fire, To deal out retribution (chastisement and vengeance) upon those who do not know or perceive or become acquainted with God, and [upon those] who ignore and refuse to obey the Gospel of our Lord Jesus Christ. Such people will pay the penalty and suffer the punishment of everlasting ruin (destruction and perdition) and eternal exclusion and banishment from the presence of the Lord and from the glory of His power, When He comes to be glorified in His saints [on that day He will be made more glorious in His consecrated people], and [He will] be marveled at and admired [in His glory reflected] in all who have believed [who have adhered to, trusted in, and relied on Him], because our witnessing among you was confidently accepted and believed [and confirmed in your lives] (2 Thessalonians 1:7-10, AMP).

1.16 On the day he comes to be glorified in his holy people and to be marveled at among all those who have believed. This includes you, because you believed our testimony to you (2 Thessalonians 1:10, NIV).

1.17 But rejoice, inasmuch as ye are partakers of Christ's sufferings; that, when his glory shall be revealed, ye may be glad also with exceeding joy (1 Peter 4:13, KJV).

1.18 Beloved, we are [even here and] now God's children; it is not yet disclosed (made clear) what we shall be [hereafter], but we know that when He comes and is manifested, we shall [as God's children] resemble and be like Him, for we shall see Him just as He [really] is (1 John 3:2, AMP).

1.19 Dear friends, now we are children of God, and what we will be has not yet been made known. But we know that when he appears, we shall be like him, for we shall see him as he is (1 John 3:2, NIV).

REFERENCE 2 — You Will Be Changed to Be Like Jesus

2.1 If a man die, shall he live again? all the days of my appointed time will I wait, till my change come (Job 14:14, KJV).

2.2 For those whom He foreknew [of whom He was aware and loved beforehand], He also destined from the beginning [foreordaining them] to be molded into the image of His Son [and share inwardly His likeness], that He might become the firstborn among many brethren (Romans 8:29, AMP).

2.3 Behold, I tell you a mystery; we will not all sleep, but we will all be changed, in a moment, in the twinkling of an eye, at the last trumpet; for the trumpet will sound, and the dead will be raised imperishable, and we will be changed (1 Corinthians 15:51-52, NASB).

2.4 But we all, with unveiled face, beholding as in a mirror the glory of the Lord, are being transformed into the same image from glory to glory, just as from the Lord, the Spirit (2 Corinthians 3:18, NASB).

2.5 Who will transform and fashion anew the body of our humiliation to conform to and be like the body of His glory and majesty, by exerting that power which enables Him even to subject everything to Himself (Philippians 3:21, AMP).

2.6 Dear friends, now we are children of God, and what we will be has not yet been made known. But we know that when he appears, we shall be like him, for we shall see him as he is (1 John 3:2, NIV).

2.7 May he strengthen your hearts so that you will be blameless and holy in the presence of our God and Father when our Lord Jesus comes with all his holy ones (1 Thessalonians 3:13, NIV).

REFERENCE 3 — His Appearing and Return Is in You

3.1 When the Lord shall build up Zion, he shall appear in his glory (Psalm 102:16, KJV).

3.2 But who can endure the day of his coming? Who can stand when he appears? For he will be like a refiner's fire or a launderer's soap (Malachi 3:2, NIV).

3.3 At that time the sign of the Son of Man will appear in the sky, and all the nations of the earth will mourn. They will see the Son of Man coming on the clouds of the sky, with power and great glory (Matthew 24:30, NIV).

3.4 Keep the commandment without stain or reproach until the appearing of our Lord Jesus Christ (1 Timothy 6:14, NASB).

3.5 When Christ, Who is our life, appears, then you also will appear with Him in [the splendor of His] glory (Colossians 3:4, AMP).

3.6 Even so it is that Christ, having been offered to take upon Himself and bear as a burden the sins of many once and once for all, will appear a second time, not to carry any burden of sin nor to deal with sin, but to bring to full salvation those who are [eagerly, constantly, and patiently] waiting for and expecting Him (Hebrews 9:28, AMP).

3.7 I charge thee therefore before God, and the Lord Jesus Christ, who shall judge the quick and the dead at his appearing and his kingdom (2 Timothy 4:1, KJV).

3.8 Awaiting and looking for the [fulfillment, the realization of our] blessed hope, even the glorious appearing of our great God and Savior Christ Jesus (the Messiah, the Anointed One) (Titus 2:13, AMP).

3.9 The trial of your faith, being much more precious than of gold that perisheth, though it be tried with fire, might be found unto praise and honour and glory at the appearing of Jesus Christ (1 Peter 1:7, KJV).

3.10 And when the Chief Shepherd appears, you will receive the crown of glory that will never fade away (1 Peter 5:4, NIV).

3.11 Now, little children, abide in Him, so that when He appears, we may have confidence and not shrink away from Him in shame at His coming (1 John 2:28, NASB).

3.12 Beloved, now we are children of God, and it has not appeared as yet what we will be. We know that when He appears, we will be like Him, because we will see Him just as He is (1 John 3:2, NASB).

REFERENCE 4 — Your Inheritance Is Received at the Return of Jesus

4.1 Now if we are children, then we are heirs—heirs of God and co-heirs with Christ, if indeed we share in his sufferings in order that we may also share in his glory (Romans 8:17, NIV).

4.2 For all who are led by the Spirit of God are sons of God. For [the Spirit which] you have now received [is] not a spirit of slavery to put you once more in bondage to fear, but you have received the Spirit of adoption [the Spirit producing sonship] in [the bliss of] which we cry, Abba (Father)! Father! The Spirit Himself [thus] testifies together with our own spirit, [assuring us] that we are children of God. And if we are [His] children, then we are [His] heirs also: heirs of God and fellow heirs with Christ [sharing His inheritance with Him]; only we must share His suffering if we are to share His glory. [But what of that?] For I consider that the sufferings of this present time (this present life) are not worth being compared with the glory that is about to be revealed to us and in us and for us and conferred on us! For [even the whole] creation (all nature) waits expectantly and longs earnestly for God's sons to be made known [waits for the revealing, the disclosing of their sonship]. For the creation (nature) was subjected to frailty (to futility, condemned to frustration), not because of some intentional fault on its part, but by the will of Him Who so subjected it—[yet] with the hope [Eccl. 1:2] That nature (creation) itself will be set free from its bondage to decay and corruption [and gain an entrance] into the glorious freedom of God's children. We know that the whole creation [of irrational creatures] has been moaning together in the pains of labor until now. [Jer. 12:4, 11] And not only the creation, but we ourselves too, who have and enjoy the firstfruits of the [Holy] Spirit [a foretaste of the blissful things to come] groan inwardly as we wait for the redemption of our bodies [from sensuality and the grave, which will reveal] our adoption (our manifestation as God's sons) (Romans 8:14-23, AMP).

4.3 For those whom He foreknew, He also predestined to become conformed to the image of His Son, so that He would be the firstborn among many brethren (Romans 8:29, NASB).

4.4 But Christ (the Messiah) was faithful over His [own Father's] house as a Son [and Master of it]. And it is we who are [now members] of this house, if we hold fast and firm to the end our joyful and exultant confidence and sense of triumph in our hope [in Christ] (Hebrews 3:6, AMP).

PART II

IMMORTALITY
WHEN JESUS RETURNS

REFERENCE 5 — Immortality and the Redemption of Your Body at the Return of Jesus

5.1 Then they will go away into eternal punishment, but those who are just and upright and in right standing with God into eternal life (Matthew 25:46, AMP).

5.2 But because of your stubbornness and your unrepentant heart, you are storing up wrath against yourself for the day of God's wrath, when his righteous judgment will be revealed. God "will give to each person according to what he has done." To those who by persistence in doing good seek glory, honor and immortality, he will give eternal life. But for those who are self-seeking and who reject the truth and follow evil, there will be wrath and anger (Romans 2:5-8, NIV).

5.3 I consider that our present sufferings are not worth comparing with the glory that will be revealed in us. The creation waits in eager expectation for the sons of God to be revealed. For the creation was subjected to frustration, not by its own choice, but by the will of the one who subjected it, in hope that the creation itself will be liberated from its bondage to decay and brought into the glorious freedom of the children of God. We know that the whole creation has been groaning as in the pains of childbirth right up to the present time. Not only so, but we ourselves, who have the firstfruits of the Spirit, groan inwardly as we wait eagerly for our adoption as sons, the redemption of our bodies (Romans 8:18-23, NIV).

5.4 And do not grieve the Holy Spirit of God [do not offend or vex or sadden Him], by Whom you were sealed (marked, branded as God's own, secured) for the day of redemption (of final deliverance through Christ from evil and the consequences of sin) (Ephesians 4:30, AMP).

5.5 That He might present to Himself the church in all her glory, having no spot or wrinkle or any such thing; but that she would be holy and blameless (Ephesians 5:27, NASB).

5.6 But it has now been revealed through the appearing of our Savior, Christ Jesus, who has destroyed death and has brought life and immortality to light through the gospel (2 Timothy 1:10, NIV).

5.7 Now if Christ is preached, that He has been raised from the dead, how do some among you say that there is no resurrection of the dead? But if there is no resurrection of the dead, not even Christ has been raised; and if Christ has not been raised, then our preaching is vain, your faith also is vain. Moreover we are even found to be false witnesses of God, because we testified against God that He raised Christ, whom He did not raise, if in fact the dead are not raised. For if the dead are not raised, not even Christ has been raised; and if Christ has not been raised, your faith is worthless; you are still in your sins. Then those also who have fallen asleep in Christ have perished. If we have hoped in Christ in this life only, we are of all men most to be pitied (1 Corinthians 15:12-19, NASB).

5.8 Behold, I tell you a mystery; we will not all sleep, but we will all be changed, in a moment, in the twinkling of an eye, at the last trumpet; for the trumpet will sound, and the dead will be raised imperishable, and we will be changed. For this perishable must put on the imperishable, and this mortal must put on immortality (1 Corinthians 15:51-53, NASB).

REFERENCE 6 — Humanity and the Majority of Christians Are Not Ready

6.1 Multitudes, multitudes in the valley of decision: for the day of the Lord is near in the valley of decision (Joel 3:14, KJV).

6.2 As it was in the days of Noah, so it will be at the coming of the Son of Man. For in the days before the flood, people were eating and drinking, marrying and giving in marriage, up to the day Noah entered the ark; and they knew nothing about what would happen until the flood came and took them all away. That is how it will be at the coming of the Son of Man (Matthew 24:37-39, NIV).

6.3 So you also must be ready, because the Son of Man will come at an hour when you do not expect him (Matthew 24:44, NIV).

6.4 Watch therefore [give strict attention and be cautious and active], for you know neither the day nor the hour when the Son of Man will come (Matthew 25:13, AMP).

6.5 "For whoever is ashamed of Me and My words, the Son of Man will be ashamed of him when He comes in His glory, and the glory of the Father and of the holy angels (Luke 9:26, NASB).

6.6 You also must be ready, for the Son of Man is coming at an hour and a moment when you do not anticipate it (Luke 12:40, AMP).

6.7 Exclaiming, Would that you had known personally, even at least in this your day, the things that make for peace (for freedom from all the distresses that are experienced as the result of sin and upon which your peace—your security, safety, prosperity, and happiness—depends)! But now they are hidden from your eyes (Luke 19:42, AMP).

6.8 Keep awake then and watch at all times [be discreet, attentive, and ready], praying that you may have the full strength and ability and be accounted worthy to escape all these things [taken together] that will take place, and to stand in the presence of the Son of Man (Luke 21:36, AMP).

6.9 And, "If it is hard for the righteous to be saved, what will become of the ungodly and the sinner? (1 Peter 4:18, NIV).

6.10 And did not spare the ancient world, but preserved Noah, a preacher of righteousness, with seven others, when He brought a flood upon the world of the ungodly; and if He condemned the cities of Sodom and Gomorrah to destruction by reducing them to ashes, having made them an example to those who would live ungodly lives thereafter (2 Peter 2:5-6, NASB).

6.11 Now I want to remind you, though you were fully informed once for all, that though the Lord [at one time] delivered a people out of the land of Egypt, He subsequently destroyed those [of them] who did not believe [who refused to adhere to, trust in, and rely upon Him]. And angels who did not keep (care for, guard, and hold to) their own first place of power but abandoned their proper dwelling place—these He has reserved in custody in eternal chains (bonds) under the thick gloom of utter darkness until the judgment and doom of the great day. [The wicked are sentenced to suffer] just as Sodom and Gomorrah and the adjacent towns—which likewise gave themselves over to impurity and indulged in unnatural vice and sensual perversity—are laid out [in plain sight] as an exhibit of perpetual punishment [to warn] of everlasting fire (Jude 1:5-7, AMP).

6.12 So then because thou art lukewarm, and neither cold nor hot, I will spew thee out of my mouth (Revelation 3:16, KJV).

6.13 The harvest is past, the summer is ended, and we are not saved (Jeremiah 8:20, NIV).

REFERENCE 7 — When Will Jesus Return?

7.1 When the Lord shall build up Zion, he shall appear in his glory (Psalm 102:16, KJV).

7.2 Behold, I will send you Elijah the prophet before the coming of the great and dreadful day of the Lord (Malachi 4:5, KJV).

7.3 Another parable put he forth unto them, saying, The kingdom of heaven is likened unto a man which sowed good seed in his field: But while men slept, his enemy came and sowed tares among the wheat, and went his way. But when the blade was sprung up, and brought forth fruit, then appeared the tares also. So the servants of the householder came and said unto him, Sir, didst not thou sow good seed in thy field? from whence then hath it tares? He said unto them, An enemy hath done this. The servants said unto him, Wilt thou then that we go and gather them up? But he said, Nay; lest while ye gather up the tares, ye root up also the wheat with them. Let both grow together until the harvest: and in the time of harvest I will say to the reapers, Gather ye together first the tares, and bind them in bundles to burn them: but gather the wheat into my barn (Matthew 13:24-30, KJV).

7.4 Then he left the crowd and went into the house. His disciples came to him and said, "Explain to us the parable of the weeds in the field." He answered, "The one who sowed the good seed is the Son of Man. The field is the world, and the good seed stands for the sons of the kingdom. The weeds are the sons of the evil one, and the enemy who sows them is the devil. The harvest is the end of the age, and the harvesters are angels. "As the weeds are pulled up and burned in the fire, so it will be at the end of the age. The Son of Man will send out his angels, and they will weed out of his kingdom everything that causes sin and all who do evil. They will throw them into the fiery furnace, where there will be weeping and gnashing of teeth. Then the righteous will shine like the sun in the kingdom of their Father. He who has ears, let him hear (Matthew 13:36-43, NIV).

7.5 This is how it will be at the end of the age. The angels will come and separate the wicked from the righteous and throw them into the fiery furnace, where there will be weeping and gnashing of teeth (Matthew 13:49-50, NIV).

7.6 For the Son of Man is going to come in the glory of His Father with His angels, and will then repay every man according to his deeds. Truly I say to you, there are some of those who are standing here who will not taste death until they see the Son of Man coming in His kingdom (Matthew 16:27-28, NASB).

7.7 But he who endures to the end will be saved (Matthew 24:13, AMP).

7.8 Immediately after the distress of those days the sun will be darkened, and the moon will not give its light; the stars will fall from the sky, and the heavenly bodies will be shaken.' "At that time the sign of the Son of Man will appear in the sky, and all the nations of the earth will mourn. They will see the Son of Man coming on the clouds of the sky, with power and great glory. And he will send his angels with a loud trumpet call, and they will gather his elect from the four winds, from one end of the heavens to the other (Matthew 24:29-31, NIV).

7.9 Then shall two be in the field; the one shall be taken, and the other left. Two women shall be grinding at the mill; the one shall be taken, and the other left (Matthew 24:40-41, KJV).

7.10 I tell you, on that night there will be two in one bed; one will be taken and the other will be left. There will be two women grinding at the same place; one will be taken and the other will be left [Two men will be in the field; one will be taken and the other will be left.] (Luke 17:34-36, NASB).

7.11 And you will be hated and detested by everybody for My name's sake, but he who patiently perseveres and endures to the end will be saved (made a partaker of the salvation by Christ, and delivered from spiritual death) (Mark 13:13, AMP).

7.12 But in those days, after that tribulation, the sun shall be darkened, and the moon shall not give her light, And the stars of heaven shall fall, and the powers that are in heaven shall be shaken. And then shall they see the Son of Man coming in the clouds with great power and glory. And then shall he send his angels, and shall gather together his elect from the four winds, from the uttermost part of the earth to the uttermost part of heaven (Mark 13:24-27, KJV).

7.13 For like the lightning, that flashes and lights up the sky from one end to the other, so will the Son of Man be in His [own] day. But first He must suffer many things and be disapproved and repudiated and rejected by this age and generation. And [just] as it was in the days of Noah, so will it be in the time of the Son of Man. [People] ate, they drank, they married, they were given in marriage, right up to the day when Noah went into the ark, and the flood came and destroyed them all. [Gen. 6:5-8; 7:6-24] So also [it was the same] as it was in the days of Lot. [People] ate, they drank, they bought, they sold, they planted, they built; But on the [very] day that Lot went out of Sodom, it rained fire and brimstone from heaven and destroyed [them] all. That is the way it will be on the day that the Son of Man is revealed (Luke 17:24-30, AMP).

7.14 But each in his own rank and turn: Christ (the Messiah) [is] the firstfruits, then those who are Christ's [own will be resurrected] at His coming. After that comes the end (the completion), when He delivers over the kingdom to God the Father after rendering inoperative and abolishing every [other] rule and every authority and power (1 Corinthians 15:23-24, AMP).

7.15 Take notice! I tell you a mystery (a secret truth, an event decreed by the hidden purpose or counsel of God). We shall not all fall asleep [in death], but we shall all be changed (transformed) In a moment, in the twinkling of an eye, at the [sound of the] last trumpet call. For a trumpet will sound, and the dead [in Christ] will be raised imperishable (free and immune from decay), and we shall be changed (transformed) (1 Corinthians 15:51-52, AMP).

7.16 When Christ, who is our life, shall appear, then shall ye also appear with him in glory (Colossians 3:4, KJV).

7.17 For the Lord Himself will descend from heaven with a loud cry of summons, with the shout of an archangel, and with the blast of the trumpet of God. And those who have departed this life in Christ will rise first. Then we, the living ones who remain [on the earth], shall simultaneously be caught up along with [the resurrected dead] in the clouds to meet the Lord in the air; and so always (through the eternity of the eternities) we shall be with the Lord! (1 Thessalonians 4:16-17, AMP).

7.18 But as to the suitable times and the precise seasons and dates, brethren, you have no necessity for anything being written to you. For you yourselves know perfectly well that the day of the [return of the] Lord will come [as unexpectedly and suddenly] as a thief in the night. When people are saying, All is well and secure, and, There is peace and safety, then in a moment unforeseen destruction (ruin and death) will come upon them as suddenly as labor pains come upon a woman with child; and they shall by no means escape, for there will be no escape. But you are not in [given up to the power of] darkness, brethren, for that day to overtake you by surprise like a thief. For you are all sons of light and sons of the day; we do not belong either to the night or to darkness. Accordingly then, let us not sleep, as the rest do, but let us keep wide awake (alert, watchful, cautious, and on our guard) and let us be sober (calm, collected, and circumspect) (1 Thessalonians 5:1-6, AMP).

7.19 And give relief to you who are troubled, and to us as well. This will happen when the Lord Jesus is revealed from heaven in blazing fire with his powerful angels. He will punish those who do not know God and do not obey the gospel of our Lord Jesus. They will be punished with everlasting destruction and shut out from the presence of the Lord and from the majesty of his power on the day he comes to be glorified in his holy people and to be marveled at among all those who have believed. This includes you, because you believed our testimony to you (2 Thessalonians 1:7-10, NIV).

7.20 But relative to the coming of our Lord Jesus Christ (the Messiah) and our gathering together to [meet] Him, we beg you, brethren, Not to allow your minds to be quickly unsettled or disturbed or kept excited or alarmed, whether it be by some [pretended] revelation of [the] Spirit or by word or by letter [alleged to be] from us, to the effect that the day of the Lord has [already] arrived and is here. Let no one deceive or beguile you in any way, for that day will not come except the apostasy comes first [unless the predicted great falling away of those who have professed to be Christians has come], and the man of lawlessness (sin) is revealed, who is the son of doom (of perdition), [Dan. 7:25; 8:25; 1 Tim. 4:1] Who opposes and exalts himself so proudly and insolently against and over all that is called God or that is worshiped, [even to his actually] taking his seat in the temple of God, proclaiming that he himself is God. [Ezek. 28:2; Dan. 11:36, 37] Do you not recollect that when I was still with you, I told you these things? And now you know what is restraining him [from being revealed at this time]; it is so that he may be manifested (revealed) in his own [appointed] time. And then the lawless one (the antichrist) will be revealed and the Lord Jesus will slay him with the breath of His mouth and bring him to an end by His appearing at His coming. [Isa. 11:4] The coming [of the lawless one, the antichrist] is through the activity and working of Satan and will be attended by great power and with all sorts of [pretended] miracles and signs and delusive marvels—[all of them] lying wonders (2 Thessalonians 2:1-9,, AMP).

7.21 I solemnly charge you in the presence of God and of Christ Jesus, who is to judge the living and the dead, and by His appearing and His kingdom (2 Timothy 4:1, NASB).

7.22 [As to what remains] henceforth there is laid up for me the [victor's] crown of righteousness [for being right with God and doing right], which the Lord, the righteous Judge, will award to me and recompense me on that [great] day—and not to me only, but also to all those who have loved and yearned for and welcomed His appearing (His return) (2 Timothy 4:8, AMP).

7.23 But rejoice, inasmuch as ye are partakers of Christ's sufferings; that, when his glory shall be revealed, ye may be glad also with exceeding joy (1 Peter 4:13, KJV).

7.24 But the day of the Lord will come like a thief, and then the heavens will vanish (pass away) with a thunderous crash, and the [material] elements [of the universe] will be dissolved with fire, and the earth and the works that are upon it will be burned up. Since all these things are thus in the process of being dissolved, what kind of person ought [each of] you to be [in the meanwhile] in consecrated and holy behavior and devout and godly qualities, While you wait and earnestly long for (expect and hasten) the coming of the day of God by reason of which the flaming heavens will be dissolved, and the [material] elements [of the universe] will flare and melt with fire? [Isa. 34:4]. But we look for new heavens and a new earth according to His promise, in which righteousness (uprightness, freedom from sin, and right standing with God) is to abide [Isa. 65:17; 66:22]. (2 Peter 3:10-13).

7.25 So, beloved, since you are expecting these things, be eager to be found by Him [at His coming] without spot or blemish and at peace [in serene confidence, free from fears and agitating passions and moral conflicts] (2 Peter 3:10-14, AMP).

7.26 And he who overcomes (is victorious) and who obeys My commands to the [very] end [doing the works that please Me], I will give him authority and power over the nations (Revelation 2:26, AMP).

7.27 Where is the promise of His coming? For since the forefathers fell asleep, all things have continued exactly as they did from the beginning of creation (2 Peter 3:4, AMP).

REFERENCE 8 — Characteristics of His Return

8-a: The Day Of

8.1 Behold, the day of the Lord is coming!—fierce, with wrath and raging anger—to make the land and the [whole] earth a desolation and to destroy out of it its sinners [Isa. 2:10-22; Rev. 19:11-21]. For the stars of the heavens and their constellations will not give their light; the sun will be darkened at its rising and the moon will not shed its light. And I, the Lord, will punish the world for its evil, and the wicked for their guilt and iniquity; I will cause the arrogance of the proud to cease and will lay low the haughtiness of the terrible and the boasting of the violent and ruthless. I will make a man more rare than fine gold, and mankind scarcer than the pure gold of Ophir. Therefore I will make the heavens tremble; and the earth shall be shaken out of its place at the wrath of the Lord of hosts in the day of His fierce anger (Isaiah 13:9-13, AMP).

8.2 Blow the trumpet in Zion; sound an alarm on My holy Mount [Zion]. Let all the inhabitants of the land tremble, for the day of [the judgment of] the Lord is coming; it is close at hand (Joel 2:1, AMP).

8.3 The sun will be turned to darkness and the moon to blood before the coming of the great and dreadful day of the Lord (Joel 2:31, NIV).

8.4 Multitudes, multitudes in the valley of decision: for the day of the Lord is near in the valley of decision. The sun and the moon shall be darkened, and the stars shall withdraw their shining (Joel 3:14-15, KJV).

8.5 Near is the great day of the Lord, Near and coming very quickly; Listen, the day of the Lord! In it the warrior cries out bitterly. A day of wrath is that day, A day of trouble and distress, A day of destruction and desolation, A day of darkness and gloom, A day of clouds and thick darkness, A day of trumpet and battle cry Against the fortified cities And the high corner towers. I will bring distress on men So that they will walk like the blind, Because they have sinned against the Lord; And their blood will be poured out like dust And their flesh like dung. Neither their silver nor their gold Will be able to deliver them On the day of the Lord's wrath; And all the earth will be devoured In the fire of His jealousy, For He will make a complete end, Indeed a terrifying one, Of all the inhabitants of the earth (Zephaniah 1:14-18, NASB).

8.6 Collect your thoughts, yes, unbend yourselves [in submission and see if there is no sense of shame and no consciousness of sin left in you], O shameless nation [not desirous or desired]! [The time for repentance is speeding by like chaff whirled before the wind!] Therefore consider, before God's decree brings forth [the curse upon you], before the time [to repent] is gone like the drifting chaff, before the fierce anger of the Lord comes upon you—yes, before the day of the wrath of the Lord comes upon you! Seek the Lord [inquire for Him, inquire of Him, and require Him as the foremost necessity of your life], all you humble of the land who have acted in compliance with His revealed will and have kept His commandments; seek righteousness, seek humility [inquire for them, require them as vital]. It may be you will be hidden in the day of the Lord's anger (Zephaniah 2:1-3, AMP).

8.7 For, behold, the day cometh, that shall burn as an oven; and all the proud, yea, and all that do wickedly, shall be stubble: and the day that cometh shall burn them up, saith the Lord of hosts, that it shall leave them neither root nor branch Mal 4:1, KJV).

8.8 For like the lightning, that flashes and lights up the sky from one end to the other, so will the Son of Man be in His [own] day (Luke 17:24, AMP).

8.9 But because of your stubbornness and unrepentant heart you are storing up wrath for yourself in the day of wrath and revelation of the righteous judgment of God, who will render to each according to His deeds (Romans 2:5-6, NASB).

8.10 Therefore you do not lack any spiritual gift as you eagerly wait for our Lord Jesus Christ to be revealed. He will keep you strong to the end, so that you will be blameless on the day of our Lord Jesus Christ (1 Corinthians 1:7-8, NIV).

8.11 And I am convinced and sure of this very thing, that He Who began a good work in you will continue until the day of Jesus Christ [right up to the time of His return], developing [that good work] and perfecting and bringing it to full completion in you (Philippians 1:6, AMP).

8.12 And this is my prayer: that your love may abound more and more in knowledge and depth of insight, so that you may be able to discern what is best and may be pure and blameless until the day of Christ (Philippians 1:9-10, NIV).

8.13 Holding forth the word of life; that I may rejoice in the day of Christ, that I have not run in vain, neither laboured in vain (Philippians 2:16, KJV).

8.14 For you yourselves know perfectly well that the day of the [return of the] Lord will come [as unexpectedly and suddenly] as a thief in the night (1 Thessalonians 5:2, AMP).

8.15 Concerning the coming of our Lord Jesus Christ and our being gathered to him, we ask you, brothers, not to become easily unsettled or alarmed by some prophecy, report or letter supposed to have come from us, saying that the day of the Lord has already come (2 Thessalonians 2:1-2, NIV).

8.16 But the day of the Lord will come like a thief, and then the heavens will vanish (pass away) with a thunderous crash, and the [material] elements [of the universe] will be dissolved with fire, and the earth and the works that are upon it will be burned up (2 Peter 3:10, AMP).

8.17 Since all these things are to be destroyed in this way, what sort of people ought you to be in holy conduct and godliness, looking for and hastening the coming of the day of God, because of which the heavens will be destroyed by burning, and the elements will melt with intense heat! (2 Peter 3:12, NASB).

8.18 Behold, I will send my messenger, and he shall prepare the way before me: and the Lord, whom ye seek, shall suddenly come to his temple, even the messenger of the covenant, whom ye delight in: behold, he shall come, saith the Lord of hosts (Malachi 3:2 But who may abide the day of his coming? and who shall stand when he appeareth? for he is like a refiner's fire, and like fullers' soap (Malachi 3:1-2, KJV).

8-b: His Coming

8.19 Behold, I will send you Elijah the prophet before the coming of the great and dreadful day of the Lord (Malachi 4:5, KJV).

8.20 Truly I say to you, there are some of those who are standing here who will not taste death until they see the Son of Man coming in His kingdom (Matthew 16:28, NASB).

8.21 And as he sat upon the mount of Olives, the disciples came unto him privately, saying, Tell us, when shall these things be? and what shall be the sign of thy coming, and of the end of the world? (Matthew 24:3, KJV).

8.22 For just as the lightning flashes from the east and shines and is seen as far as the west, so will the coming of the Son of Man be. Wherever there is a fallen body (a corpse), there the vultures (or eagles) will flock together. [Job 39:30] Immediately after the tribulation of those days the sun will be darkened, and the moon will not shed its light, and the stars will fall from the sky, and the powers of the heavens will be shaken. [Isa. 13:10; 34:4; Joel 2:10, 11; Zeph. 1:15] Then the sign of the Son of Man will appear in the sky, and then all the tribes of the earth will mourn and beat their breasts and lament in anguish, and they will see the Son of Man coming on the clouds of heaven with power and great glory [in brilliancy and splendor] (Matthew 24:27-30, AMP).

8.23 No one knows about that day or hour, not even the angels in heaven, nor the Son, but only The Father. As it was in the days of Noah, so it will be at the coming of the Son of Man. For in the days before the flood, people were eating and drinking, marrying and giving in marriage, up to the day Noah entered the ark; and they knew nothing about what would happen until the flood came and took them all away. That is how it will be at the coming of the Son of Man (Matthew 24:36-39, NIV).

8.24 For this reason you also must be ready; for the Son of Man is coming at an hour when you do not think He will (Matthew 24:44, NASB).

8.25 But if that servant is wicked and says to himself, My master is delayed and is going to be gone a long time, And begins to beat his fellow servants and to eat and drink with the drunken, The master of that servant will come on a day when he does not expect him and at an hour of which he is not aware, And will punish him [cut him up by scourging] and put him with the pretenders (hypocrites); there will be weeping and grinding of teeth (Matthew 24:48-51, AMP).

8.26 When the Son of Man comes in his glory, and all the angels with him, he will sit on his throne in heavenly glory. All the nations will be gathered before him, and he will separate the people one from another as a shepherd separates the sheep from the goats (Matthew 25:31-2, NIV).

8.27 Jesus said to him, "You have said it yourself; nevertheless I tell you, hereafter you will see the Son of Man sitting at the right hand of power, and coming on the clouds of heaven" (Matthew 26:64, NASB).

8.28 Whosoever therefore shall be ashamed of me and of my words in this adulterous and sinful generation; of him also shall the Son of Man be ashamed, when he cometh in the glory of his Father with the holy angels (Mark 8:38, KJV).

8.29 And then they will see the Son of Man coming in clouds with great (kingly) power and glory (majesty and splendor) (Mark 13:26, AMP).

8.30 It is like a man [already] going on a journey; when he leaves home, he puts his servants in charge, each with his particular task, and he gives orders to the doorkeeper to be constantly alert and on the watch. Therefore watch (give strict attention, be cautious and alert), for you do not know when the Master of the house is coming—in the evening, or at midnight, or at cockcrowing, or in the morning— [Watch, I say] lest He come suddenly and unexpectedly and find you asleep. And what I say to you I say to everybody: Watch (give strict attention, be cautious, active, and alert) (Mark 13:34-37, AMP).

8.31 And Jesus said, I AM; and you will [all] see the Son of Man seated at the right hand of Power (the Almighty) and coming on the clouds of heaven (Mark 14:62, AMP).

8.32 And then shall they see the Son of Man coming in a cloud with power and great glory (Luke 21:27, KJV).

8.33 Be on guard, so that your hearts will not be weighted down with dissipation and drunkenness and the worries of life, and that day will not come on you suddenly like a trap; for it will come upon all those who dwell on the face of all the earth. But keep on the alert at all times, praying that you may have strength to escape all these things that are about to take place, and to stand before the Son of Man (Luke 21:34-36, NASB).

8.34 That you are not [consciously] falling behind or lacking in any special spiritual endowment or Christian grace [the reception of which is due to the power of divine grace operating in your souls by the Holy Spirit], while you wait and watch [constantly living in hope] for the coming of our Lord Jesus Christ and [His] being made visible to all. And He will establish you to the end [keep you steadfast, give you strength, and guarantee your vindication; He will be your warrant against all accusation or indictment so that you will be] guiltless and irreproachable in the day of our Lord Jesus Christ (the Messiah) (1 Corinthians 1:7-8, AMP).

8.35 But each in his own rank and turn: Christ (the Messiah) [is] the firstfruits, then those who are Christ's [own will be resurrected] at His coming. After that comes the end (the completion), when He delivers over the kingdom to God the Father after rendering inoperative and abolishing every [other] rule and every authority and power (1 Corinthians 15:23-24, AMP).

8.36 For what is our hope, our joy, or the crown in which we will glory in the presence of our Lord Jesus when he comes? Is it not you? (1 Thessalonians 2:19, NIV).

8.37 So that He may strengthen and confirm and establish your hearts faultlessly pure and unblamable in holiness in the sight of our God and Father, at the coming of our Lord Jesus Christ (the Messiah) with all His saints (the holy and glorified people of God)! Amen, (so be it)! (1 Thessalonians 3:13, AMP).

8.38 For this we say to you by the word of the Lord, that we who are alive and remain until the coming of the Lord, will not precede those who have fallen asleep (1 Thessalonians 4:15, NASB).

8.39 And may the God of peace Himself sanctify you through and through [separate you from profane things, make you pure and wholly consecrated to God]; and may your spirit and soul and body be preserved sound and complete [and found] blameless at the coming of our Lord Jesus Christ (the Messiah) (1 Thessalonians 5:23, AMP).

8.40 Concerning the coming of our Lord Jesus Christ and our being gathered to him, we ask you, brothers, not to become easily unsettled or alarmed by some prophecy, report or letter supposed to have come from us, saying that the day of the Lord has already come (2 Thessalonians 2:1-2, NIV).

8.41 I charge [you] in the presence of God and of Christ Jesus, Who is to judge the living and the dead, and by (in the light of) His coming and His kingdom (2 Timothy 4:1, AMP).

8.42 And then the lawless one will be revealed, whom the Lord Jesus will overthrow with the breath of his mouth and destroy by the splendor of his coming (2 Thessalonians 2:8, NIV).

8.43 So be patient, brethren, [as you wait] till the coming of the Lord. See how the farmer waits expectantly for the precious harvest from the land. [See how] he keeps up his patient [vigil] over it until it receives the early and late rains. So you also must be patient. Establish your hearts [strengthen and confirm them in the final certainty], for the coming of the Lord is very near (James 5:7-8, AMP).

8.44 They will say, "Where is this 'coming' he promised? Ever since our fathers died, everything goes on as it has since the beginning of creation." But they deliberately forget that long ago by God's word the heavens existed and the earth was formed out of water and by water. By these waters also the world of that time was deluged and

Part II - Scripture References 207

destroyed. By the same word the present heavens and earth are reserved for fire, being kept for the day of judgment and destruction of ungodly men (2 Peter 3:4-7, NIV).

8.45 And now, little children, abide in him; that, when he shall appear, we may have confidence, and not be ashamed before him at his coming (1 John 2:28, KJV).

8.46 Enoch, the seventh from Adam, prophesied about these men: "See, the Lord is coming with thousands upon thousands of his holy ones to judge everyone, and to convict all the ungodly of all the ungodly acts they have done in the ungodly way, and of all the harsh words ungodly sinners have spoken against him" (Jude 1:14-15, NIV).

8-c: With Glory

8.47 And the glory of the Lord will be revealed, and all mankind together will see it. For the mouth of the Lord has spoken (Isaiah 40:5, NIV).

8.48 For the Son of Man is going to come in his Father's glory with his angels, and then he will reward each person according to what he has done (Matthew 16:27, NIV).

8.49 Then the sign of the Son of Man will appear in the sky, and then all the tribes of the earth will mourn and beat their breasts and lament in anguish, and they will see the Son of Man coming on the clouds of heaven with power and great glory [in brilliancy and splendor] (Matthew 24:30, AMP).

8.50 When the Son of Man shall come in his glory, and all the holy angels with him, then shall he sit upon the throne of his glory (Matthew 25:31, KJV).

8.51 Whosoever therefore shall be ashamed of me and of my words in this adulterous and sinful generation; of him also shall the Son of Man be ashamed, when he cometh in the glory of his Father with the holy angels (Mark 8:38, KJV).

8.52 Then the sign of the Son of Man will appear in the sky, and then all the tribes of the earth will mourn and beat their breasts and lament in anguish, and they will see the Son of Man coming on the clouds of heaven with power and great glory [in brilliancy and splendor] (Matthew 24:30, AMP).

8.53 For whoever is ashamed of Me and My words, the Son of Man will be ashamed of him when He comes in His glory, and the glory of the Father and of the holy angels (Luke 9:26, NASB).

8.54 And then they will see the Son of Man coming in a cloud with great (transcendent and overwhelming) power and [all His kingly] glory (majesty and splendor) (Luke 21:27, AMP).

8.55 I consider that our present sufferings are not worth comparing with the glory that will be revealed in us (Romans 8:18, NIV).

8.56 But we all, with unveiled face, beholding as in a mirror the glory of the Lord, are being transformed into the same image from glory to glory, just as from the Lord, the Spirit (2 Corinthians 3:18, NASB).

8.57 That He might present the church to Himself in glorious splendor, without spot or wrinkle or any such things [that she might be holy and faultless] (Ephesians 5:27, AMP).

8.58 For our citizenship is in heaven, from which also we eagerly wait for a Savior, the Lord Jesus Christ; who will transform the body of our humble state into conformity with the body of His glory, by the exertion of the power that He has even to subject all things to Himself (Philippians 3:20-21, NASB).

8.59 When He comes to be glorified in His saints [on that day He will be made more glorious in His consecrated people], and [He will] be marveled at and admired [in His glory reflected] in all who have believed [who have adhered to, trusted in, and relied on Him], because our witnessing among you was confidently accepted and believed [and confirmed in your lives](2 Thessalonians 1:10, AMP).

8.60 It teaches us to say "No" to ungodliness and worldly passions, and to live self-controlled, upright and godly lives in this present age, while we wait for the blessed hope—the glorious appearing of our great God and Savior, Jesus Christ (Titus 2:12-13, NIV).

8.61 But insofar as you are sharing Christ's sufferings, rejoice, so that when His glory [full of radiance and splendor] is revealed, you may also rejoice with triumph [exultantly] (1 Peter 4:13, AMP).

8.62 To the elders among you, I appeal as a fellow elder, a witness of Christ's sufferings and one who also will share in the glory to be revealed (1 Peter 5:1, NIV).

8-d: Is Revealed

8.63 And the glory of the Lord will be revealed, and all mankind together will see it. For the mouth of the Lord has spoken (Isaiah 40:5, NIV).

8.64 It will be just the same on the day that the Son of Man is revealed (Luke 17:30, NASB).

8.65 I consider that our present sufferings are not worth comparing with the glory that will be revealed in us (Romans 8:18, NIV).

8.66 The work of each [one] will become [plainly, openly] known (shown for what it is); for the day [of Christ] will disclose and declare it, because it will be revealed with fire, and the fire will test and critically appraise the character and worth of the work each person has done (1 Corinthians 3:13, AMP).

8.67 God is just: He will pay back trouble to those who trouble you and give relief to you who are troubled, and to us as well. This will happen when the Lord Jesus is revealed from heaven in blazing fire with his powerful angels (2 Thessalonians 1:6-7, NIV).

8.68 Who are being guarded (garrisoned) by God's power through [your] faith [till you fully inherit that final] salvation that is ready to be revealed [for you] in the last time (1 Peter 1:5, AMP).

8.69 But rejoice that you participate in the sufferings of Christ, so that you may be overjoyed when his glory is revealed (1 Peter 4:13, NIV).

8.70 Therefore, I exhort the elders among you, as your fellow elder and witness of the sufferings of Christ, and a partaker also of the glory that is to be revealed (1 Peter 5:1, NASB

8-e: With His Angels

8.71 The enemy that sowed them is the devil; the harvest is the end of the world; and the reapers are the angels. As therefore the tares are gathered and burned in the fire; so shall it be in the end of this world. The Son of Man shall send forth his angels, and they shall gather out of his kingdom all things that offend, and them which do iniquity (Matthew 13:39-41, KJV).

8.72 This is how it will be at the end of the age. The angels will come and separate the wicked from the righteous (Matthew 13:49, NIV).

8.73 And he shall send his angels with a great sound of a trumpet, and they shall gather together his elect from the four winds, from one end of heaven to the other (Matthew 24:31, KJV).

8.74 For whoever is ashamed of Me and My words in this adulterous and sinful generation, the Son of Man will also be ashamed of him when He comes in the glory of His Father with the holy angels (Mark 8:38, NASB).

8.75 And he will send his angels and gather his elect from the four winds, from the ends of the earth to the ends of the heavens (Mark 13:27, NIV).

8.76 For the Lord Himself will descend from heaven with a loud cry of summons, with the shout of an archangel, and with the blast of the trumpet of God. And those who have departed this life in Christ will rise first (1 Thessalonians 4:16, AMP).

8.77 God is just: He will pay back trouble to those who trouble you and give relief to you who are troubled, and to us as well. This will happen when the Lord Jesus is revealed from heaven in blazing fire with his powerful angels (2 Thessalonians 1:7, NIV).

8-f: Coming in the Clouds of Heaven

8.78 In my vision at night I looked, and there before me was one like a son of man, coming with the clouds of heaven. He approached the Ancient of Days and was led into his presence. He was given authority, glory and sovereign power; all peoples, nations and men of every language worshiped him. His dominion is an everlasting dominion that will not pass away, and his kingdom is one that will never be destroyed (Daniel 7:13-14, NIV).

8.79 And then the sign of the Son of Man will appear in the sky, and then all the tribes of the earth will mourn, and they will see the Son of Man coming on the clouds of the sky with power and great glory (Matthew 24:30, NASB).

8.80 Jesus saith unto him, Thou hast said: nevertheless I say unto you, Hereafter shall ye see the Son of Man sitting on the right hand of power, and coming in the clouds of heaven (Matthew 26:64, KJV).

8.81 And then they will see the Son of Man coming in clouds with great (kingly) power and glory (majesty and splendor) (Mark 13:26, AMP).

8.82 "I am," said Jesus. "And you will see the Son of Man sitting at the right hand of the Mighty One and coming on the clouds of heaven" (Mark 14:62, NIV).

8.83 And then shall they see the Son of Man coming in a cloud with power and great glory (Luke 21:27, KJV).

8.84 After that, we who are still alive and are left will be caught up together with them in the clouds to meet the Lord in the air. And so we will be with the Lord forever (1 Thessalonians 4:17, NIV).

Part II - Scripture References 211

8.85 Behold, He is coming with the clouds, and every eye will see Him, even those who pierced Him; and all the tribes of the earth will mourn over Him. So it is to be. Amen (Revelation 1:7, NASB).

8.86 Then the righteous will shine forth as the sun in the kingdom of their Father. He who has ears, let him hear (Matthew 13:43, NASB).

8-g: Gather His Flock

8.87 Then I Myself will gather the remnant of My flock out of all the countries where I have driven them and bring them back to their pasture, and they will be fruitful and multiply (Jeremiah 23:3, NASB).

8.88 I will surely gather all of you, O Jacob; I will surely collect the remnant of Israel. I will bring them [Israel] together like sheep in a fold, like a flock in the midst of their pasture. They [the fold and the pasture] shall swarm with men and hum with much noise (Micah 2:12, AMP).

8.89 His winnowing fork is in His hand, and He will thoroughly clear His threshing floor; and He will gather His wheat into the barn, but He will burn up the chaff with unquenchable fire (Matthew 3:12, NASB).

8.90 Let both grow together until the harvest: and in the time of harvest I will say to the reapers, Gather ye together first the tares, and bind them in bundles to burn them: but gather the wheat into my barn (Matthew 13:30, KJV).

8.91 And He will send out His angels with a loud trumpet call, and they will gather His elect (His chosen ones) from the four winds, [even] from one end of the universe to the other (Matthew 24:31, AMP).

8.92 And he will send his angels and gather his elect from the four winds, from the ends of the earth to the ends of the heavens (Mark 13:27, NIV).

8.93 Whose fan is in his hand, and he will thoroughly purge his floor, and will gather the wheat into his garner; but the chaff he will burn with fire unquenchable (Luke 3:17, KJV).

8.94 And not for that nation only, but that also he should gather together in one the children of God that were scattered abroad (John 11:52, KJV).

8.95 That in the dispensation of the fulness of times he might gather together in one all things in Christ, both which are in heaven, and which are on earth; even in him (Ephesians 1:10, KJV).

8.96 Concerning the coming of our Lord Jesus Christ and our being gathered to him, we ask you, brothers, not to become easily unsettled or alarmed by some prophecy, report or letter supposed to have come from us, saying that the day of the Lord has already come. (2 Thessalonians 2:1-2, NIV).

8-h: Like a Thief in the Night

8.97 "Behold, I am going to send My messenger, and he will clear the way before Me. And the Lord, whom you seek, will suddenly come to His temple; and the messenger of the covenant, in whom you delight, behold, He is coming," says the Lord of hosts (Malachi 3:1, NASB).

8.98 Therefore be on the alert, for you do not know which day your Lord is coming. But be sure of this, that if the head of the house had known at what time of the night the thief was coming, he would have been on the alert and would not have allowed his house to be broken into. For this reason you also must be ready; for the Son of Man is coming at an hour when you do not think He will (Matthew 24:42-44, NASB).

8.99 Watch therefore [give strict attention and be cautious and active], for you know neither the day nor the hour when the Son of Man will come (Matthew 25:13, AMP).

8.100 No one knows about that day or hour, not even the angels in heaven, nor the Son, but only the Father. Be on guard! Be alert! You do not know when that time will come. It's like a man going away: He leaves his house and puts his servants in charge, each with his assigned task, and tells the one at the door to keep watch. Therefore keep watch because you do not know when the owner of the house will come back—whether in the evening, or at midnight, or when the rooster crows, or at dawn. If he comes suddenly, do not let him find you sleeping. What I say to you, I say to everyone: "Watch!" (Mark 13:32-37, NIV).

8.101 It will be good for those servants whose master finds them watching when he comes. I tell you the truth, he will dress himself to serve, will have them recline at the table and will come and wait on them. It will be good for those servants whose master finds them ready, even if he comes in the second or third watch of the night. But understand this: If the owner of the house had known at what hour the thief was coming, he would not have let his house be broken into. You also must be ready, because the Son of Man will come at an hour when you do not expect him (Luke 12:37-40, NIV).

8.102 But suppose the servant says to himself, 'My master is taking a long time in coming,' and he then begins to beat the menservants and maidservants and to eat and drink and get drunk. The master of that servant will come on a day when he does not expect him and at an hour he is not aware of. He will cut him to pieces and assign him a place with the unbelievers (Luke 12:45-46, NIV).

8.103 Be on guard, so that your hearts will not be weighted down with dissipation and drunkenness and the worries of life, and that day will not come on you suddenly like a trap; for it will come upon all those who dwell on the face of all the earth. But keep on the alert at all times, praying that you may have strength to escape all these things that are about to take place, and to stand before the Son of Man (Luke 21:34-36, NASB).

8.104 For you yourselves know perfectly well that the day of the [return of the] Lord will come [as unexpectedly and suddenly] as a thief in the night. When people are saying, All is well and secure, and, There is peace and safety, then in a moment unforeseen destruction (ruin and death) will come upon them as suddenly as labor pains come upon a woman with child; and they shall by no means escape, for there will be no escape. But you are not in [given up to the power of] darkness, brethren, for that day to overtake you by surprise like a thief (1 Thessalonians 5:2-4, AMP).

8.105 But the day of the Lord will come like a thief, in which the heavens will pass away with a roar and the elements will be destroyed with intense heat, and the earth and its works will be burned up (2 Peter 3:10, NASB).

8.106 Remember, therefore, what you have received and heard; obey it, and repent. But if you do not wake up, I will come like a thief, and you will not know at what time I will come to you (Revelation 3:3, NIV).

8.107 Behold, I come as a thief. Blessed is he that watcheth, and keepeth his garments, lest he walk naked, and they see his shame (Revelation 16:15, KJV)

8-i: Day of the Trumpet

8.108 The great day of the Lord is near, it is near, and hasteth greatly, even the voice of the day of the Lord: the mighty man shall cry there bitterly. That day is a day of wrath, a day of trouble and distress, a day of wasteness and desolation, a day of darkness and gloominess, a day of clouds and thick darkness, A day of the trumpet and alarm against the fenced cities, and against the high towers (Zephaniah 1:14-16, KJV).

8.109 Blow the trumpet in Zion; sound an alarm on My holy Mount [Zion]. Let all the inhabitants of the land tremble, for the day of [the judgment of] the Lord is coming; it is close at hand (Joel 2:1, AMP).

8.110 Take notice! I tell you a mystery (a secret truth, an event decreed by the hidden purpose or counsel of God). We shall not all fall asleep [in death], but we shall all be changed (transformed) In a moment, in the twinkling of an eye, at the [sound of the] last trumpet call. For a trumpet will sound, and the dead [in Christ] will be raised imperishable (free and immune from decay), and we shall be changed (transformed). For this perishable [part of us] must put on the imperishable [nature], and this mortal [part of us, this nature that is capable of dying] must put on immortality (freedom from death) (1 Corinthians 15:51-53, AMP).

8.111 For the Lord Himself will descend from heaven with a loud cry of summons, with the shout of an archangel, and with the blast of the trumpet of God. And those who have departed this life in Christ will rise first (1 Thessa-lonians 4:16, AMP).

8.112 And he will send his angels with a loud trumpet call, and they will gather his elect from the four winds, from one end of the heavens to the other (Matthew 24:31, NIV).

8-j: Severing the Wicked from the Just

8.113 For the upright will live in the land and the blameless will remain in it; But the wicked will be cut off from the land and the treacherous will be uprooted from it (Proverbs 2:21-22, NASB).

8.114 For evildoers shall be cut off, but those who wait and hope and look for the Lord [in the end] shall inherit the earth. [Isa. 57:13c] For yet a little while, and the evildoers will be no more; though you look with care where they used to be, they will not be found. [Heb. 10:36, 37; Rev. 21:7, 8] But the meek [in the end] shall inherit the earth and shall delight themselves in the abundance of peace (Psalm 37:9-11, AMP).

8.115 Let the sinners be consumed out of the earth, and let the wicked be no more. Bless thou the Lord, O my soul. Praise ye the Lord (Psalm 104:35, KJV).

8.116 Behold, the day of the Lord cometh, cruel both with wrath and fierce anger, to lay the land desolate: and he shall destroy the sinners thereof out of it (Isaiah 13:9, KJV).

8.117 As it was in the days of Noah, so it will be at the coming of the Son of Man. For in the days before the flood, people were eating and drinking, marrying and giving in marriage, up to the day Noah entered the ark; and they knew nothing about what would happen until the flood came and took them all away. That is how it will be at the coming of the Son of Man. Two men will be in the field; one will be taken and the other left. Two women will be grinding with a hand mill; one will be taken and the other left (Matthew 24:37-41, NIV).

8.118 When the Son of Man comes in his glory, and all the angels with him, he will sit on his throne in heavenly glory. All the nations will be gathered before him, and he will separate the people one from another as a shepherd separates the sheep from the goats. He will put the sheep on his right and the goats on his left. Then the King will say to those on his right, 'Come, you who are blessed by my Father; take your inheritance, the kingdom prepared for you since the creation of the world' (Matthew 25:31-34, NIV).

8.119 I tell you, on that night there will be two in one bed; one will be taken and the other will be left. There will be two women grinding at the same place; one will be taken and the other will be left. ["Two men will be in the field; one will be taken and the other will be left."] (Luke 17:34-36, NASB).

8.120 Just as the darnel (weeds resembling wheat) is gathered and burned with fire, so it will be at the close of the age. The Son of Man will send forth His angels, and they will gather out of His kingdom all causes of offense [persons by whom others are drawn into error or sin] and all who do iniquity and act wickedly, And will cast them into the furnace of fire; there will be weeping and wailing and grinding of teeth (Matthew 13:40-42, AMP).

8.121 So shall it be at the end of the world: the angels shall come forth, and sever the wicked from among the just (Matthew 13:49, KJV).

8.122 My prayer is not that you take them out of the world but that you protect them from the evil one (John 17:15, NIV).

8-k: Every Knee Shall Bow

8.123 I have sworn by myself, the word is gone out of my mouth in righteousness, and shall not return, That unto me every knee shall bow, every tongue shall swear (Isaiah 45:23, KJV).

8.124 For it is written, As I live, says the Lord, every knee shall bow to Me, and every tongue shall confess to God [acknowledge Him to His honor and to His praise] (Romans 14:11, AMP).

8.125 so that at the name of Jesus every knee will bow, of those who are in heaven and on earth and under the earth, and that every tongue will confess that Jesus Christ is Lord, to the glory of God the Father (Philippians 2:10-11, NASB).

8.126 Look, he is coming with the clouds, and every eye will see him, even those who pierced him; and all the peoples of the earth will mourn because of him. So shall it be! Amen (Revelation 1:7, NIV).

8-l: Fire

8.127 But who may abide the day of his coming? and who shall stand when he appeareth? for he is like a refiner's fire, and like fullers' soap: And he shall sit as a refiner and purifier of silver: and he shall purify the sons of Levi, and purge them as gold and silver, that they may offer unto the Lord an offering in righteousness (Malachi 3:2-3, KJV).

8.128 For behold, the day comes that shall burn like an oven, and all the proud and arrogant, yes, and all that do wickedly and are lawless, shall be stubble; the day that comes shall burn them up, says the Lord of hosts, so that it will leave them neither root nor branch (Malachi 4:1, AMP).

8.129 His winnowing fork is in His hand, and He will thoroughly clear His threshing floor; and He will gather His wheat into the barn, but He will burn up the chaff with unquenchable fire (Matthew 3:12, NASB).

8.130 Let both grow together until the harvest: and in the time of harvest I will say to the reapers, Gather ye together first the tares, and bind them in bundles to burn them: but gather the wheat into my barn (Matthew 13:30, KJV).

8.131 Just as the darnel (weeds resembling wheat) is gathered and burned with fire, so it will be at the close of the age. The Son of Man will send forth His angels, and they will gather out of His kingdom all causes of offense [persons by whom others are drawn into error or sin] and all who do iniquity and act wickedly, and will cast them into the furnace of fire; there will be weeping and wailing and grinding of teeth (Matthew 13:40-42, AMP).

8.132 Whose fan is in his hand, and he will thoroughly purge his floor, and will gather the wheat into his garner; but the chaff he will burn with fire unquenchable (Luke 3:17, KJV).

8.133 But the same day that Lot went out of Sodom it rained fire and brimstone from heaven, and destroyed them all. Even thus shall it be in the day when the Son of Man is revealed (Luke 17:29-30, KJV).

8.134 And to [recompense] you who are so distressed and afflicted [by granting you] relief and rest along with us [your fellow sufferers] when the Lord Jesus is revealed from heaven with His mighty angels in a flame of fire, To deal out retribution (chastisement and vengeance) upon those who do not know or perceive or become acquainted with God, and [upon those] who ignore and refuse to obey the Gospel of our Lord Jesus Christ (2 Thessalonians 1:7-8, AMP).

8.135 So that the proof of your faith, being more precious than gold which is perishable, even though tested by fire, may be found to result in praise and glory and honor at the revelation of Jesus Christ (1 Peter 1:7, NASB).

8.136 But the day of the Lord will come like a thief. The heavens will disappear with a roar; the elements will be destroyed by fire, and the earth and everything in it will be laid bare. Since every-thing will be destroyed in this way, what kind of people ought you to be? You ought to live holy and godly lives as you look forward to the day of God and speed its coming. That day will bring about the destruction of the heavens by fire, and the elements will melt in the heat (2 Peter 3:10-12, NIV).

8.137 They will say, "Where is this 'coming' he promised? Ever since our fathers died, everything goes on as it has since the beginning of creation." But they deliberately forget that long ago by God's word the heavens existed and the earth was formed out of water and by water. By these waters also the world of that time was deluged and destroyed. By the same word the present heavens and earth are reserved for fire, being kept for the day of judgment and destruction of ungodly men (2 Peter 3:4-7, NIV).

REFERENCE 9 — Judgment Day

9.1 But the Lord shall remain and continue forever; He has prepared and established His throne for judgment. [Heb. 1:11] And He will judge the world in righteousness (rightness and Equity); He will minister justice to the peoples in uprightness (Psalm 9:7-8, AMP).

9.2 The wicked shall be turned into hell, and all the nations that forget God (Psalm 9:17, KJV).

9.3 For the Lord loves justice And does not forsake His godly ones; They are preserved forever, But the descendants of the wicked will be cut off (Psalm 37:28, NASB).

9.4 Rejoice, O young man, in thy youth; and let thy heart cheer thee in the days of thy youth, and walk in the ways of thine heart, and in the sight of thine eyes: but know thou, that for all these things God will bring thee into judgment (Ecclesiastes 11:9, KJV).

9.5 For God will bring every deed into judgment, including every hidden thing, whether it is good or evil (Ecclesiastes 12:14, NIV).

9.6 Wail, for the day of the Lord is near! It will come as destruction from the Almighty. Therefore all hands will fall limp, And every man's heart will melt. They will be terrified, Pains and anguish will take hold of them; They will writhe like a woman in labor, They will look at one another in astonishment, Their faces aflame. Behold, the day of the Lord is coming, Cruel, with fury and burning anger, To make the land a desolation; And He will exterminate its sinners from it. For the stars of heaven and their constellations Will not flash forth their light; The sun will be dark when it rises And the moon will not shed its light. Thus I will punish the world for its evil And the wicked for their iniquity; I will also put an end to the arrogance of the proud And abase the haughtiness of the ruthless. I will make mortal man scarcer than pure gold And mankind than the gold of Ophir. Therefore I will make the heavens tremble, And the earth will be shaken from its place At the fury of the Lord of hosts In the day of His burning anger (Isaiah 13:6-13, NASB).

9.7 See, the Lord is coming out of his dwelling to punish the people of the earth for their sins. The earth will disclose the blood shed upon her; she will conceal her slain no longer (Isaiah 26:21, NIV).

9.8 But let him who glories glory in this: that he understands and knows Me [personally and practically, directly discerning and recognizing My character], that I am the Lord, Who practices loving-kindness, judgment, and righteousness in the earth, for in these things I delight, says the Lord (Jeremiah 9:24, AMP).

9.9 A stream of fire came forth from before Him; a thousand thousands ministered to Him and ten thousand times ten thousand rose up and stood before Him; the Judge was seated [the court was in session] and the books were opened (Daniel 7:10, AMP).

9.10 For, behold, the day cometh, that shall burn as an oven; and all the proud, yea, and all that do wickedly, shall be stubble: and the day that cometh shall burn them up, saith the Lord of hosts, that it shall leave them neither root nor branch (Malachi 4:1, KJV).

9.11 Enter through the narrow gate; for wide is the gate and spacious and broad is the way that leads away to destruction, and many are those who are entering through it. But the gate is narrow (contracted by pressure) and the way is straitened and compressed that leads away to life, and few are those who find it (Matthew 7:13-14, AMP).

9.12 But I tell you that every careless word that people speak, they shall give an accounting for it in the day of judgment (Matthew 12:36, NASB).

9.13 The Son of Man will send out his angels, and they will weed out of his kingdom everything that causes sin and all who do evil. They will throw them into the fiery furnace, where there will be weeping and gnashing of teeth (Matthew 13:41-42, NIV).

9.14 So shall it be at the end of the world: the angels shall come forth, and sever the wicked from among the just, And shall cast them into the furnace of fire: there shall be wailing and gnashing of teeth (Matthew 13:49-50, KJV).

9.15 Then shall he say also unto them on the left hand, Depart from me, ye cursed, into everlasting fire, prepared for the devil and his angels (Matthew 25:41, KJV).

9.16 If your hand causes you to sin, cut it off. It is better for you to enter life maimed than with two hands to go into hell, where the fire never goes out (Mark 9:43, NIV).

9.17 But I will warn you whom to fear: fear the One who, after He has killed, has authority to cast into hell; yes, I tell you, fear Him! (Luke 12:5, NASB).

9.18 That servant who knows his master's will and does not get ready or does not do what his master wants will be beaten with many blows (Luke 12:47, NIV).

9.19 But you, why do you judge your brother? Or you again, why do you regard your brother with contempt? For we will all stand before the judgment seat of God (Romans 14:10, NASB).

9.20 For we must all appear and be revealed as we are before the judgment seat of Christ, so that each one may receive [his pay] according to what he has done in the body, whether good or evil [considering what his purpose and motive have been, and what he has achieved, been busy with, and given himself and his attention to accomplishing] (2 Corinthians 5:10, AMP).

9.21 He will punish those who do not know God and do not obey the gospel of our Lord Jesus. They will be punished with everlasting destruction and shut out from the presence of the Lord and from the majesty of his power (2 Thessalonians 1:8-9, NIV).

9.22 Just as man is destined to die once, and after that to face judgment (Hebrews 9:27, NIV).

9.23 I solemnly charge you in the presence of God and of Christ Jesus, who is to judge the living and the dead, and by His appearing and His kingdom (2 Timothy 4:1, NASB).

9.24 For the time is come that judgment must begin at the house of God: and if it first begin at us, what shall the end be of them that obey not the gospel of God? (1 Peter 4:17, KJV).

9.25 For if God did not spare angels when they sinned, but cast them into hell and committed them to pits of darkness, reserved for judgment (2 Peter 2:4, NASB).

9.26 The Lord knows how to rescue the godly from temptation, and to keep the unrighteous under punishment for the day of judgment (2 Peter 2:9, NASB).

9.27 By the same word the present heavens and earth are reserved for fire, being kept for the day of judgment and destruction of ungodly men (2 Peter 3:7, NIV).

9.28 Though you already know all this, I want to remind you that the Lord delivered his people out of Egypt, but later destroyed those who did not believe. And the angels who did not keep their positions of authority but abandoned their own home—these he has kept in darkness, bound with everlasting chains for judgment on the great Day. In a similar way, Sodom and Gomorrah and the surrounding towns gave themselves up to sexual immorality and perversion. They serve as an example of those who suffer the punishment of eternal fire (Jude 1:57, NIV).

9.29 He said in a loud voice, "Fear God and give him glory, because the hour of his judgment has come. Worship him who made the heavens, the earth, the sea and the springs of water (Revelation 14:7, NIV).

9.30 I [also] saw the dead, great and small; they stood before the throne, and books were opened. Then another book was opened, which is [the Book] of Life. And the dead were judged (sentenced) by what they had done [their whole way of feeling and acting, their aims and endeavors] in accordance with what was recorded in the books (Revelation 20:12, AMP).

9.31 And if anyone's name was not found written in the book of life, he was thrown into the lake of fire (Revelation 20:15, NIV).

9.32 But as for the cowards and the ignoble and the contemptible and the cravenly lacking in courage and the cowardly submissive, and as for the unbelieving and faithless, and as for the depraved and defiled with abominations, and as for murderers and the lewd and adulterous and the practicers of magic arts and the idolaters (those who give supreme devotion to anyone or anything other than God) and all liars (those who knowingly convey untruth by word or deed)—[all of these shall have] their part in the lake that blazes with fire and brimstone. This is the second death (Revelation 21:8, AMP).

9.33 And the angels who did not keep their positions of authority but abandoned their own home—these he has kept in darkness, bound with everlasting chains for judgment on the great Day (Jude 1:6, NIV).

REFERENCE 10 — Only a Remnant Will Be Saved

10.1 Except the Lord of hosts had left us a very small remnant [of survivors], we should have been like Sodom, and we should have been like Gomorrah (Isaiah 1:9, AMP).

10.2 And it shall come to pass, that whosoever shall call on the name of the Lord shall be delivered: for in mount Zion and in Jerusalem shall be deliverance, as the Lord hath said, and in the remnant whom the Lord shall call (Joel 2:32, KJV).

10.3 And I will make her that halted a remnant, and her that was cast far off a strong nation: and the Lord shall reign over them in mount Zion from henceforth, even for ever (Micah 4:7, KJV).

10.4 And Isaiah calls out (solemnly cries aloud) over Israel: Though the number of the sons of Israel be like the sand of the sea, only the remnant (a small part of them) will be saved [from perdition, condemnation, judgment] (Romans 9:27, AMP).

REFERENCE 11 — The Kingdom of God

11.1 But seek ye first the kingdom of God, and his righteousness; and all these things shall be added unto you (Matthew 6:33, KJV).

11.2 But if I drive out demons by the Spirit of God, then the kingdom of God has come upon you (Matthew 12:28, NIV).

11.3 And again I say unto you, It is easier for a camel to go through the eye of a needle, than for a rich man to enter into the kingdom of God (Matthew 19:24, KJV).

11.4 "Which of the two did the will of his father?" They said, "The first." Jesus said to them, "Truly I say to you that the tax collectors and prostitutes will get into the kingdom of God before you (Matthew 21:31, NASB).

11.5 Therefore I tell you that the kingdom of God will be taken away from you and given to a people who will produce its fruit (Matthew 21:43, NIV).

11.6 Now after that John was put in prison, Jesus came into Galilee, preaching the gospel of the kingdom of God, And saying, The time is fulfilled, and the kingdom of God is at hand: repent ye, and believe the gospel (Mark 1:14-15, KJV).

11.7 Now after John was arrested and put in prison, Jesus came into Galilee, preaching the good news (the Gospel) of the kingdom of God, And saying, The [appointed period of] time is fulfilled (completed), and the kingdom of God is at hand; repent (have a change of mind which issues in regret for past sins and in change of conduct for the better) and believe (trust in, rely on, and adhere to) the good news (the Gospel) (Mark 1:14-15, AMP).

11.8 He also said, "This is what the kingdom of God is like. A man scatters seed on the ground. night and day, whether he sleeps or gets up, the seed sprouts and grows, though he does not know how. All by itself the soil produces grain—first the stalk, then the head, then the full kernel in the head. As soon as the grain is ripe, he puts the sickle to it, because the harvest has come." Again he said, "What shall we say the kingdom of God is like, or what parable shall we use to describe it? It is like a mustard seed, which is the smallest seed you plant in the ground. Yet when planted, it grows and becomes the largest of all garden plants, with such big branches that the birds of the air can perch in its shade (Mark 4:26-32, NIV).

11.9 And he said unto them, Verily I say unto you, That there be some of them that stand here, which shall not taste of death, till they have seen the kingdom of God come with power (Mark 9:1, KJV).

11.10 And if thine eye offend thee, pluck it out: it is better for thee to enter into the kingdom of God with one eye, than having two eyes to be cast into hell fire (Mark 9:47, KJV).

11.11 When Jesus saw this, he was indignant. He said to them, "Let the little children come to me, and do not hinder them, for the kingdom of God belongs to such as these. I tell you the truth, anyone who will not receive the kingdom of God like a little child will never enter it (Mark 10:14-15, NIV).

11.12 And Jesus looked around and said to His disciples, With what difficulty will those who possess wealth and keep on holding it enter the kingdom of God! And the disciples were amazed and bewildered and perplexed at His words. But Jesus said to them again, Children, how hard it is for those who trust (place their confidence, their sense of safety) in riches to enter the kingdom of God! It is easier for a camel to go through the eye of a needle than for a rich man to enter the kingdom of God (Mark 10:23-25, AMP).

11.13 And when Jesus saw that he answered discreetly, he said unto him, Thou art not far from the kingdom of God. And no man after that durst ask him any question (Mark 12:34, KJV).

11.14 Solemnly and surely I tell you, I shall not again drink of the fruit of the vine till that day when I drink it of a new and a higher quality in God's kingdom (Mark 14:25, AMP).

11.15 Joseph of Arimathaea, an honourable counsellor, which also waited for the kingdom of God, came, and went in boldly unto Pilate, and craved the body of Jesus (Mark 15:43, KJV).

11.16 But He said to them, "I must preach the kingdom of God to the other cities also, for I was sent for this purpose (Luke 4:43, NASB).

11.17 And solemnly lifting up His eyes on His disciples, He said: Blessed (happy—with life-joy and satisfaction in God's favor and salvation, apart from your outward condition—and to be envied) are you poor and lowly and afflicted (destitute of wealth, influence, position, and honor), for the kingdom of God is yours (Luke 6:20, AMP).

11.18 After this, Jesus traveled about from one town and village to another, proclaiming the good news of the kingdom of God. The Twelve were with him (Luke 8:1, NIV).

11.19 And he sent them to preach the kingdom of God, and to heal the sick (Luke 9:2, KJV).

11.20 But the crowds learned about it and followed him. He welcomed them and spoke to them about the kingdom of God, and healed those who needed healing (Luke 9:11, NIV).

11.21 But I tell you of a truth, there be some standing here, which shall not taste of death, till they see the kingdom of God (Luke 9:27, KJV).

11.22 And Jesus said unto him, No man, having put his hand to the plough, and looking back, is fit for the kingdom of God (Luke 9:62, KJV).

11.23 And heal those in it who are sick, and say to them, "The kingdom of God has come near to you." But whatever city you enter and they do not receive you, go out into its streets and say, "Even the dust of your city which clings to our feet we wipe off in protest against you; yet be sure of this, that the kingdom of God has come near" (Luke 10:9-11, NASB).

11.24 But if I drive out demons by the finger of God, then the kingdom of God has come to you (Luke 11:20, NIV).

11.25 But rather seek ye the kingdom of God; and all these things shall be added unto you (Luke 12:31, KJV).

11.26 Then said he, Unto what is the kingdom of God like? and whereunto shall I resemble it? It is like a grain of mustard seed, which a man took, and cast into his garden; and it grew, and waxed a great tree; and the fowls of the air lodged in the branches of it. And again he said, Whereunto shall I liken the kingdom of God? It is like leaven, which a woman took and hid in three measures of meal, till the whole was leavened (Luke 13:18-21, KJV).

11.27 There will be weeping there, and gnashing of teeth, when you see Abraham, Isaiah and Jacob and all the prophets in the kingdom of God, but you yourselves thrown out (Luke 13:29, NIV).

11.28 People will come from east and west and north and south, and will take their places at the feast in the kingdom of God (Luke 13:28-29, NIV).

11.29 Until John came, there were the Law and the Prophets; since then the good news (the Gospel) of the kingdom of God is being preached, and everyone strives violently to go in [would force his own way rather than God's way into it] (Luke 16:16, AMP).

11.30 Asked by the Pharisees when the kingdom of God would come, He replied to them by saying, The kingdom of God does not come with signs to be observed or with visible display, Nor will people say, Look! Here [it is]! or, See, [it is] there! For behold, the kingdom of God is within you [in your hearts] and among you [surrounding you] (Luke 17:20-21, AMP).

11.31 But Jesus called the children to him and said, "Let the little children come to me, and do not hinder them, for the kingdom of God belongs to such as these. I tell you the truth, anyone who will not receive the kingdom of God like a little child will never enter it (Luke 18:16-17, NIV).

11.32 And Jesus looked at him and said, "How hard it is for those who are wealthy to enter the kingdom of God! For it is easier for a camel to go through the eye of a needle than for a rich man to enter the kingdom of God" (Luke 18:24-25, NASB).

11.33 Even so, when you see these things happening, you know that the kingdom of God is near (Luke 21:31, NIV).

11.34 For I say unto you, I will not any more eat thereof, until it be fulfilled in the kingdom of God (Luke 22:16, KJV).

11.35 For I say unto you, I will not drink of the fruit of the vine, until the kingdom of God shall come (Luke 22:18, KJV).

11.36 Who had not consented to their decision and action. He came from the Judean town of Arimathea and he was waiting for the kingdom of God (Luke 23:51, NIV).

11.37 Jesus answered and said unto him, Verily, verily, I say unto thee, Except a man be born again, he cannot see the kingdom of God. Nicodemus saith unto him, How can a man be born when he is old? can he enter the second time into his mother's womb, and be born? Jesus answered, Verily, verily, I say unto thee, Except a man be born of water and of the Spirit, he cannot enter into the kingdom of God (John 3:3-5, KJV).

11.38 To them also He showed Himself alive after His passion (His suffering in the garden and on the cross) by [a series of] many convincing demonstrations [unquestionable evidences and infallible proofs], appearing to them during forty days and talking [to them] about the things of the kingdom of God (Acts 1:3, AMP).

11.39 But when they believed Philip as he preached the good news of the kingdom of God and the name of Jesus Christ, they were baptized, both men and women (Acts 8:12, NIV).

11.40 Strengthening the souls of the disciples, encouraging them to continue in the faith, and saying, "Through many tribulations we must enter the kingdom of God" (Acts 14:22, NASB).

11.41 And he went into the synagogue, and spake boldly for the space of three months, disputing and persuading the things concerning the kingdom of God (Acts 19:8, KJV).

11.42 And now, behold, I know that ye all, among whom I have gone preaching the kingdom of God, shall see my face no more (Acts 20:25, KJV).

11.43 They arranged to meet Paul on a certain day, and came in even larger numbers to the place where he was staying. From morning till evening he explained and declared to them the kingdom of God and tried to convince them about Jesus from the Law of Moses and from the Prophets (Acts 28:23, NIV).

11.44 Preaching the kingdom of God, and teaching those things which concern the Lord Jesus Christ, with all confidence, no man forbidding him (Acts 28:31, KJV).

11.45 [After all] the kingdom of God is not a matter of [getting the] food and drink [one likes], but instead it is righteousness (that state which makes a person acceptable to God) and [heart] peace and joy in the Holy Spirit (Romans 14:17, AMP).

11.46 For the kingdom of God is not a matter of talk but of power (1 Corinthians 4:20, NIV).

11.47 Or do you not know that the unrighteous will not inherit the kingdom of God? Do not be deceived; neither fornicators, nor idolaters, nor adulterers, nor effeminate, nor homosexuals, nor thieves, nor the covetous, nor drunkards, nor revilers, nor swindlers, will inherit the kingdom of God (1 Corinthians 6:9-10, NASB).

11.48 I declare to you, brothers, that flesh and blood cannot inherit the kingdom of God, nor does the perishable inherit the imperishable (1 Corin-thians 15:50, NIV).

11.49 Envyings, murders, drunkenness, revellings, and such like: of the which I tell you before, as I have also told you in time past, that they which do such things shall not inherit the kingdom of God (Galatians 5:21, KJV).

11.50 This is a plain indication of God's righteous judgment so that you will be considered worthy of the kingdom of God, for which indeed you are suffering (2 Thessalonians 1:5, NASB).

REFERENCE 12 — The City of God

12.1 There is a river, the streams whereof shall make glad the city of God, the holy place of the tabernacles of the most High (Psalm 46:4, KJV).

12.2 As we have heard, so have we seen in the city of the Lord of hosts, in the city of our God: God will establish it for ever. Selah (Psalm 48:8, KJV).

12.3 Morning after morning I will root up all the wicked in the land, that I may eliminate all the evildoers from the city of the Lord (Psalm 101:8, AMP).

12.4 Unless the Lord builds the house, They labor in vain who build it; Unless the Lord guards the city, The watchman keeps awake in vain (Psalm 127:1, NASB).

12.5 Then shall there enter into the gates of this city kings and princes sitting upon the throne of David, riding in chariots and on horses, they, and their princes, the men of Judah, and the inhabitants of Jerusalem: and this city shall remain for ever (Jeremiah 17:25, KJV).

12.6 The gates of the city will be named after the tribes of Israel. The three gates on the north side will be the gate of Reuben, the gate of Judah and the gate of Levi (Ezekiel 48:31, KJV).

12.7 The distance around the city shall be 18,000 [4 x 4,500] measures; and the name of the city from that day and ever after shall be, The Lord Is There (Ezekiel 48:35, AMP).

12.8 For he was looking forward to the city with foundations, whose architect and builder is God (Hebrews 11:10, NIV).

12.9 Instead, they were longing for a better country—a heavenly one. Therefore God is not ashamed to be called their God, for he has prepared a city for them (Hebrews 11:16, NIV).

12.10 But you have come to Mount Zion, to the heavenly Jerusalem, the city of the living God. You have come to thousands upon thousands of angels in joyful assembly (Hebrews 12:22, NIV).

12.11 For here we have no permanent city, but we are looking for the one which is to come (Hebrews 13:14, AMP).

12.12 Him who overcomes I will make a pillar in the temple of my God. Never again will he leave it. I will write on him the name of my God and the name of the city of my God, the new Jerusalem, which is coming down out of heaven from my God; and I will also write on him my new name (Revelation 3:12, NIV).

12.13 And they swarmed up over the broad plain of the earth and encircled the fortress (camp) of God's people (the saints) and the beloved city; but fire descended from heaven and consumed them (Revelation 20:9, AMP).

12.14 I saw the Holy City, the new Jerusalem, coming down out of heaven from God, prepared as a bride beautifully dressed for her husband (Revelation 21:2, NIV).

12.15 And he carried me away in the spirit to a great and high mountain, and showed me that great city, the holy Jerusalem, descending out of heaven from God (Revelation 21:10, KJV).

12.16 And the wall of the city had twelve foundation stones, and on them were the twelve names of the twelve apostles of the Lamb. The one who spoke with me had a gold measuring rod to measure the city, and its gates and its wall. The city is laid out as a square, and its length is as great as the width; and he measured the city with the rod, fifteen hundred miles; its length and width and height are equal. And he measured its wall, seventy-two yards, according to human measurements, which are also angelic measurements. The material of the wall was jasper; and the city was pure gold, like clear glass. The foundation stones of the city wall were adorned with every kind of precious stone. The first foundation stone was jasper; the second, sapphire; the third, chalcedony; the fourth, emerald; the fifth, sardonyx; the sixth, sardius; the seventh, chrysolite; the eighth, beryl; the ninth, topaz; the tenth, chrysoprase; the eleventh, jacinth; the twelfth, amethyst. And the twelve gates were twelve pearls; each one of the gates was a single pearl. And the street of the city was pure gold, like transparent glass. I saw no temple in it, for the Lord God the Almighty and the Lamb are its temple. And the city has no need of the sun or of the moon to shine on it, for the glory of God has illumined it, and its lamp is the Lamb. The nations will walk by its light, and the kings of the earth will bring their glory into it. In the daytime (for there will be no night there) its gates will never be closed; and they will bring the glory and the honor of the nations into it; and nothing unclean, and no one who practices abomination and lying, shall ever come into it, but only those whose names are written in the Lamb's book of life (Revelation 21:14-27, NASB).

REFERENCE 13 — The End: Matthew, Mark and Luke Parallel Accounts

The following three gospel books record Jesus's teaching when he answered the apostles' question: "What shall be the sign of thy coming, and of the end of the world?" The answers are too lengthy to include in this REFERENCE section, but their chapters and verses are listed for your REFERENCE:

13.1   Matthew 24:1-31

13.2   Mark 15:1-37

13.3   Luke 21:1-38

Part III

Only Jesus...

REFERENCE 14 — Only Jesus Can Save You

14.1 And straightway the father of the child cried out, and said with tears, Lord, I believe; help thou mine unbelief (Mark 9:24, KJV).

14.2 I bring you good tiding of great joy which will be to all people. For there is born to you this day in the city of David a Savior, who is Christ the Lord (Luke 2:10-11 (NKJ)

14.3 Those along the traveled road are the people who have heard; then the devil comes and carries away the message out of their hearts, that they may not believe (acknowledge Me as their Savior and devote themselves to Me) and be saved [here and hereafter] (Luke 8:12, AMP).

14.4 Jesus answered and said to him, "Truly, truly, I say to you, unless one is born again he cannot see the kingdom of God" (John 3:3, NASB).

14.5 Do not be amazed that I said to you, "You must be born again. The wind blows where it wishes and you hear the sound of it, but do not know where it comes from and where it is going; so is everyone who is born of the Spirit (John 3:7-8, NASB).

14.6 For God so loved the world that he gave his one and only Son, that whoever believes in him shall not perish but have eternal life (John 3:16, NIV).

14.7 But whoever takes a drink of the water that I will give him shall never, no never, be thirsty any more. But the water that I will give him shall become a spring of water welling up (flowing, bubbling) [continually] within him unto (into, for) eternal life (John 4:14, NIV).

14.8 I assure you, most solemnly I tell you, the person whose ears are open to My words [who listens to My message] and believes and trusts in and clings to and relies on Him Who sent Me has (possesses now) eternal life. And he does not come into judgment [does not incur sentence of judgment, will not come under condemnation], but he has already passed over out of death into life (John 5:24, AMP).

14.9 Do not work for food that spoils, but for food that endures to eternal life, which the Son of Man will give you. On him God the Father has placed his seal of approval (John 6:27, NIV).

14.10 They then said, What are we to do, that we may [habitually] be working the works of God? [What are we to do to carry out what God requires?] Jesus replied, This is the work (service) that God asks of you: that you believe in the One Whom He has sent [that you cleave to, trust, rely on, and have faith in His Messenger] (John 6:28-29, AMP).

14.11 I am the door; if anyone enters through Me, he will be saved, and will go in and out and find pasture (John 10:9, NASB).

14.12 My sheep hear my voice, and I know them, and they follow me: And I give unto them eternal life; and they shall never perish, neither shall any man pluck them out of my hand (John 10:27-28, KJV).

14.13 I know that His commandment is eternal life; therefore the things I speak, I speak just as the Father has told Me (John 12:50, NASB).

14.14 Jesus answered, "I am the way and the truth and the life. No one comes to the Father except through me" (John 14:6, NIV).

14.15 For you granted him authority over all people that he might give eternal life to all those you have given him. Now this is eternal life: that they may know you, the only true God, and Jesus Christ, whom you have sent (John 17:2-3, NIV).

14.16 Let it be known to all of you and to all the people of Israel, that by the name of Jesus Christ the Nazarene, whom you crucified, whom God raised from the dead— by this name this man stands here before you in good health. He is the stone which was rejected by you, the builders, but which became the chief cornerstone. And there is salvation in no one else; for there is no other name under heaven that has been given among men by which we must be saved (Acts 4:10-12, NASB).

14.17 And there is salvation in no one else; for there is no other name under heaven that has been given among men by which we must be saved (Acts 4:12, NASB).

14.18 Therefore, my brothers, I want you to know that through Jesus the forgiveness of sins is proclaimed to you. Through him everyone who believes is justified from everything you could not be justified from by the law of Moses (Acts 13:38-39, NIV).

14.19 But God demonstrates His own love toward us, in that while we were yet sinners, Christ died for us. Much more then, having now been justified by His blood, we shall be saved from the wrath of God through Him. For if while we were enemies we were reconciled to God through the death of His Son, much more, having been reconciled, we shall be saved by His life. And not only this, but we also exult in God through our Lord Jesus Christ, through whom we have now received the reconciliation (Romans 5:8-11, NASB).

14.20 But God's free gift is not at all to be compared to the trespass [His grace is out of all proportion to the fall of man]. For if many died through one man's falling away (his lapse, his offense), much more profusely did God's grace and the free gift [that comes] through the undeserved favor of the one Man Jesus Christ abound and overflow to and for [the benefit of] many (Romans 5:15, AMP).

14.21 The law was added so that the trespass might increase. But where sin increased, grace increased all the more, so that, just as sin reigned in death, so also grace might reign through righteousness to bring eternal life through Jesus Christ our Lord (Romans 5:20-21, NIV).

14.22 But now being made free from sin, and become servants to God, ye have your fruit unto holiness, and the end everlasting life. For the wages of sin is death; but the gift of God is eternal life through Jesus Christ our Lord (Romans 6:22-23, KJV).

14.23 For those who are according to the flesh and are controlled by its unholy desires set their minds on and pursue those things which gratify the flesh, but those who are according to the Spirit and are controlled by the desires of the Spirit set their minds on and seek those things which gratify the [Holy] Spirit. Now the mind of the flesh [which is sense and reason without the Holy Spirit] is death [death that comprises all the miseries arising from sin, both here and hereafter]. But the mind of the [Holy] Spirit is life and [soul] peace [both now and forever]. [That is] because the mind of the flesh [with its carnal thoughts and purposes] is hostile to God, for it does not submit itself to God's Law; indeed it cannot. So then those who are living the life of the flesh [catering to the appetites and impulses of their carnal nature] cannot please or satisfy God, or be acceptable to Him. But you are not living the life of the flesh, you are living the life of the Spirit, if the [Holy] Spirit of God [really] dwells within you [directs and controls you]. But if anyone does not possess the [Holy] Spirit of Christ, he is none of His [he does not belong to Christ, is not truly a child of God (Romans 8:5-9, AMP).

14.24 Because if you acknowledge and confess with your lips that Jesus is Lord and in your heart believe (adhere to, trust in, and rely on the truth) that God raised Him from the dead, you will be saved (Romans 10:9, AMP).

14.25 This righteousness from God comes through faith in Jesus Christ to all who believe. There is no difference, for all have sinned and fall short of the glory of God, and are justified freely by his grace through the redemption that came by Christ Jesus. God presented him as a sacrifice of atonement, through faith in his blood. He did this to demonstrate his justice, because in his forbearance he had left the sins committed beforehand unpunished—he did it to demonstrate his justice at the present time, so as to be just and the one who justifies those who have faith in Jesus (Romans 3:22-26, NIV).

14.26 But it is from Him that you have your life in Christ Jesus, Whom God made our Wisdom from God, [revealed to us a knowledge of the divine plan of salvation previously hidden, manifesting itself as] our Righteousness [thus making us upright and putting us in right standing with God], and our Consecration [making us pure and holy], and our Redemption [providing our ransom from eternal penalty for sin] (1 Corinthians 1:30, AMP).

14.27 And such some of you were [once]. But you were washed clean (purified by a complete atonement for sin and made free from the guilt of sin), and you were consecrated (set apart, hallowed), and you were justified [pronounced righteous, by trusting] in the name of the Lord Jesus Christ and in the [Holy] Spirit of our God. Everything is permissible (1 Corinthians 6:11-12, AMP).

14.28 For since [it was] through a man that death [came into the world, it is] also through a Man that the resurrection of the dead [has come]. For just as [because of their union of nature] in Adam all people die, so also [by virtue of their union of nature] shall all in Christ be made alive (1 Corinthians 15:21-22, AMP).

14.29 Therefore if any person is [ingrafted] in Christ (the Messiah) he is a new creation (a new creature altogether); the old [previous moral and spiritual condition] has passed away. Behold, the fresh and new has come! But all things are from God, Who through Jesus Christ reconciled us to Himself [received us into favor, brought us into harmony with Himself] and gave to us the ministry of reconciliation [that by word and deed we might aim to bring others into harmony with Him]. It was God [personally present] in Christ, reconciling and restoring the world to favor with Himself, not counting up and holding against [men] their trespasses [but cancelling them], and committing to us the message of reconciliation (of the restoration to favor) (2 Corinthians 5:17-19, AMP).

14.30 In whom we have redemption through his blood, the forgiveness of sins According to the riches of his grace; Wherein he hath abounded toward us in all wisdom and prudence; Having made known unto us the mystery of his will According to his good pleasure which he hath purposed in himself: That in the dispensation of the fulness [sic] of times he might gather together in one all things in Christ, both which are in heaven, and which are on earth; even in him (Ephesians 1:7-10, KJV).

14.31 But because of his great love for us, God, who is rich in mercy, made us alive with Christ even when we were dead in transgressions—it is by grace you have been saved. And God raised us up with Christ and seated us with him in the heavenly realms in Christ Jesus, in order that in the coming ages he might show the incomparable riches of his grace, expressed in his kindness to us in Christ Jesus. For it is by grace you have been saved, through faith—and this not from yourselves, it is the gift of God (Ephesians 2:4-8, NIV).

14.32 [The Father] has delivered and drawn us to Himself out of the control and the dominion of darkness and has transferred us into the kingdom of the Son of His love, In Whom we have our redemption through His blood, [which means] the forgiveness of our sins (Colossians 1:13-14, AMP).

14.33 For God was pleased to have all his fullness dwell in him, and through him to reconcile to himself all things, whether things on earth or things in heaven, by making peace through his blood, shed on the cross. Once you were alienated from God and were enemies in your minds because of your evil behavior. But now he has reconciled you by Christ's physical body through death to present you holy in his sight, without blemish and free from accusation (Colossians 1:19-22, NIV).

14.34 For God has not appointed us to [incur His] wrath [He did not select us to condemn us], but [that we might] obtain [His] salvation through our Lord Jesus Christ (the Messiah) Who died for us so that whether we are still alive or are dead [at Christ's appearing], we might live together with Him and share His life (1 Thessalonians 5:9-10, AMP).

14.35 But we, brethren beloved by the Lord, ought and are obligated [as those who are in debt] to give thanks always to God for you, because God chose you from the beginning as His firstfruits (first converts) for salvation through the sanctifying work of the [Holy] Spirit and [your] belief in (adherence to, trust in, and reliance on) the Truth. [It was] to this end that He called you through our Gospel, so that you may obtain and share in the glory of our Lord Jesus Christ (the Messiah (2 Thessalonians 2:13-14, AMP).

14.36 For this is good and acceptable in the sight of God our Saviour; Who will have all men to be saved, and to come unto the knowledge of the truth. For there is one God, and one mediator between God and men, the man Christ Jesus; Who gave himself a ransom for all, to be testified in due time (1 Timothy 2:3-6, KJV).

14.37 For the grace of God that brings salvation has appeared to all men. It teaches us to say "No" to ungodliness and worldly passions, and to live self-controlled, upright and godly lives in this present age, while we wait for the blessed hope—the glorious appearing of our great God and Savior, Jesus Christ (Titus 2:11-13, NIV).

14.38 But when the goodness and loving-kindness of God our Savior to man [as man] appeared, He saved us, not because of any works of righteousness that we had done, but because of His own pity and mercy, by [the] cleansing [bath] of the new birth (regeneration) and renewing of the Holy Spirit, Which He poured out [so] richly upon us through Jesus Christ our Savior. [And He did it in order] that we might be justified by His grace (by His favor, wholly undeserved), [that we might be acknowledged and counted as conformed to the divine will in purpose, thought, and action], and that we might become heirs of eternal life according to [our] hope (Titus 3:4-7, AMP).

14.39 How shall we escape [appropriate retribution] if we neglect and refuse to pay attention to such a great salvation [as is now offered to us, letting it drift past us forever]? For it was declared at first by the Lord [Himself], and it was confirmed to us and proved to be real and genuine by those who personally heard [Him speak]. [Besides this evidence] it was also established and plainly endorsed by God, Who showed His approval of it by signs and wonders and various miraculous manifestations of [His] power and by imparting the gifts of the Holy Spirit [to the believers] according to His own will (Hebrews 2:3-4, AMP).

14.40 And being made perfect, he became the author of eternal salvation unto all them that obey him (Hebrews 5:9, KJV).

14.41 How much more surely shall the blood of Christ, Who by virtue of [His] eternal Spirit [His own preexistent divine personality] has offered Himself as an unblemished sacrifice to God, purify our consciences from dead works and lifeless observances to serve the [ever] living God? [Christ, the Messiah] is therefore the Negotiator and Mediator of an [entirely] new agreement (testament, covenant), so that those who are called and offered it may receive the fulfillment of the promised everlasting inheritance—since a death has taken place which rescues and delivers and redeems them from the transgressions committed under the [old] first agreement (Hebrews 9:14-15, AMP).

14.42 Blessed be the God and Father of our Lord Jesus Christ, who according to His great mercy has caused us to be born again to a living hope through the resurrection of Jesus Christ from the dead (1 Peter 1:3, NASB).

14.43 Obtaining as the outcome of your faith the salvation of your souls. As to this salvation, the prophets who prophesied of the grace that would come to you made careful searches and inquiries (1 Peter 1:9-10, NASB).

14.44 For you know that it was not with perishable things such as silver or gold that you were redeemed from the empty way of life handed down to you from your forefathers, but with the precious blood of Christ, a lamb without blemish or defect (1 Peter 1:18-19, NIV).

14.45 For you have been born again, not of perishable seed, but of imperishable, through the living and enduring word of God (1 Peter 1:23, NIV).

14.46 But if we walk in the light, as he is in the light, we have fellowship with one another, and the blood of Jesus, his Son, purifies us from all sin (1 John 1:7, NIV).

14.47 And the testimony is this, that God has given us eternal life, and this life is in His Son (He who has the Son has the life; he who does not have the Son of God does not have the life (1 John 5:11-12, NASB).

14.48 Guard and keep yourselves in the love of God; expect and patiently wait for the mercy of our Lord Jesus Christ (the Messiah)—[which will bring you] unto life eternal (Jude 1:21, AMP).

REFERENCE 15 — Fulfills Your Heart's Desire for Love

15.1 Come to me, all you who are weary and burdened, and I will give you rest. Take my yoke upon you and learn from me, for I am gentle and humble in heart, and you will find rest for your souls. For my yoke is easy and my burden is light (Matthew 11:28-30, NIV).

15.2 "Teacher, which is the greatest commandment in the Law?" Jesus replied: "Love the Lord your God with all your heart and with all your soul and with all your mind. This is the first and greatest commandment" (Matthew 22:36-38, NIV).

15.3 As Jesus and his disciples were on their way, he came to a village where a woman named Martha opened her home to him. She had a sister called Mary, who sat at the Lord's feet listening to what he said. But Martha was distracted by all the preparations that had to be made. She came to him and asked, "Lord, don't you care that my sister has left me to do the work by myself? Tell her to help me!" "Martha, Martha," the Lord answered, "you are worried and upset about many things, but only one thing is needed. Mary has chosen what is better, and it will not be taken away from her" (Luke 10:38-42, NIV).

15.4 As the Father has loved me, so have I loved you. Now remain in my love. If you obey my commands, you will remain in my love, just as I have obeyed my Father's commands and remain in his love (John 15:9-10, NIV).

15.5 And hope does not disappoint, because the love of God has been poured out within our hearts through the Holy Spirit who was given to us (Romans 5:5, NASB).

15.6 But God shows and clearly proves His [own] love for us by the fact that while we were still sinners, Christ (the Messiah, the Anointed One) died for us (Romans 5:8, AMP).

15.7 Who shall ever separate us from Christ's love? Shall suffering and affliction and tribulation? Or calamity and distress? Or persecution or hunger or destitution or peril or sword? Even as it is written, For Thy sake we are put to death all the day long; we are regarded and counted as sheep for the slaughter [Ps. 44:22] (Romans 8:35-36, AMP).

15.8 Yet amid all these things we are more than conquerors and gain a surpassing victory through Him Who loved us. For I am persuaded beyond doubt (am sure) that neither death nor life, nor angels nor principalities, nor things impending and threatening nor things to come, nor powers, Nor height nor depth, nor anything else in all creation will be able to separate us from the love of God which is in Christ Jesus our Lord (Romans 8:37-39, AMP).

15.9 For in Christ Jesus neither circumcision nor uncircumcision has any value. The only thing that counts is faith expressing itself through love (Galatians 5:6, NIV)

15.10 But the fruit of the [Holy] Spirit [the work which His presence within accomplishes] is love, joy (gladness), peace, patience (an even temper, forbearance), kindness, goodness (benevolence), faithfulness, Gentleness (meekness, humility), self-control (self-restraint, continence). Against such things there is no law [that can bring a charge] (Galatians 5:22-23, AMP).

15.11 Just as He chose us in Him before the foundation of the world, that we would be holy and blameless before Him. In love (Ephesians 1:4, NASB).

15.12 But because of his great love for us, God, who is rich in mercy, made us alive with Christ even when we were dead in transgressions—it is by grace you have been saved (Ephesians 2:4-5, NIV).

15.13 May Christ through your faith [actually] dwell (settle down, abide, make His permanent home) in your hearts! May you be rooted deep in love and founded securely on love, That you may have the power and be strong to apprehend and grasp with all the saints [God's devoted people, the experience of that love] what is the breadth and length and height and depth [of it]; [That you may really come] to know [practically, through experience for yourselves] the love of Christ, which far surpasses mere knowledge [without experience]; that you may be filled [through all your being] unto all the fullness of God [may have the richest measure of the divine Presence, and become a body wholly filled and flooded with God Himself]! (Ephesians 3:17-19, AMP).

15.14 And walk in love, just as Christ also loved you and gave Himself up for us, an offering and a sacrifice to God as a fragrant aroma (Ephesians 5:2, NASB).

15.15 And over all these virtues put on love, which binds them all together in perfect unity (Colossians 3:14, NIV).

15.16 May the Lord direct your hearts into [realizing and showing] the love of God and into the steadfastness and patience of Christ and in waiting for His return (2 Thessalonians 3:5, AMP).

15.17 For God hath not given us the spirit of fear; but of power, and of love, and of a sound mind (2 Timothy 1:7, KJV).

15.18 But when the goodness and loving-kindness of God our Savior to man [as man] appeared, He saved us, not because of any works of righteousness that we had done, but because of His own pity and mercy, by [the] cleansing [bath] of the new birth (regeneration) and renewing of the Holy Spirit, Which He poured out [so] richly upon us through Jesus Christ our Savior (Titus 3:4-6, AMP).

15.19 Though you have not seen him, you love him; and even though you do not see him now, you believe in him and are filled with an inexpressible and glorious joy (1 Peter1:8, NIV).

15.20 How great is the love the Father has lavished on us, that we should be called children of God! And that is what we are! The reason the world does not know us is that it did not know him (1 John 3:1, NIV).

15.21 This is how God showed his love among us: He sent his one and only Son into the world that we might live through him. This is love: not that we loved God, but that he loved us and sent his Son as an atoning sacrifice for our sins (1 John 4:9-10, NIV).

15.22 We know that we live in him and he in us, because he has given us of his Spirit. And we have seen and testify that the Father has sent his Son to be the Savior of the world. If anyone acknowledges that Jesus is the Son of God, God lives in him and he in God. And so we know and rely on the love God has for us. God is love. Whoever lives in love lives in God, and God in him (1 John 4:13-16, NIV).

15.23 There is no fear in love. But perfect love drives out fear, because fear has to do with punishment. The one who fears is not made perfect in love. We love because he first loved us (1 John 4:18-19, NIV).

15.24 Keep yourselves in God's love as you wait for the mercy of our Lord Jesus Christ to bring you to eternal life (Jude 1:21, NIV).

REFERENCE 16 — Ransoms You from Sin

16.1 I have blotted out, as a thick cloud, thy transgressions, and, as a cloud, thy sins: return unto me; for I have redeemed thee. Sing, O ye heavens; for the Lord hath done it: shout, ye lower parts of the earth: break forth into singing, ye mountains, O forest, and every tree therein: for the Lord hath redeemed Jacob, and glorified himself in Israel (Isaiah 44:22-23, KJV).

16.2 The Son of Man will send forth His angels, and they will gather out of His kingdom all causes of offense [persons by whom others are drawn into error or sin] and all who do iniquity and act wickedly (Matthew 13:41, AMP).

16.3 And you, little one, shall be called a prophet of the Most High; for you shall go on before the face of the Lord to make ready His ways, [Isa. 40:3; Mal. 4:5] To bring and give the knowledge of salvation to His people in the forgiveness and remission of their sins (Luke 1:76-77, AMP).

16.4 Jesus answered him, I assure you, most solemnly I tell you, that unless a person is born again (anew, from above), he cannot ever see (know, be acquainted with, and experience) the kingdom of God (John 3:3, AMP).

16.5 For God so loved the world that he gave his one and only Son, that whoever believes in him shall not perish but have eternal life. For God did not send his Son into the world to condemn the world, but to save the world through him (John 3:16-17, NIV).

16.6 Jesus answered them, "Truly, truly, I say to you, everyone who commits sin is the slave of sin" (John 8:34, NASB).

16.7 And when He comes, He will convict and convince the world and bring demonstration to it about sin and about righteousness (uprightness of heart and right standing with God) and about judgment. (John 16:8, AMP).

16.8 Knowing this, that our old self was crucified with Him, in order that our body of sin might be done away with, so that we would no longer be slaves to sin (Romans 6:6, NASB).

16.9 Therefore do not let sin reign in your mortal body so that you obey its evil desires. Do not offer the parts of your body to sin, as instruments of wickedness, but rather offer yourselves to God, as those who have been brought from death to life; and offer the parts of your body to him as instruments of righteousness. For sin shall not be your master, because you are not under law, but under grace (Romans 6:12-14, NIV).

16.10 Do you not know that if you continually surrender yourselves to anyone to do his will, you are the slaves of him whom you obey, whether that be to sin, which leads to death, or to obedience which leads to righteousness (right doing and right standing with God)? (Romans 6:16, AMP).

16.11 But now that you have been set free from sin and have become slaves to God, the benefit you reap leads to holiness, and the result is eternal life. For the wages of sin is death, but the gift of God is eternal life in Christ Jesus our Lord (Romans 6:22-23, NIV).

16.12 But if Christ lives in you, [then although] your [natural] body is dead by reason of sin and guilt, the spirit is alive because of [the] righteousness [that He imputes to you] (Romans 8:10, AMP).

16.13 Therefore if any person is [ingrafted] in Christ (the Messiah) he is a new creation (a new creature altogether); the old [previous moral and spiritual condition] has passed away. Behold, the fresh and new has come! (2 Corinthians 5:17, AMP).

16.14 As for you, you were dead in your transgressions and sins, in which you used to live when you followed the ways of this world and of the ruler of the kingdom of the air, the spirit who is now at work in those who are disobedient. All of us also lived among them at one time, gratifying the cravings of our sinful nature and following its desires and thoughts. Like the rest, we were by nature objects of wrath. But because of his great love for us, God, who is rich in mercy, made us alive with Christ even when we were dead in transgressions—it is by grace you have been saved (Ephesians 2:1-5, NIV).

16.15 Strip yourselves of your former nature [put off and discard your old unrenewed self] which characterized your previous manner of life and becomes corrupt through lusts and desires that spring from delusion; And be constantly renewed in the spirit of your mind [having a fresh mental and spiritual attitude], And put on the new nature (the regenerate self) created in God's image, [Godlike] in true righteousness and holiness (Ephesians 4:22-24, AMP).

16.16 This is the covenant I will make with the house of Israel after that time, declares the Lord. I will put my laws in their minds and write them on their hearts. I will be their God, and they will be my people. No longer will a man teach his neighbor, or a man his brother, saying, 'Know the Lord,' because they will all know me, from the least of them to the greatest. For I will forgive their wickedness and will remember their sins no more (Hebrews 8:10-12, NIV).

16.17 Even so it is that Christ, having been offered to take upon Himself and bear as a burden the sins of many once and once for all, will appear a second time, not to carry any burden of sin nor to deal with sin, but to bring to full salvation those who are [eagerly, constantly, and patiently] waiting for and expecting Him (Hebrews 9:28, AMP).

16.18 But if we walk in the Light as He Himself is in the Light, we have fellowship with one another, and the blood of Jesus His Son cleanses us from all sin (1 John 1:7, NASB).

16.19 [But] he who commits sin [who practices evildoing] is of the devil [takes his character from the evil one], for the devil has sinned (violated the divine law) from the beginning. The reason the Son of God was made manifest (visible) was to undo (destroy, loosen, and dissolve) the works the devil [has done] (1 John 3:8, AMP).

16.20 Those whom I [dearly and tenderly] love, I tell their faults and convict and convince and reprove and chasten [I discipline and instruct them]. So be enthusiastic and in earnest and burning with zeal and repent [changing your mind and attitude] (Revelation 3:19, AMP).

REFERENCE 17 — Lives within Your Heart

17.1 Blessed and enviably happy [with a happiness produced by the experience of God's favor and especially conditioned by the revelation of His matchless grace] are those who mourn, for they shall be comforted (Matthew 5:4, AMP).

17.2 Blessed (happy, enviably fortunate, and spiritually prosperous—possessing the happiness produced by the experience of God's favor and especially conditioned by the revelation of His grace, regardless of their outward conditions) are the pure in heart, for they shall see God (Matthew 5:8, AMP).

17.3 Heal the sick, raise the dead, cleanse those who have leprosy, drive out demons. Freely you have received, freely give (Matthew 10:8, NIV).

17.4 If you then, evil as you are, know how to give good gifts [gifts that are to their advantage] to your children, how much more will your heavenly Father give the Holy Spirit to those who ask and continue to ask Him (Luke 11:13, AMP).

17.5 Jesus answered him, I assure you, most solemnly I tell you, that unless a person is born again (anew, from above), he cannot ever see (know, be acquainted with, and experience) the kingdom of God (John 3:3, AMP).

17.6 And he who believes in (has faith in, clings to, relies on) the Son has (now possesses) eternal life. But whoever disobeys (is unbelieving toward, refuses to trust in, disregards, is not subject to) the Son will never see (experience) life, but [instead] the wrath of God abides on him. [God's displeasure remains on him; His indignation hangs over him continually (J John 3:36, AMP).

17.7 In the last day, that great day of the feast, Jesus stood and cried, saying, If any man thirst, let him come unto me, and drink (John 7:37, KJV).

17.8 Remain in me, and I will remain in you. No branch can bear fruit by itself; it must remain in the vine. Neither can you bear fruit unless you remain in me. "I am the vine; you are the branches. If a man remains in me and I in him, he will bear much fruit; apart from me you can do nothing (John 15:4-5, NIV).

17.9 And now I am coming to You; I say these things while I am still in the world, so that My joy may be made full and complete and perfect in them [that they may experience My delight fulfilled in them, that My enjoyment may be perfected in their own souls, that they may have My gladness within them, filling their hearts] (John 17:13, AMP).

17.10 May the God of your hope so fill you with all joy and peace in believing [through the experience of your faith] that by the power of the Holy Spirit you may abound and be overflowing (bubbling over) with hope (Romans 15:13, AMP).

17.11 And my language and my message were not set forth in persuasive (enticing and plausible) words of wisdom, but they were in demonstration of the [Holy] Spirit and power [a proof by the Spirit and power of God, operating on me and stirring in the minds of my hearers the most holy emotions and thus persuading them], So that your faith might not rest in the wisdom of men (human philosophy), but in the power of God (1 Corinthians 2:4-5, AMP).

17.12 For the kingdom of God does not consist in words but in power (1 Corinthians 4:20, NASB).

17.13 For just as Christ's [own] sufferings fall to our lot [as they overflow upon His disciples, and we share and experience them] abundantly, so through Christ comfort (consolation and encouragement) is also [shared and experienced] abundantly by us (2 Corinthians 1:5, AMP).

17.14 Examine and test and evaluate your own selves to see whether you are holding to your faith and showing the proper fruits of it. Test and prove yourselves [not Christ]. Do you not yourselves realize and know [thoroughly by an ever-increasing experience] that Jesus Christ is in you—unless you are [counterfeits] disapproved on trial and rejected? (2 Corinthians 13:5, AMP).

17.15 That you may have the power and be strong to apprehend and grasp with all the saints [God's devoted people, the experience of that love] what is the breadth and length and height and depth [of it]; [That you may really come] to know [practically, through experience for yourselves] the love of Christ, which far surpasses mere knowledge [without experience]; that you may be filled [through all your being] unto all the fullness of God [may have the richest measure of the divine Presence, and become a body wholly filled and flooded with God Himself]! (Ephesians 3:18-19, AMP).

17.16 Finally, be strong in the Lord and in his mighty power (Ephesians 6:10, NIV).

17.17 And we know (understand, recognize, are conscious of, by observation and by experience) and believe (adhere to and put faith in and rely on) the love God cherishes for us. God is love, and he who dwells and continues in love dwells and continues in God, and God dwells and continues in him (1 John 4:16, AMP).

17.18 Seeing that His divine power has granted to us everything pertaining to life and godliness, through the true knowledge of Him who called us by His own glory and excellence (2 Peter 1:3, NIV).

17.19 Behold, I stand at the door and knock; if anyone hears My voice and opens the door, I will come in to him and will dine with him, and he with Me (Revelation 3:20, NASB).

17.20 "This is the covenant that I will make with them after those days," says the lord: "I will put my laws upon their heart, and on their mind I will write them" (Hebrews 10:16, NASB).

17.21 By faith Abel offered God a better sacrifice than Cain did. By faith he was commended as a righteous man, when God spoke well of his offerings. And by faith he still speaks, even though he is dead (Hebrews 11:4, NIV).

REFERENCE 18 — Fulfills the Scripture regarding the Savior

18.1 And beginning at Moses and all the Prophets, he expounded to them in all the Scriptures the things concerning Himself (Luke 24:27, NKJ)

18.2 Therefore the Lord himself shall give you a sign; Behold, a virgin shall conceive, and bear a son, and shall call his name Immanuel (Isaiah 7:14, KJV).

18.3 For unto us a child is born, unto us a son is given: and the government shall be upon his shoulder: and his name shall be called Wonderful, Counsellor [sic], The mighty God, The everlasting Father, The Prince of Peace. Of the increase of his government and peace there shall be no end, upon the throne of David, and upon his kingdom, to order it, and to establish it with judgment and with justice from henceforth even forever. The zeal of the Lord of hosts will perform this (Isaiah 9:6-7, KJV).

18.4 Behold, the Lord God will come with strong hand, and his arm shall rule for him: behold, his reward is with him, and his work before him. He shall feed his flock like a shepherd: he shall gather the lambs with his arm, and carry them in his bosom, and shall gently lead those that are with young (Isaiah 40:10-11, KJV).

18.5 A bruised reed He will not break And a dimly burning wick He will not extinguish; He will faithfully bring forth justice. He will not be disheartened or crushed until He has established justice in the earth; And the coastlands will wait expectantly for His law (Isaiah 42:3-4, NASB).

18.6 He is despised and rejected of men; a man of sorrows, and acquainted with grief: and we hid as it were our faces from him; he was despised, and we esteemed him not. Surely he hath borne our griefs, and carried our sorrows: yet we did esteem him stricken, smitten of God, and afflicted. But he was wounded for our transgressions, he was bruised for our iniquities: the chastisement of our peace was upon him; and with his stripes we are healed. All we like sheep have gone astray; we have turned every one to his own way; and the Lord hath laid on him the iniquity of us all. He was oppressed, and he was afflicted, yet he opened not his mouth: he is brought as a lamb to the slaughter, and as a sheep before her shearers is dumb, so he openeth not his mouth. He was taken from prison and from judgment: and who shall declare his generation? for he was cut off out of the land of the living: for the transgression of my people was he stricken. And he made his grave with the wicked, and with the rich in his death; because he had done no violence, neither was any deceit in his mouth. Yet it pleased the Lord to bruise him; he hath put him to grief: when thou shalt make his soul an offering for sin, he shall see his seed, he shall prolong his days, and the pleasure of the Lord shall prosper in his hand. He shall see of the travail of his soul, and shall be satisfied: by his knowledge shall my righteous servant justify many; for he shall bear their iniquities. Therefore will I divide him a portion with the great, and he shall divide the spoil with the strong; because he hath poured out his soul unto death: and he was numbered with the transgressors; and he bare the sin of many, and made intercession for the transgressors (Isaiah 53:3-12, KJV).

18.7 The Spirit of the Lord God is upon me, because the Lord has anointed and qualified me to preach the Gospel of good tidings to the meek, the poor, and afflicted; He has sent me to bind up and heal the brokenhearted, to proclaim liberty to the [physical and spiritual] captives and the opening of the prison and of the eyes to those who are bound (Isaiah 61:1, AMP).

18.8 Behold, the Lord has proclaimed to the end of the earth: Say to the Daughter of Zion, Behold, your salvation comes [in the person of the Lord]; behold, His reward is with Him, and His work and recompense before Him. And they shall call them the Holy People, the Redeemed of the Lord; and you shall be called Sought Out, a City Not Forsaken (Isaiah 62:11-12, AMP).

18.9 But thou, Bethlehem Ephratah, though thou be little among the thousands of Judah, yet out of thee shall he come forth unto me that is to be ruler in Israel; whose goings forth have been from of old, from everlasting (Micah 5:2, KJV).

18.10 Rejoice greatly, O daughter of Zion! Shout in triumph, O daughter of Jerusalem! Behold, your king is coming to you; He is just and endowed with salvation, Humble, and mounted on a donkey, Even on a colt, the foal of a donkey (Zechariah 9:9, NASB).

18.11 She will bear a Son, and you shall call His name Jesus [the Greek form of the Hebrew Joshua, which means Savior], for He will save His people from their sins [that is, prevent them from failing and missing the true end and scope of life, which is God]. All this took place that it might be fulfilled which the Lord had spoken through the prophet, Behold, the virgin shall become pregnant and give birth to a Son, and they shall call His name Emmanuel—which, when translated, means, God with us (Matthew 1:21-23, AMP).

18.12 So he called together all the chief priests and learned men (scribes) of the people and anxiously asked them where the Christ was to be born. They replied to him, In Bethlehem of Judea, for so it is written by the prophet: And you Bethlehem, in the land of Judah, you are not in any way least or insignificant among the chief cities of Judah; for from you shall come a

Ruler (Leader) Who will govern and shepherd My people Israel (Matthew 2:4-6, AMP).

18.13 He went and dwelt in a town called Nazareth, so that what was spoken through the prophets might be fulfilled: He shall be called a Nazarene [Branch, Separated One] (Matthew 2:23, AMP).

18.14 And leaving Nazareth, He went and dwelt in Capernaum by the sea, in the country of Zebulun and Naphtali— That what was spoken by the prophet Isaiah might be brought to pass: The land of Zebulun and the land of Naphtali, in the way to the sea, beyond the Jordan, Galilee of the Gentiles [of the peoples who are not of Israel]—[Isa. 9:1-2] The people who sat (dwelt enveloped) in darkness have seen a great Light, and for those who sat in the land and shadow of death Light has dawned (Matthew 4:13-16, AMP).

18.15 Do not think that I have come to abolish the Law or the Prophets; I have not come to abolish them but to fulfill them (Matthew 5:17, NIV).

18.16 When evening came, they brought to Him many who were under the power of demons, and He drove out the spirits with a word and restored to health all who were sick. And thus He fulfilled what was spoken by the prophet Isaiah, He Himself took [in order to carry away] our weaknesses and infirmities and bore away our diseases (Matthew 8:16-17, AMP).

18.17 This was in fulfillment of what was spoken by the prophet Isaiah. Behold, My Servant Whom I have chosen, My Beloved in and with Whom My soul is well pleased and has found its delight. I will put My Spirit upon Him, and He shall proclaim and show forth Justice to the nations. He will not strive or wrangle or cry out loudly; nor will anyone hear His voice in the streets. A bruised reed He will not break, and a moldering (dimly burning) wick He will not quench, till He brings justice and a just cause to victory. And in and on His name will the Gentiles (the peoples outside of Israel) set their hopes (Matthew 12:17-21, AMP).

18.18 That it might be fulfilled which was spoken by the prophet, saying, I will open my mouth in parables; I will utter things which have been kept secret from the foundation of the world (Matthew 13:35, KJV).

18.19 This happened that what was spoken by the prophet might be fulfilled, saying, Say to the Daughter of Zion [inhabitants of Jerusalem], Behold, your King is coming to you, lowly and riding on a donkey, and on a colt, the foal of a donkey [a beast of burden] (Matthew 21:4-5, AMP).

18.20 Jesus said to them, "Did you never read in the Scriptures, 'The stone which the builders rejected, this became the chief corner stone; this came about from the Lord, and it is marvelous in our eyes? Therefore I say to you, the kingdom of God will be taken away from you and given to a people, producing the fruit of it. And he who falls on this stone will be broken to pieces; but on whomever it falls, it will scatter him like dust" (Matthew 21:42-44, NASB).

18.21 But how then would the Scriptures be fulfilled that say it must happen in this way? (Matthew 26:54, NIV).

18.22 Wherefore that field was called, The field of blood, unto this day. Then was fulfilled that which was spoken by Jeremy the prophet, saying, And they took the thirty pieces of silver, the price of him that was valued, whom they of the children of Israel did value; And gave them for the potter's field, as the Lord appointed me (Matthew 27:8-10, KJV).

18.23 The beginning of the gospel of Jesus Christ, the Son of God. As it is written in Isaiah the prophet: "Behold, I send my messenger ahead of you, who will prepare your way; the voice of one crying in the wilderness, `make ready the way of the Lord, make his paths straight'" (Mark 1:1-3, NASB).

18.24 Blessed (praised and extolled and thanked) be the Lord, the God of Israel, because He has come and brought deliverance and redemption to His people! And He has raised up a Horn of salvation [a mighty and valiant Helper, the Author of salvation] for us in the house of David His servant— This is as He promised by the mouth of His holy prophets from the most ancient times [in the memory of man] (Luke 1:68-70, AMP).

18.25 And, behold, there was a man in Jerusalem, whose name was Simeon; and the same man was just and devout, waiting for the consolation of Israel: and the Holy Ghost was upon him. And it was revealed unto him by the Holy Ghost, that he should not see death, before he had seen the Lord's Christ. And he came by the Spirit into the temple: and when the parents brought in the child Jesus, to do for him after the custom of the law, Then took he him up in his arms, and blessed God, and said, Lord, now lettest thou thy servant depart in peace according to thy word: For mine eyes have seen thy salvation, Which thou hast prepared before the face of all people; A light to lighten the Gentiles, and the glory of thy people Israel (Luke 2:25-32, KJV).

18.26 So He came to Nazareth, [that Nazareth] where He had been brought up, and He entered the synagogue, as was His custom on

Part III - Scripture References 249

the Sabbath day. And He stood up to read. And there was handed to Him [the roll of] the book of the prophet Isaiah. He opened (unrolled) the book and found the place where it was written, [Isa. 61:1, 2] The Spirit of the Lord [is] upon Me, because He has anointed Me [the Anointed One, the Messiah] to preach the good news (the Gospel) to the poor; He has sent Me to announce release to the captives and recovery of sight to the blind, to send forth as delivered those who are oppressed [who are downtrodden, bruised, crushed, and broken down by calamity], To proclaim the accepted and acceptable year of the Lord [the day when salvation and the free favors of God profusely abound. [Isa. 61:1, 2] Then He rolled up the book and gave it back to the attendant and sat down; and the eyes of all in the synagogue were gazing [attentively] at Him. And He began to speak to them: Today this Scripture has been fulfilled while you are present and hearing (Luke 4:16-21, AMP).

18.27 Jesus took the Twelve aside and told them, "We are going up to Jerusalem, and everything that is written by the prophets about the Son of Man will be fulfilled (Luke 18:31, NIV).

18.28 For I tell you that this Scripture must yet be fulfilled in Me: And He was counted and classed among the wicked (the outlaws, the criminals); for what is written about Me has its fulfillment [has reached its end and is finally settled] (Luke 22:37, AMP).

18.29 And He said to them, "O foolish men and slow of heart to believe in all that the prophets have spoken! Was it not necessary for the Christ to suffer these things and to enter into His glory?" Then beginning with Moses and with all the prophets, He explained to them the things concerning Himself in all the Scriptures (Luke 24:25-27, NASB).

18.30 Then He said to them, This is what I told you while I was still with you: everything which is written concerning Me in the Law of Moses and the Prophets and the Psalms must be fulfilled. Then He [thoroughly] opened up their minds to understand the Scriptures (Luke 24:44-46, AMP).

18.31 So when He was raised from the dead, His disciples remembered that He said this; and they believed the Scripture and the word which Jesus had spoken (John 2:22, NASB).

18.32 He who believes in Me [who cleaves to and trusts in and relies on Me] as the Scripture has said, From his innermost being shall flow [continuously] springs and rivers of living water. But He was speaking here of the Spirit, Whom those who believed (trusted, had faith) in Him were afterward to receive. For the [Holy] Spirit had not yet been given, because Jesus was not yet glorified (raised to honor). Listening to those words, some of the multitude said, This is certainly and beyond doubt the Prophet! [Deut. 18:15, 18; John 1:21; 6:14; Acts 3:22] Others said, This is the Christ (the Messiah, Anointed One)! But some said, What? Does the Christ come out of Galilee? Does not the Scripture tell us that the Christ will come from the offspring of David and from Bethlehem, the village where David lived? (John 7:38-42, AMP).

18.33 "I do not speak of all of you. I know the ones I have chosen; but it is that the Scripture may be fulfilled, 'he who eats my bread has lifted up his heel against me.'" (John 13:18, NASB).

18.34 But this cometh to pass, that the word might be fulfilled that is written in their law, They hated me without a cause (John 15:25, KJV).

18.35 While I was with them, I kept and preserved them in Your Name [in the knowledge and worship of You]. Those You have given Me I guarded and protected, and not one of them has perished or is lost except the son of perdition [Judas Iscariot—the one who is now doomed to destruction, destined to be lost], that the Scripture might be fulfilled (John 17:12, AMP).

18.36 This happened so that the words he had spoken would be fulfilled: "I have not lost one of those you gave me" (John 18:9, NIV).

18.37 This was to fulfill the word which Jesus had spoken to show (indicate, predict) by what manner of death He was to die (John 18:32, AMP).

18.38 So they said to one another, Let us not tear it, but let us cast lots to decide whose it shall be. This was to fulfill the Scripture, They parted My garments among them, and for My clothing they cast lots. So the soldiers did these things (John 19:24, AMP).

18.39 So they said to one another, Let us not tear it, but let us cast lots to decide whose it shall be. This was to fulfill the Scripture, They parted My garments among them, and for My clothing they cast lots. So the soldiers did these things (John 19:24, KJV).

18.40 For these things came to pass to fulfill the Scripture, "Not a bone of Him shall be broken." And again another Scripture says, "They shall look on Him whom they pierced" (John 19:36-37, NASB).

18.41 For as yet they did not understand the Scripture, that He must rise again from the dead (John 20:9, NASB).

18.42 Brethren, the Scripture had to be fulfilled, which the Holy Spirit foretold by the mouth of David concerning Judas, who became a guide to those who arrested Jesus (Acts 1:16, NASB).

18.43 Then the Spirit said to Philip, "Go up and join this chariot." Philip ran up and heard him reading Isaiah the prophet, and said, "Do you understand what you are reading?" And he said, "Well, how could I, unless someone guides me?" And he invited Philip to come up and sit with him. Now the passage of Scripture which he was reading was this: "He was led as a sheep to slaughter; and as a lamb before its shearer is silent, so He does not open His mouth. In humiliation His judgment was taken away; who will relate His generation? For His life is removed from the earth." The eunuch answered Philip and said, "Please tell me, of whom does the prophet say this? Of himself or of someone else?" Then Philip opened his mouth, and beginning from this Scripture he preached Jesus to him (Acts 8:29-35, NASB).

18.44 And Paul entered, as he usually did, and for three Sabbaths he reasoned and argued with them from the Scriptures, Explaining [them] and [quoting passages] setting forth and proving that it was necessary for the Christ to suffer and to rise from the dead, and saying, This Jesus, Whom I proclaim to you, is the Christ (the Messiah) (Acts 17:2-3, AMP).

18.45 Now these [Jews] were better disposed and more noble than those in Thessalonica, for they were entirely ready and accepted and welcomed the message [concerning the attainment through Christ of eternal salvation in the kingdom of God] with inclination of mind and eagerness, searching and examining the Scriptures daily to see if these things were so (Acts 17:11, AMP).

18.46 For with great power he refuted the Jews in public [discussions], showing and proving by the Scriptures that Jesus is the Christ (the Messiah) (Acts 18:28, AMP).

18.47 Paul, a bond-servant of Christ Jesus, called as an apostle, set apart for the gospel of God, which He promised beforehand through His prophets in the holy Scriptures, concerning His Son, who was born of a descendant of David according to the flesh, who was declared the Son of God with power by the resurrection from the dead, according to the Spirit of holiness, Jesus Christ our Lord (Romans 1:1-4, NASB).

18.48 The Scripture says, No man who believes in Him [who adheres to, relies on, and trusts in Him] will [ever] be put to shame or be disappointed (Romans 10:11, AMP).

18.49 For what I received I passed on to you as of first importance: that Christ died for our sins according to the Scriptures, that he was buried, that he was raised on the third day according to the Scriptures (1 Corinthians 15:3-4, NIV).

18.50 But the Scripture declares that the whole world is a prisoner of sin, so that what was promised, being given through faith in Jesus Christ, might be given to those who believe (Galatians 3:22, NIV).

18.51 And that from a child thou hast known the holy Scriptures, which are able to make thee wise unto salvation through faith which is in Christ Jesus (2 Timothy 3:15, KJV).

18.52 Then I said, Behold, here I am, coming to do Your will, O God—[to fulfill] what is written of Me in the volume of the Book [Ps. 40:6-8] (Hebrews 10:7, AMP).

18.53 Wherefore also it is contained in the Scripture, Behold, I lay in Zion a chief corner stone, elect, precious: and he that believeth on him shall not be confounded (1 Peter 2:6, KJV).

18.54 We did not follow cleverly invented stories when we told you about the power and coming of our Lord Jesus Christ, but we were eyewitnesses of his majesty (2 Peter 1:16, NIV).

18.55 As to this salvation, the prophets who prophesied of the grace that would come to you made careful searches and inquiries, seeking to know what person or time the Spirit of Christ within them was indicating as He predicted the sufferings of Christ and the glories to follow. It was revealed to them that they were not serving themselves, but you, in these things which now have been announced to you through those who preached the gospel to you by the Holy Spirit sent from heaven--things into which angels long to look (1 Peter 1:10-12, NASB).

REFERENCE 19 — Created the Heavens and the Earth

19.1 In the beginning God (prepared, formed, fashioned, and) created the heavens and the earth (Genesis 1:1, AMP).

19.2 You alone are the Lord. You have made the heavens, The heaven of heavens with all their host, The earth and all that is on it, The seas and all that is in them. You give life to all of them And the heavenly host bows down before You (Nehemiah 9:6, NASB).

19.3 Thus says God the Lord—He Who created the heavens and stretched them forth, He Who spread abroad the earth and that which comes out of it, He Who gives breath to the people on it and spirit to those who walk in it (Isaiah 42:5, AMP).

19.4 Thus says the Lord, your Redeemer, and He Who formed you from the womb: I am the Lord, Who made all things, Who alone stretched out the heavens, Who spread out the earth by Myself [who was with Me]? (Isaiah 44:24, AMP).

19.5 I made the earth and created man upon it. I, with My hands, stretched out the heavens, and I commanded all their host (Isaiah 45:12, AMP).

19.6 For thus saith the Lord that created the heavens; God himself that formed the earth and made it; he hath established it, he created it not in vain, he formed it to be inhabited: I am the Lord; and there is none else (Isaiah 45:18, KJV).

19.7 God made the earth by His power; He established the world by His wisdom and by His understanding and skill stretched out the heavens (Jere-miah 10:12, AMP).

19.8 Alas, Lord God! Behold, You have made the heavens and the earth by Your great power and by Your outstretched arm! There is nothing too hard or too wonderful for You (Jeremiah 32:17, AMP).

19.9 He made the earth by his power; he founded the world by his wisdom and stretched out the heavens by his understanding (Jeremiah 51:15, NIV).

19.10 And he answered and said unto them, Have ye not read, that he which made them at the beginning made them male and female (Matthew 19:4, KJV).

19.11 In the beginning [before all time] was the Word (Christ), and the Word was with God, and the Word was God Himself. [Isa. 9:6] He was present originally with God. All things were made and came into existence through Him; and without Him was not even one thing made that has come into being (John 1:1-3, AMP).

19.12 He came into the world, and though the world was made through Him, the world did not recognize Him [did not know Him] (John 1:10, AMP).

19.13 And now, Father, glorify Me along with Yourself and restore Me to such majesty and honor in Your presence as I had with You before the world existed (John 17:5, AMP).

19.14 The God who made the world and all things in it, since He is Lord of heaven and earth, does not dwell in temples made with hands (Acts 17:24, NASB).

19.15 Just as He chose us in Him before the foundation of the world, that we would be holy and blameless before Him. In love (Ephesians 1:4, NASB).

19.16 Also to enlighten all men and make plain to them what is the plan [regarding the Gentiles and providing for the salvation of all men] of the mystery kept hidden through the ages and concealed until now in [the mind of] God Who created all things by Christ Jesus (Ephesians 3:9, AMP).

19.17 He is the image of the invisible God, the firstborn of all creation. For by Him all things were created, both in the heavens and on earth, visible and invisible, whether thrones or dominions or rulers or authorities—all things have been created through Him and for Him. He is before all things, and in Him all things hold together (Colossians 1:15-17, NASB).

19.18 [But] in the last of these days He has spoken to us in [the person of a] Son, Whom He appointed Heir and lawful Owner of all things, also by and through Whom He created the worlds and the reaches of space and the ages of time [He made, produced, built, operated, and arranged them in order] (Hebrews 1:2, AMP).

19.19 But in these last days he has spoken to us by his Son, whom he appointed heir of all things, and through whom he made the universe (Hebrews 1:2, NIV).

19.20 For it was an act worthy [of God] and fitting [to the divine nature] that He, for Whose sake and by Whom all things have their existence, in bringing many sons into glory, should make the Pioneer of their salvation perfect [should bring to maturity the human experience necessary to be perfectly equipped for His office as High Priest] through suffering (Hebrews 2:10, AMP).

19.21 Worthy are You, our Lord and God, to receive the glory and the honor and dominion, for You created all things; by Your will they were [brought into being] and were created (Revelation 4:11, AMP).

19.22 He said to me: "It is done. I am the Alpha and the Omega, the Beginning and the End. To him who is thirsty I will give to drink without cost from the spring of the water of life (Revelation 21:6, NIV).

19.23 By faith we understand that the universe was formed at God's command, so that what is seen was not made out of what was visible (Hebrews 11:3, NIV).

PART IV

HOW TO BE READY

REFERENCE 20 — Watch and Be Ready

20.1 You also must be ready therefore, for the Son of Man is coming at an hour when you do not expect Him (Matthew 24:44, AMP).

20.2 Watch therefore, for ye know neither the day nor the hour wherein the Son of Man cometh (Matthew 25:13, KJV).

20.3 You also must be ready, because the Son of Man will come at an hour when you do not expect him (Luke 12:40, NIV).

20.4 Watch ye therefore, and pray always, that ye may be accounted worthy to escape all these things that shall come to pass, and to stand before the Son of Man (Luke 21:36, KJV).

20.5 But take heed to yourselves and be on your guard, lest your hearts be overburdened and depressed (weighed down) with the giddiness and headache and nausea of self-indulgence, drunkenness, and worldly worries and cares pertaining to [the business of] this life, and [lest] that day come upon you suddenly like a trap or a noose; For it will come upon all who live upon the face of the entire earth. Keep awake then and watch at all times [be discreet, attentive, and ready], praying that you may have the full strength and ability and be accounted worthy to escape all these things [taken together] that will take place, and to stand in the presence of the Son of Man (Luke 21:34-36, AMP).

20.6 So then because thou art lukewarm, and neither cold nor hot, I will spew thee out of my mouth (Revelation 3:16, KJV).

REFERENCE 21 — You Are the Temple of God

21.1 Jesus answered and said to them, "Destroy this temple, and in three days I will raise it up." The Jews therefore said, "It took forty-six years to build this temple, and will You raise it up in three days?" But He was speaking of the temple of His body (John 2:19-21, NASB).

21.2 However, you are not in the flesh but in the Spirit, if indeed the Spirit of God dwells in you. But if anyone does not have the Spirit of Christ, he does not belong to Him (Romans 8:9, NASB).

21.3 Do you not know that you are a temple of God, and that the Spirit of God dwells in you? If any man destroys the temple of God, God will destroy him, for the temple of God is holy, and that is what you are (1 Corinthians 3:16-17, NASB).

21.4 Or do you not know that your body is a temple of the Holy Spirit who is in you, whom you have from God, and that you are not your own? (1 Corinthians 6:19, NASB).

21.5 Or what agreement has the temple of God with idols? For we are the temple of the living God; just as God said, "I will dwell in them and walk among them; and I will be their God, and they shall be my people" (2 Corinthians 6:16, NASB).

21.6 In whom the whole building, being fitted together, is growing into a holy temple in the Lord, in whom you also are being built together into a dwelling of God in the Spirit (Ephesians 2:21-22, NASB).

21.7 The God who made the world and all things in it, since He is Lord of heaven and earth, does not dwell in temples made with hands (Acts 17:24, NASB).

21.8 They serve at a sanctuary that is a copy and shadow of what is in heaven. This is why Moses was warned when he was about to build the tabernacle: "See to it that you make everything according to the pattern shown you on the mountain" (Hebrews 8.5, NIV).

21.9 Seeing that that first [outer portion of the] tabernacle was a parable (a visible symbol or type or picture of the present age). In it gifts and sacrifices are offered, and yet are incapable of perfecting the conscience or of cleansing and renewing the inner man of the worshiper (Hebrews 9:9, AMP).

21.10 If they shall fall away, to renew them again unto repentance; seeing they crucify to themselves the Son of God afresh, and put him to an open shame. (Hebrews 6:6 KJV).

REFERENCE 22 — Keep Your Heart Holy

22.1 But let judgment run down as waters, and righteousness as a mighty stream (Amos 5:24, KJV).

22.2 Blessed are the pure in heart: for they shall see God (Matthew 5:8, KJV).

22.3 Neither shall they say, Lo here! or, lo there! for, behold, the kingdom of God is within you (Luke 17:21, KJV).

22.4 I urge you therefore, brethren, by the mercies of God, to present your bodies a living and holy sacrifice acceptable to God, which is your spiritual service of worship (Romans 12:1, NASB).

22.5 For the kingdom of God is not a matter of eating and drinking, but of righteousness, peace and joy in the Holy Spirit (Romans 14:17, NIV).

22.6 If any man defile the temple of God, him shall God destroy; for the temple of God is holy, which temple ye are (1st Corinthians 3:17, KJV).

22.7 Shun immorality and all sexual looseness [flee from impurity in thought, word, or deed]. Any other sin which a man commits is one outside the body, but he who commits sexual immorality sins against his own body (1 Corinthians 6:18, AMP).

22.8 For no temptation (no trial regarded as enticing to sin), [no matter how it comes or where it leads] has overtaken you and laid hold on you that is not common to man [that is, no temptation or trial has come to you that is beyond human resistance and that is not adjusted and adapted and belonging to human experience, and such as man can bear]. But God is faithful [to His Word and to His compassionate nature], and He [can be trusted] not to let you be tempted and tried and assayed beyond your ability and strength of resistance and power to endure, but with the temptation He will [always] also provide the way out (the means of escape to a landing place), that you may be capable and strong and powerful to bear up under it patiently. Therefore, my dearly beloved, shun (keep clear away from, avoid by flight if need be) any sort of idolatry (of loving or venerating anything more than God). (1 Corinthians 10:13-14, AMP).

22.9 Casting down imaginations, and every high thing that exalteth itself against the knowledge of God, and bringing into captivity every thought to the obedience of Christ (2 Corinthians 10:5, KJV).

22.10 This I say then, Walk in the Spirit, and ye shall not fulfil [sic] the lust of the flesh (Galatians 5:16, KJV).

22.11 And grieve not the holy Spirit of God, whereby ye are sealed unto the day of redemption (Ephesians 4:30, KJV).

22.12 But immorality (sexual vice) and all impurity [of lustful, rich, wasteful living] or greediness must not even be named among you, as is fitting and proper among saints (God's consecrated people). Let there be no filthiness (obscenity, indecency) nor foolish and sinful (silly and corrupt) talk, nor coarse jesting, which are not fitting or becoming; but instead voice your thankfulness [to God]. For be sure of this: that no person practicing sexual vice or impurity in thought or in life, or one who is covetous [who has lustful desire for the property of others and is greedy for gain]—for he [in effect] is an idolater—has any inheritance in the kingdom of Christ and of God. Let no one delude and deceive you with empty excuses and groundless arguments [for these sins], for through these things the wrath of God comes upon the sons of rebellion and disobedience. So do not associate or be sharers with them (Ephesians 5:3-7, AMP).

22.13 If you have died with Christ to the elementary principles of the world, why, as if you were living in the world, do you submit yourself to decrees, such as, "Do not handle, do not taste, do not touch! (which all refer to things destined to perish with use)—in accordance with the commandments and teachings of men? These are matters which have, to be sure, the appearance of wisdom in self-made religion and self-abasement and severe treatment of the body, but are of no value against fleshly indulgence (Colossians 2:20-23, NASB).

22.14 So kill (deaden, deprive of power) the evil desire lurking in your members [those animal impulses and all that is earthly in you that is employed in sin]: sexual vice, impurity, sensual appetites, unholy desires, and all greed and covetousness, for that is idolatry (the deifying of self and other created things instead of God). It is on account of these [very sins] that the [holy] anger of God is ever coming upon the sons of disobedience (those who are obstinately opposed to the divine will) (Colossians 3:5-6, AMP).

22.15 Furthermore, brethren, we beg and admonish you in [virtue of our union with] the Lord Jesus, that [you follow the instructions which] you learned from us about how you ought to walk so as to please and gratify God, as indeed you are doing, [and] that you do so even more and more abundantly [attaining yet greater perfection in living this life]. For you know what charges and precepts we gave you [on the authority and by the inspiration of] the Lord Jesus. For this is the will of God, that you should be consecrated (separated and set apart for pure and holy living): that you should abstain and shrink from all sexual vice (1 Thessalonians 4:1-3, AMP).

22.16 For God did not call us to be impure, but to live a holy life (1 Thessalonians 4:7, NIV).

22.17 But thou, O man of God, flee these things; and follow after righteousness, godliness, faith, love, patience, meekness (1 Timothy 6:11, KJV).

22.18 Not by works of righteousness which we have done, but according to his mercy he saved us, by the washing of regeneration, and renewing of the Holy Ghost (Titus 3:5, KJV).

22.19 Follow peace with all men, and holiness, without which no man shall see the Lord (Hebrews 12:14, KJV).

22.20 Let marriage be held in honor among all, and let the marriage bed be undefiled; for fornicators and adulterers God will judge (Hebrews 13:4, NASB).

22.21 Then when lust hath conceived, it bringeth forth sin: and sin, when it is finished, bringeth forth death (James 1:15, KJV).

22.22 As obedient children, do not be conformed to the former lusts which were yours in your ignorance, but like the Holy One who called you, be holy yourselves also in all your behavior; because it is written, "You shall be holy, for I am holy (1 Peter 1:14-16, NASB).

22.23 For the eyes of the Lord are over the righteous, and his ears are open unto their prayers: but the face of the Lord is against them that do evil (1 Peter 3:12, KJV).

22.24 By this the children of God and the children of the devil are obvious: anyone who does not practice righteousness is not of God, nor the one who does not love his brother (1 John 3:10, NASB).

22.25 But whoever causes one of these little ones who believe in and acknowledge and cleave to Me to stumble and sin [that is, who entices him or hinders him in right conduct or thought], it would be better (more expedient and profitable or advantageous) for him to have a great millstone fastened around his neck and to be sunk in the depth of the sea (Matthew 18:6, AMP).

REFERENCE 23 — Maintain Sexual Purity

23.1 Blessed are the pure in heart: for they shall see God (Matthew 5:8, KJV).

23.2 But I say unto you, That whosoever looketh on a woman to lust after her hath committed adultery with her already in his heart (Matthew 5:28, KJV).

23.3 But the things that come out of the mouth come from the heart, and these make a man 'unclean.' For out of the heart come evil thoughts, murder, adultery, sexual immorality, theft, false testimony, slander. These are what make a man 'unclean'; but eating with unwashed hands does not make him 'unclean' (Matthew 15:18-20, NIV).

23.4 "Are you so dull?" he asked. "Don't you see that nothing that enters a man from the outside can make him 'unclean'? For it doesn't go into his heart but into his stomach, and then out of his body. (In saying this, Jesus declared all foods "clean.") He went on: "What comes out of a man is what makes him 'unclean.' For from within, out of men's hearts, come evil thoughts, sexual immorality, theft, murder, adultery, greed, malice, deceit, lewdness, envy, slander, arrogance and folly. All these evils come from inside and make a man 'unclean'" (Mark 7:18-23, NIV).

23.5 For it has seemed good to the Holy Spirit and to us not to lay upon you any greater burden than these indispensable requirements: That you abstain from what has been sacrificed to idols and from [tasting] blood and from [eating the meat of animals] that have been strangled and from sexual impurity. If you keep yourselves from these things, you will do well. Farewell [be strong]! (Acts 15:28-29, AMP).

23.6 Therefore God gave them up in the lusts of their [own] hearts to sexual impurity, to the dishonoring of their bodies among themselves [abandoning them to the degrading power of sin], Because they exchanged the truth of God for a lie and worshiped and served the creature rather than the Creator, Who is blessed forever! Amen (so be it). For this reason God gave them over and abandoned them to vile affections and degrading passions. For their women exchanged their natural function for an unnatural and abnormal one, And the men also turned from natural relations with women and were set ablaze (burning out, consumed) with lust for one another—men committing shameful acts with men and suffering in their own bodies and personalities the inevitable consequences and penalty of their wrong-doing and going astray, which was [their] fitting retribution (Romans 1:24-27, AMP).

23.7 Do you not know that you are a temple of God and that the Spirit of God dwells in you? If any man destroys the temple of God, God will destroy him, for the temple of God is holy, and that is what you are (1 Corinthians 3:16-17, NASB).

23.8 I have written you in my letter not to associate with sexually immoral people—not at all meaning the people of this world who are immoral, or the greedy and swindlers, or idolaters. In that case you would have to leave this world. But now I am writing you that you must not associate with anyone who calls himself a brother but is sexually immoral or greedy, an idolater or a slanderer, a drunkard or a swindler. With such a man do not even eat (1 Corinthians 5:9-11, NIV).

23.9 Do you not know that the unrighteous and the wrongdoers will not inherit or have any share in the kingdom of God? Do not be deceived (misled): neither the impure and immoral, nor idolaters, nor adulterers, nor those who participate in homosexuality, Nor cheats (swindlers and thieves), nor greedy graspers, nor drunkards, nor foulmouthed revilers and slanderers, nor extortioners and robbers will inherit or have any share in the kingdom of God (1 Corinthians 6:9-10, AMP).

23.10 Food [is intended] for the stomach and the stomach for food, but God will finally end [the functions of] both and bring them to nothing. The body is not intended for sexual immorality, but [is intended] for the Lord, and the Lord [is intended] for the body [to save, sanctify, and raise it again] (1 Corinthians 6:13, AMP).

23.11 Or do you not know that the one who joins himself to a harlot is one body with her? For He says, "The two will become one flesh" (1 Corinthians 6:16, NASB).

23.12 Shun immorality and all sexual looseness [flee from impurity in thought, word, or deed]. Any other sin which a man commits is one outside the body, but he who commits sexual immorality sins against his own body (1 Corinthians 6:18, AMP).

23.13 But because of the temptation to impurity and to avoid immorality, let each [man] have his own wife and let each [woman] have her own husband (1 Corinthians 7:2, AMP).

23.14 But because of immoralities, each man is to have his own wife, and each woman is to have her own husband (1 Corinthians 7:2, NASB).

23.15 But if they have not self-control (restraint of their passions), they should marry. For it is better to marry than to be aflame [with passion and tortured continually with ungratified desire] (1 Corinthians 7:9, AMP).

23.16 We should not commit sexual immorality, as some of them did—and in one day twenty-three thousand of them died (1 Corinthians 10:8, NIV).

23.17 I am afraid that when I come again my God will humble me before you, and I will be grieved over many who have sinned earlier and have not repented of the impurity, sexual sin and debauchery in which they have indulged (2 Corinthians 12:21, NIV).

23.18 Now the deeds of the flesh are evident, which are: immorality, impurity, sensuality, idolatry, sorcery, enmities, strife, jealousy, outbursts of anger, disputes, dissensions, factions, envying, drunkenness, carousing, and things like these, of which I forewarn you just as I have forewarned you that those who practice such things shall not inherit the kingdom of God (Gala-tians 5:19-21, NASB).

23.19 But among you there must not be even a hint of sexual immorality, or of any kind of impurity, or of greed, because these are improper for God's holy people. Nor should there be obscenity, foolish talk or coarse joking, which are out of place, but rather thanksgiving. For of this you can be sure: No immoral, impure or greedy person—such a man is an idolater—has any inheritance in the kingdom of Christ and of God. Let no one deceive you with empty words, for because of such things God's wrath comes on those who are disobedient (Ephesians 5:3-6, NIV).

23.20 Finally, brethren, whatsoever things are true, whatsoever things are honest, whatsoever things are just, whatsoever things are pure, whatsoever things are lovely, whatsoever things are of good report; if there be any virtue, and if there be any praise, think on these things (Philippians 4:8, KJV).

23.21 Put to death, therefore, whatever belongs to your earthly nature: sexual immorality, impurity, lust, evil desires and greed, which is idolatry. Because of these, the wrath of God is coming (Colossians 3:5-6, NIV).

23.22 For you know what commandments we gave you by the authority of the Lord Jesus. For this is the will of God, your sanctification; that is, that you abstain from sexual immorality; that each of you know how to possess his own vessel in sanctification and honor, not in lustful passion, like the Gentiles who do not know God; and that no man transgress and defraud his brother in the matter because the Lord is the avenger in all these things, just as we also told you before and solemnly warned you. For God has not called us for the purpose of impurity, but in sanctification. Consequently, he who rejects this is not rejecting man but the God who gives His Holy Spirit to you (1 Thessalonians 4:2-8, NASB).

23.23 But the goal of our instruction is love from a pure heart and a good conscience and a sincere faith (1 Timothy 1:5, NASB).

23.24 Knowing this, that the law is not made for a righteous man, but for the lawless and disobedient, for the ungodly and for sinners, for unholy and profane, for murderers of fathers and murderers of mothers, for manslayers, For whoremongers, for them that defile themselves with mankind, for menstealers, for liars, for perjured persons, and if there be any other thing that is contrary to sound doctrine (1 Timothy 1:9-10, KJV).

23.25 Flee also youthful lusts: but follow righteousness, faith, charity, peace, with them that call on the Lord out of a pure heart (2 Timothy 2:22, KJV).

23.26 Marriage should be honored by all, and the marriage bed kept pure, for God will judge the adulterer and all the sexually immoral (Hebrews 13:4, NIV).

23.27 Blessed (happy, to be envied) is the man who is patient under trial and stands up under temptation, for when he has stood the test and been approved, he will receive [the victor's] crown of life which God has promised to those who love Him (James 1:12, AMP).

23.28 Seeing ye have purified your souls in obeying the truth through the Spirit unto unfeigned love of the brethren, see that ye love one another with a pure heart fervently (1 Peter1:22, KJV).

23.29 For by these He has granted to us His precious and magnificent promises, so that by them you may become partakers of the divine nature, having escaped the corruption that is in the world by lust (2 Peter 1:4, NASB).

23.30 Many will follow their sensuality, and because of them the way of the truth will be maligned; and in their greed they will exploit you with false words; their judgment from long ago is not idle, and their destruction is not asleep. For if God did not spare angels when they sinned, but cast them into hell and committed them to pits of darkness, reserved for judgment; and did not spare the ancient world, but preserved Noah, a preacher of righteousness, with seven others, when He brought a flood upon the world of the ungodly; and if He condemned the cities of Sodom and Gomorrah to destruction by reducing them to ashes, having made them an example to those who would live ungodly lives thereafter; and if He rescued righteous Lot, oppressed by the sensual conduct of unprincipled men (for by what he saw and heard that righteous man, while living among them, felt his righteous soul tormented day after day by their lawless deeds), then the Lord knows how to rescue the godly from temptation, and to keep the unrighteous under punishment for the day of judgment (2 Peter 2:2-9, NASB).

23.31 And everyone who has this hope fixed on Him purifies himself, just as He is pure (1 John 3:3, NASB).

23.32 [The wicked are sentenced to suffer] just as Sodom and Gomorrah and the adjacent towns—which likewise gave themselves over to impurity and indulged in unnatural vice and sensual perversity—are laid out [in plain sight] as an exhibit of perpetual punishment [to warn] of everlasting fire (Jude 1:7, AMP).

23.33 But the cowardly, the unbelieving, the vile, the murderers, the sexually immoral, those who practice magic arts, the idolaters and all liars—their place will be in the fiery lake of burning sulfur. This is the second death (Revelation 21:8, NIV).

REFERENCE 24 — Forgive Everyone Always

24.1 You have heard that it was said, "Love your neighbor and hate your enemy." But I tell you: Love your enemies and pray for those who persecute you, that you may be sons of your Father in heaven. He causes his sun to rise on the evil and the good, and sends rain on the righteous and the unrighteous. If you love those who love you, what reward will you get? Are not even the tax collectors doing that? And if you greet only your brothers, what are you doing more than others? Do not even pagans do that? Be perfect, therefore, as your heavenly Father is perfect (Matthew 5:43-48, NIV).

24.2 And forgive us our debts, as we also have forgiven (left, remitted, and let go of the debts, and have given up resentment against) our debtors. And lead (bring) us not into temptation, but deliver us from the evil one. For Yours is the kingdom and the power and the glory forever. Amen. For if you forgive people their trespasses [their reckless and willful sins, leaving them, letting them go, and giving up resentment], your heavenly Father will also forgive you. But if you do not forgive others their trespasses [their reckless and willful sins, leaving them, letting them go, and giving up resentment], neither will your Father forgive you your trespasses (Matthew 6:12, AMP).

24.3 Then Peter came to Jesus and asked, "Lord, how many times shall I forgive my brother when he sins against me? Up to seven times?" Jesus answered, "I tell you, not seven times, but seventy-seven times. Therefore, the kingdom of heaven is like a king who wanted to settle accounts with his servants. As he began the settlement, a man who owed him ten thousand talents was brought to him. Since he was not able to pay, the master ordered that he and his wife and his children and all that he had be sold to repay the debt. The servant fell on his knees before him. 'Be patient with me,' he begged, 'and I will pay back everything.' The servant's master took pity on him, canceled the debt and let him go. But when that servant went out, he found one of his fellow servants who owed him a hundred denarii. He grabbed him and began to choke him. 'Pay back what you owe me!' he demanded. His fellow servant fell to his knees and begged him, 'Be patient with me, and I will pay you back.' But he refused. Instead, he went off and had the man thrown into prison until he could pay the debt. When the other servants saw what had happened, they were greatly distressed and went and told their master everything that had happened. Then the master called the servant in. 'You wicked servant,' he said, 'I canceled all that debt of yours because you begged me to. Shouldn't you have had mercy on your fellow servant just as I had on you?' In anger his master turned him over to the jailers to be tortured, until he should pay back all he owed. This is how my heavenly Father will treat each of you unless you forgive your brother from your heart (Matthew 18:21-35, NIV).

24.4 And whenever you stand praying, if you have anything against anyone, forgive him and let it drop (leave it, let it go), in order that your Father Who is in heaven may also forgive you your [own] failings and shortcomings. But if you do not forgive, neither will your Father in heaven forgive your failings and shortcomings (Mark 11:25, AMP).

24.5 But I tell you who hear me: Love your enemies, do good to those who hate you, bless those who curse you, pray for those who mistreat you. If someone strikes you on one cheek, turn to him the other also. If someone takes your cloak, do not stop him from taking your tunic.

Give to everyone who asks you, and if anyone takes what belongs to you, do not demand it back. Do to others as you would have them do to you. If you love those who love you, what credit is that to you? Even 'sinners' love those who love them. And if you do good to those who are good to you, what credit is that to you? Even 'sinners' do that. And if you lend to those from whom you expect repayment, what credit is that to you? Even 'sinners' lend to 'sinners,' expecting to be repaid in full. But love your enemies, do good to them, and lend to them without expecting to get anything back. Then your reward will be great, and you will be sons of the Most High, because he is kind to the ungrateful and wicked. Be merciful, just as your Father is merciful (Luke 6:27-36, NIV).

24.6 For this reason I say to you, her sins, which are many, have been forgiven, for she loved much; but he who is forgiven little, loves little (Luke 7:47, NASB).

24.7 And forgive us our sins, for we ourselves also forgive everyone who is indebted to us [who has offended us or done us wrong]. And bring us not into temptation but rescue us from evil (Luke 11:4, AMP).

24.8 Be on your guard! If your brother sins, rebuke him; and if he repents, forgive him. And if he sins against you seven times a day, and returns to you seven times, saying, 'I repent,' forgive him (Luke 17:3-4, NASB).

24.9 Bless those who persecute you [who are cruel in their attitude toward you]; bless and do not curse them. Rejoice with those who rejoice [sharing others' joy], and weep with those who weep [sharing others' grief]. Live in harmony with one another; do not be haughty (snobbish, high-minded, exclusive), but readily adjust yourself to [people, things] and give yourselves to humble tasks. Never overestimate yourself or be wise in your own conceits. [Prov. 3:7] Repay no one evil for evil, but take thought for what is honest and proper and noble [aiming to be above reproach] in the sight of everyone. [Prov. 20:22] If possible, as far as it depends on you, live at peace with everyone. Beloved, never avenge yourselves, but leave the way open for [God's] wrath; for it is written, Vengeance is Mine, I will repay (requite), says the Lord. [Deut. 32:35] But if your enemy is hungry, feed him; if he is thirsty, give him drink; for by so doing you will heap burning coals upon his head. [Prov. 25:21, 22] Do not let yourself be overcome by evil, but overcome (master) evil with good (Romans 12:14-21, AMP).

24.10 And we still toil unto weariness [for our living], working hard with our own hands. When men revile us [wound us with an accursed sting], we bless them. When we are persecuted, we take it patiently and endure it (1 Corinthians 4:12, AMP).

24.11 And all things are of God, who hath reconciled us to himself by Jesus Christ, and hath given to us the ministry of reconciliation; To wit, that God was in Christ, reconciling the world unto himself, not imputing their trespasses unto them; and hath committed unto us the word of reconciliation (2 Corinthians 5:18-19, KJV).

24.12 Let all bitterness and indignation and wrath (passion, rage, bad temper) and resentment (anger, animosity) and quarreling (brawling, clamor, contention) and slander (evil-speaking, abusive or blasphemous language) be banished from you, with all malice (spite, ill will, or baseness of any kind). And become useful and helpful and kind to one another, tenderhearted (compassionate, understanding, loving-hearted), forgiving one another [readily and freely], as God in Christ forgave you (Ephesians 4:31-32, AMP).

24.13 But now you must rid yourselves of all such things as these: anger, rage, malice, slander, and filthy language from your lips (Colossians 3:8, NIV).

24.14 So, as those who have been chosen of God, holy and beloved, put on a heart of compassion, kindness, humility, gentleness and patience; bearing with one another, and forgiving each other, whoever has a complaint against anyone; just as the Lord forgave you, so also should you (Colossians 3:12-13, NASB).

24.15 See that none render evil for evil unto any man; but ever follow that which is good, both among yourselves, and to all men (1 Thessalonians 5:15, KJV).

24.16 Exercise foresight and be on the watch to look [after one another], to see that no one falls back from and fails to secure God's grace (His unmerited favor and spiritual blessing), in order that no root of resentment (rancor, bitterness, or hatred) shoots forth and causes trouble and bitter torment, and the many become contaminated and defiled by it (Hebrews 12:15, AMP).

24.17 Never return evil for evil or insult for insult (scolding, tongue-lashing, berating), but on the contrary blessing [praying for their welfare, happiness, and protection, and truly pitying and loving them]. For know that to this you have been called, that you may yourselves inherit a blessing [from God—that you may obtain a blessing as heirs, bringing welfare and happiness and protection]. For let him who wants to enjoy life and see good days [good—whether apparent or not] keep his tongue free from evil and his lips from guile (treachery, deceit). Let him turn away from wickedness and shun it, and let him do right. Let him search for peace (harmony; undisturbedness from fears, agitating passions, and moral conflicts) and seek it eagerly. [Do not merely desire peaceful relations with God, with your fellowmen, and with yourself, but pursue, go after them!] (1 Peter 3:9-11, AMP).

24.18 If we confess our sins, He is faithful and righteous to forgive us our sins and to cleanse us from all unrighteousness (1 John 1:9, NASB).

REFERENCE 25 — Let Love Be Your Only Motive

25.1 Ye have heard that it hath been said, Thou shalt love thy neighbour, and hate thine enemy. But I say unto you, Love your enemies, bless them that curse you, do good to them that hate you, and pray for them which despitefully use you, and persecute you; That ye may be the children of your Father which is in heaven: for he maketh his sun to rise on the evil and on the good, and sendeth rain on the just and on the unjust. For if ye love them which love you, what reward have ye? do not even the publicans the same? (Matthew 5:43-46, KJV).

25.2 Jesus said unto him, Thou shalt love the Lord thy God with all thy heart, and with all thy soul, and with all thy mind. This is the first and great commandment. And the second is like unto it, Thou shalt love thy neighbour as thyself (Matthew 22:37-39, KJV).

25.3 And you shall love the Lord your God out of and with your whole heart and out of and with all your soul (your life) and out of and with all your mind (with your faculty of thought and your moral understanding) and out of and with all your strength. This is the first and principal commandment. [Deut. 6:4, 5] The second is like it and is this, You shall love your neighbor as yourself. There is no other commandment greater than these (Mark 12:30-31, AMP).

25.4 But I say to you who hear, love your enemies, do good to those who hate you, bless those who curse you, pray for those who mistreat you. Whoever hits you on the cheek, offer him the other also; and whoever takes away your coat, do not withhold your shirt from him either. Give to everyone who asks of you, and whoever takes away what is yours, do not demand it back. Treat others the same way you want them to treat you. If you love those who love you, what credit is that to you? For even sinners love those who love them. If you do good to those who do good to you, what credit is that to you?

For even sinners do the same. If you lend to those from whom you expect to receive, what credit is that to you? Even sinners lend to sinners in order to receive back the same amount. But love your enemies, and do good, and lend, expecting nothing in return; and your reward will be great, and you will be sons of the Most High; for He Himself is kind to ungrateful and evil men. Be merciful, just as your Father is merciful (Luke 6:27-36, NASB).

25.5 For all the law is fulfilled in one word, even in this; Thou shalt love thy neighbour as thyself (Galatians 5:14, KJV).

25.6 But the fruit of the Spirit is love, joy, peace, longsuffering, gentleness, goodness, faith (Galatians 5:22, KJV).

25.7 Just as He chose us in Him before the foundation of the world, that we would be holy and blameless before Him. In love (Ephesians 1:4, NASB).

25.8 May Christ through your faith [actually] dwell (settle down, abide, make His permanent home) in your hearts! May you be rooted deep in love and founded securely on love, That you may have the power and be strong to apprehend and grasp with all the saints [God's devoted people, the experience of that love] what is the breadth and length and height and depth [of it]; [That you may really come] to know [practically, through experience for yourselves] the love of Christ, which far surpasses mere knowledge [without experience]; that you may be filled [through all your being] unto all the fullness of God [may have the richest measure of the divine Presence, and become a body wholly filled and flooded with God Himself]! (Ephesians 3:17-19, AMP).

25.9 With all humility and gentleness, with patience, showing tolerance for one another in love (Ephesians 4:2, NASB).

25.10 But speaking the truth in love, we are to grow up in all aspects into Him who is the head, even Christ, from whom the whole body, being fitted and held together by what every joint supplies according to the proper working of each individual part, causes the growth of the body for the building up of itself in love (Ephesians 4:15-16, NASB).

25.11 and live a life of love, just as Christ loved us and gave himself up for us as a fragrant offering and sacrifice to God (Ephesians 5:2, NIV).

25.12 Fill up and complete my joy by living in harmony and being of the same mind and one in purpose, having the same love, being in full accord and of one harmonious mind and intention (Philippians 2:2, AMP).

25.13 My purpose is that they may be encouraged in heart and united in love, so that they may have the full riches of complete understanding, in order that they may know the mystery of God, namely, Christ (Colossians 2:2, NIV).

25.14 And the Lord make you to increase and abound in love one toward another, and toward all men, even as we do toward you (1 Thessalonians 3:12, KJV).

25.15 But concerning brotherly love [for all other Christians], you have no need to have anyone write you, for you yourselves have been [personally] taught by God to love one another (1 Thessalonians 4:9, AMP).

25.16 But let us, who are of the day, be sober, putting on the breastplate of faith and love; and for an helmet, the hope of salvation (1 Thessalonians 5:8, KJV).

25.17 May the Lord direct your hearts into [realizing and showing] the love of God and into the steadfastness and patience of Christ and in waiting for His return (2 Thessalonians 3:5, AMP).

25.18 But flee from these things, you man of God, and pursue righteousness, godliness, faith, love, perseverance and gentleness (1 Timothy 6:11, NASB).

25.19 For God did not give us a spirit of timidity (of cowardice, of craven and cringing and fawning fear), but [He has given us a spirit] of power and of love and of calm and well-balanced mind and discipline and self-control (2 Timothy 1:7, AMP).

25.20 Retain the standard of sound words which you have heard from me, in the faith and love which are in Christ Jesus (2 Timothy 1:13, NASB).

25.21 And let us consider how we may spur one another on toward love and good deeds (Hebrews 10:24, NIV).

25.22 Let love for your fellow believers continue and be a fixed practice with you [never let it fail] (Hebrews 13:1, AMP).

25.23 If ye fulfil [sic] the royal law according to the Scripture, Thou shalt love thy neighbour as thyself, ye do well (James 2:8, KJV).

25.24 Now that you have purified yourselves by obeying the truth so that you have sincere love for your brothers, love one another deeply, from the heart (1 Peter 1:22, NIV).

25.25 Finally, all [of you] should be of one and the same mind (united in spirit), sympathizing [with one another], loving [each other] as brethren [of one household], compassionate and courteous (tenderhearted and humble) (1 Peter 3:8, AMP).

25.26 Love not the world, neither the things that are in the world. If any man love the world, the love of the Father is not in him (1 John 2:15, KJV).

25.27 For this is the message that ye heard from the beginning, that we should love one another (1 John 3:11, KJV).

25.28 Little children, let us not love [merely] in theory or in speech but in deed and in truth (in practice and in sincerity) (1 John 3:18, AMP).

25.29 And this is his commandment, That we should believe on the name of his Son Jesus Christ, and love one another, as he gave us commandment (1 John 3:23, KJV).

25.30 Beloved, let us love one another, for love is (springs) from God; and he who loves [his fellowmen] is begotten (born) of God and is coming [progressively] to know and understand God [to perceive and recognize and get a better and clearer knowledge of Him]. He who does not love has not become acquainted with God [does not and never did know Him], for God is love. In this the love of God was made manifest (displayed) where we are concerned: in that God sent His Son, the only begotten or unique [Son], into the world so that we might live through Him. In this is love: not that we loved God, but that He loved us and sent His Son to be the propitiation (the atoning sacrifice) for our sins. Beloved, if God loved us so [very much], we also ought to love one another. No man has at any time [yet] seen God. But if we love one another, God abides (lives and remains) in us and His love (that love which is essentially His) is brought to completion (to its full maturity, runs its full course, is perfected) in us (1 John 4:7-12, AMP).

25.31 And we have come to know and have believed the love which God has for us. God is love, and the one who abides in love abides in God, and God abides in him. By this, love is perfected with us, so that we may have confidence in the day of judgment; because as He is, so also are we in this world. There is no fear in love; but perfect love casts out fear, because fear involves punishment, and the one who fears is not perfected in love. We love, because He first loved us (1 John 4:16-19, NASB).

25.32 And this command (charge, order, injunction) we have from Him: that he who loves God shall love his brother [believer] also (1 John 4:21, AMP).

25.33 By this we know that we love the children of God, when we love God, and keep his commandments (1 John 5:2, KJV).

25.34 And now, dear lady, I am not writing you a new command but one we have had from the beginning. I ask that we love one another. And this is love: that we walk in obedience to his commands. As you have heard from the beginning, his command is that you walk in love (2 John 1:5, NIV).

25.35 Keep yourselves in God's love as you wait for the mercy of our Lord Jesus Christ to bring you to eternal life (Jude 1:21, NIV).

REFERENCE 26 — Embrace Emotional Healing

26.1 As Jesus and his disciples were on their way, he came to a village where a woman named Martha opened her home to him. She had a sister called Mary, who sat at the Lord's feet listening to what he said. But Martha was distracted by all the preparations that had to be made. She came to him and asked, "Lord, don't you care that my sister has left me to do the work by myself? Tell her to help me!" "Martha, Martha," the Lord answered, "you are worried and upset about many things, but only one thing is needed. Mary has chosen what is better, and it will not be taken away from her (Luke 10:38-42, NIV).

26.2 Now the doings (practices) of the flesh are clear (obvious): they are immorality, impurity, indecency, Idolatry, sorcery, enmity, strife, jealousy, anger (ill temper), selfishness, divisions (dissensions), party spirit (factions, sects with peculiar opinions, heresies), Envy, drunkenness, carousing, and the like. I warn you beforehand, just as I did previously, that those who do such things shall not inherit the kingdom of God. But the fruit of the [Holy] Spirit [the work which His presence within accomplishes] is love, joy (gladness), peace, patience (an even temper, forbearance), kindness, goodness (benevolence), faithfulness, Gentleness (meekness, humility), self-control (self-restraint, continence). Against such things there is no law [that can bring a charge]. And those who belong to Christ Jesus (the Messiah) have crucified the flesh (the godless human nature) with its passions and appetites and desires. If we live by the [Holy] Spirit, let us also walk by the Spirit. [If by the Holy Spirit we have our life in God, let us go forward walking in line, our conduct controlled by the Spirit.] Let us not become vainglorious and self-conceited, competitive and challenging and provoking and irritating to one another, envying and being jealous of one another (Galatians 5:19-26, AMP).

26.3 Do not grieve the Holy Spirit of God, by whom you were sealed for the day of redemption. Let all bitterness and wrath and anger and clamor and slander be put away from you, along with all malice. Be kind to one another, tender-hearted, forgiving each other, just as God in Christ also has forgiven you (Ephesians 4:30-32, NASB).

26.4 For God hath not given us the spirit of fear; but of power, and of love, and of a sound mind (2 Timothy 1:7, KJV).

26.5 Exercise foresight and be on the watch to look [after one another], to see that no one falls back from and fails to secure God's grace (His unmerited favor and spiritual blessing), in order that no root of resentment (rancor, bitterness, or hatred) shoots forth and causes trouble and bitter torment, and the many become contaminated and defiled by it (Hebrews 12:15, AMP).

26.6 He heals the brokenhearted and binds up their wounds [curing their pains and their sorrows] (Psalm 147:3, AMP).

REFERENCE 27 — Follow the Shepherd as a Member of His Church

27.1 He tends his flock like a shepherd: He gathers the lambs in his arms and carries them close to his heart; he gently leads those that have young (Isaiah 40:11, NIV).

27.2 And I will set up one shepherd over them, and he shall feed them, even my servant David; he shall feed them, and he shall be their shepherd (Eze-kiel 34:23, KJV).

27.3 And you Bethlehem, in the land of Judah, you are not in any way least or insignificant among the chief cities of Judah; for from you shall come a Ruler (Leader) Who will govern and shepherd My people Israel (Matthew 2:6, AMP).

27.4 I am the good shepherd; the good shepherd lays down His life for the sheep. He who is a hired hand, and not a shepherd, who is not the owner of the sheep, sees the wolf coming, and leaves the sheep and flees, and the wolf snatches them and scatters them. He flees because he is a hired hand and is not concerned about the sheep. I am the good shepherd, and I know My own and My own know Me, even as the Father knows Me and I know the Father; and I lay down My life for the sheep (John 10:11-15, NASB).

27.5 And His gifts were [varied; He Himself appointed and gave men to us] some to be apostles (special messengers), some prophets (inspired preachers and expounders), some evangelists (preachers of the Gospel, traveling missionaries), some pastors (shepherds of His flock) and teachers. His intention was the perfecting and the full equipping of the saints (His consecrated people), [that they should do] the work of ministering toward building up Christ's body (the church), [That it might develop] until we all attain oneness in the faith and in the comprehension of the [full and accurate] knowledge of the Son of God, that [we might arrive] at really mature manhood (the completeness of personality which is nothing less than the standard height of Christ's own perfection), the measure of the stature of the fullness of the Christ and the completeness found in Him. So then, we may no longer be children, tossed [like ships] to and fro between chance gusts of teaching and wavering with every changing wind of doctrine, [the prey of] the cunning and cleverness of unscrupulous men, [gamblers engaged] in every shifting form of trickery in inventing errors to mislead. Rather, let our lives lovingly express truth [in all things, speaking truly, dealing truly, living truly]. Enfolded in love, let us grow up in every way and in all things into Him Who is the Head, [even] Christ (the Messiah, the Anointed One). For because of Him the whole body (the church, in all its various parts), closely joined and firmly knit together by the joints and ligaments with which it is supplied, when each part [with power adapted to its need] is working properly [in all its functions], grows to full maturity, building itself up in love (Ephesians 4:11-16, AMP).

27.6 Therefore, since we have a great high priest who has gone through the heavens, Jesus the Son of God, let us hold firmly to the faith we profess. For we do not have a high priest who is unable to sympathize with our weaknesses, but we have one who has been tempted in every way, just as we are—yet was without sin (Hebrews 4:14-15, NIV).

27.7 But because Jesus lives forever, he has a permanent priesthood. Therefore he is able to save completely those who come to God through him, because he always lives to intercede for them. Such a high priest meets our need—one who is holy, blameless, pure, set apart from sinners, exalted above the heavens. Unlike the other high priests, he does not need to offer sacrifices day after day, first for his own sins, and then for the sins of the people. He sacrificed for their sins once for all when he offered himself. For the law appoints as high priests men who are weak; but the oath, which came after the law, appointed the Son, who has been made perfect forever (Hebrews 7:24-28, NIV).

27.8 Not forsaking or neglecting to assemble together [as believers], as is the habit of some people, but admonishing (warning, urging, and encouraging) one another, and all the more faithfully as you see the day approaching (Hebrews 10:25, AMP).

27.9 Now the God of peace, that brought again from the dead our Lord Jesus, that great shepherd of the sheep, through the blood of the everlasting covenant, Make you perfect in every good work to do his will, working in you that which is well-pleasing in his sight, through Jesus Christ; to whom be glory for ever and ever. Amen (Hebrews 13:20-21, KJV).

27.10 For you were continually straying like sheep, but now you have returned to the Shepherd and Guardian of your souls (1 Peter 2:25, NASB).

27.11 I warn and counsel the elders among you (the pastors and spiritual guides of the church) as a fellow elder and as an eyewitness [called to testify] of the sufferings of Christ, as well as a sharer in the glory (the honor and splendor) that is to be revealed (disclosed, unfolded): Tend (nurture, guard, guide, and fold) the flock of God that is [your responsibility], not by coercion or constraint, but willingly; not dishonorably motivated by the advantages and profits [belonging to the office], but eagerly and cheerfully; Not domineering [as arrogant, dictatorial, and overbearing persons] over those in your charge, but being examples (patterns and models of Christian living) to the flock (the congregation). And [then] when the Chief Shepherd is revealed, you will win the conqueror's crown of glory. Likewise, you who are younger and of lesser rank, be subject to the elders (the ministers and spiritual guides of the church)—[giving them due respect and yielding to their counsel]. Clothe (apron) yourselves, all of you, with humility [as the garb of a servant, so that its covering cannot possibly be stripped from you, with freedom from pride and arrogance] toward one another. For God sets Himself against the proud (the insolent, the overbearing, the disdainful, the presumptuous, the boastful)—[and He opposes, frustrates, and defeats them], but gives grace (favor, blessing) to the humble (1 Peter 5:1-5, AMP).

27.12 For the Lamb Who is in the midst of the throne will be their Shepherd, and He will guide them to the springs of the waters of life; and God will wipe away every tear from their eyes (Revelation 7:17, AMP).

REFERENCE 28 — Fulfill Your Ministry

28.1 And having been set free from sin, you have become the servants of righteousness (of conformity to the divine will in thought, purpose, and action) (Romans 6:18, AMP).

28.2 Just as each of us has one body with many members, and these members do not all have the same function, so in Christ we who are many form one body, and each member belongs to all the others. We have different gifts according to the grace given us. If a man's gift is prophesying, let him use it in proportion to his faith. If it is serving, let him serve; if it is teaching, let him teach; if it is encouraging, let him encourage; if it is contributing to the needs of others, let him give generously; if it is leadership, let him govern diligently; if it is showing mercy, let him do it cheerfully (Romans 12:4-8, NIV).

28.3 Only, let each one [seek to conduct himself and regulate his affairs so as to] lead the life which the Lord has allotted and imparted to him and to which God has invited and summoned him. This is my order in all the churches (1 Corinthians 7:17, AMP).

28.4 [It is He] Who has qualified us [making us to be fit and worthy and sufficient] as ministers and dispensers of a new covenant [of salvation through Christ], not [ministers] of the letter (of legally written code) but of the Spirit; for the code [of the Law] kills, but the [Holy] Spirit makes alive (2 Corinth-ians 3:6, AMP).

28.5 But let every person carefully scrutinize and examine and test his own conduct and his own work. He can then have the personal satisfaction and joy of doing something commendable [in itself alone] without [resorting to] boastful comparison with his neighbor (Galatians 6:4, AMP).

28.6 And say to Archippus, Take heed to the ministry which thou hast received in the Lord, that thou fulfill it (Colossians 4:17, KJV).

28.7 To this end also we pray for you always, that our God will count you worthy of your calling, and fulfill every desire for goodness and the work of faith with power (2 Thessalonians 1:11, NASB).

28.8 Therefore do not be ashamed of the testimony of our Lord or of me His prisoner, but join with me in suffering for the gospel according to the power of God, who has saved us and called us with a holy calling, not according to our works, but according to His own purpose and grace which was granted us in Christ Jesus from all eternity (2 Timothy 1:8-9, NASB).

28.9 Study to show thyself approved unto God, a workman that needeth not to be ashamed, rightly dividing the word of truth (2 Timothy 2:15, KJV).

28.10 So that the man of God may be complete and proficient, well fitted and thoroughly equipped for every good work (2 Timothy 3:17, AMP).

28.11 But you, keep your head in all situations, endure hardship, do the work of an evangelist, discharge all the duties of your ministry (2 Timothy 4:5, NIV).

28.12 Wherefore seeing we also are compassed about with so great a cloud of witnesses, let us lay aside every weight, and the sin which doth so easily beset us, and let us run with patience the race that is set before us (Hebrews 12:1, KJV).

28.13 Wherefore the rather, brethren, give diligence to make your calling and election sure: for if ye do these things, ye shall never fall (2 Peter 1:10, KJV).

REFERENCE 29 — Recognize Christian Leadership

29.1 Now when they heard this they were stung (cut) to the heart, and they said to Peter and the rest of the apostles (special messengers), Brethren, what shall we do? (Acts 2:37, AMP).

29.2 They were continually devoting themselves to the apostles' teaching and to fellowship, to the breaking of bread and to prayer (Acts 2:42, NASB).

29.3 And fear came upon every soul: and many wonders and signs were done by the apostles (Acts 2:43, NASB).

29.4 And when they had ordained them elders in every church, and had prayed with fasting, they commended them to the Lord, on whom they believed (Acts 14:23, KJV).

29.5 For I think that God hath set forth us the apostles last, as it were appointed to death: for we are made a spectacle unto the world, and to angels, and to men (1 Corinthians 4:9, KJV).

29.6 Now you [collectively] are Christ's body and [individually] you are members of it, each part severally and distinct [each with his own place and function]. So God has appointed some in the church [for His own use]: first apostles (special messengers); second prophets (inspired preachers and expounders); third teachers; then wonder-workers; then those with ability to heal the sick; helpers;

administrators; [speakers in] different (unknown) tongues (1 Corinthians 12:27-28, AMP).

29.7 And he gave some, apostles; and some, prophets; and some, evangelists; and some, pastors and teachers; For the perfecting of the saints, for the work of the ministry, for the edifying of the body of Christ: Till we all come in the unity of the faith, and of the knowledge of the Son of God, unto a perfect man, unto the measure of the stature of the fullness of Christ (Ephesians 4:11-12, KJV).

29.8 But speaking the truth in love, we are to grow up in all aspects into Him who is the head, even Christ, from whom the whole body, being fitted and held together by what every joint supplies according to the proper working of each individual part, causes the growth of the body for the building up of itself in love (Ephesians 4:15-16, NASB).

29.9 It is a trustworthy statement: if any man aspires to the office of overseer, it is a fine work he desires to do. An overseer, then, must be above reproach, the husband of one wife, temperate, prudent, respectable, hospitable, able to teach, not addicted to wine or pugnacious, but gentle, peaceable, free from the love of money. He must be one who manages his own household well, keeping his children under control with all dignity (but if a man does not know how to manage his own household, how will he take care of the church of God?), and not a new convert, so that he will not become conceited and fall into the condemnation incurred by the devil. And he must have a good reputation with those outside the church, so that he will not fall into reproach and the snare of the devil. Deacons likewise must be men of dignity, not double-tongued, or addicted to much wine or fond of sordid gain, but holding to the mystery of the faith with a clear conscience. These men must also first be tested; then let them serve as deacons if they are beyond reproach. Women must likewise be dignified, not malicious gossips, but temperate, faithful in all things. Deacons must be husbands of only one wife, and good managers of their children and their own households. For those who have served well as deacons obtain for themselves a high standing and great confidence in the faith that is in Christ Jesus. Let the elders that rule well be counted worthy of double honour, especially they who labour in the word and doctrine (1 Timothy 3:1-17, NASB).

29.10 Is any sick among you? let him call for the elders of the church; and let them pray over him, anointing him with oil in the name of the Lord (James 5:14, KJV).

29.11 I warn and counsel the elders among you (the pastors and spiritual guides of the church) as a fellow elder and as an eyewitness [called to testify] of the sufferings of Christ, as well as a sharer in the glory (the honor and splendor) that is to be revealed (disclosed, unfolded): Tend (nurture, guard, guide, and fold) the flock of God that is [your responsibility], not by coercion or constraint, but willingly; not dishonorably motivated by the advantages and profits [belonging to the office], but eagerly and cheerfully; Not domineering [as arrogant, dictatorial, and overbearing persons] over those in your charge, but being examples (patterns and models of Christian living) to the flock (the congregation) (1 Peter 5:1-3, AMP).

REFERENCE 30 — Esteem God's Authority over Man's Authority

30.1 But in vain they do worship me, teaching for doctrines the commandments of men (Matthew 15:9, KJV).

30.2 For there shall arise false Christs, and false prophets, and shall show great signs and wonders; insomuch that, if it were possible, they shall deceive the very elect (Matthew 24:24, KJV).

30.3 For false Christs and false prophets shall rise, and shall show signs and wonders, to seduce, if it were possible, even the elect (Mark 13:22, KJV).

30.4 And he said unto them, Ye are they which justify yourselves before men; but God knoweth your hearts: for that which is highly esteemed among men is abomination in the sight of God (Luke 16:15, KJV).

30.5 I have come in My Father's name and with His power, and you do not receive Me [your hearts are not open to Me, you give Me no welcome]; but if another comes in his own name and his own power and with no other authority but himself, you will receive him and give him your approval. How is it possible for you to believe [how can you learn to believe], you who [are content to seek and] receive praise and honor and glory from one another, and yet do not seek the praise and honor and glory which come from Him Who alone is God? (John 5:43-44, AMP).

30.6 Now I urge you, brethren, keep your eye on those who cause dissensions and hindrances contrary to the teaching which you learned, and turn away from them. For such men are slaves, not of our Lord Christ but of their own appetites; and by their smooth and flattering speech they deceive the hearts of the unsuspecting (Romans 16:17-18, KJV).

30.7 And my speech and my preaching was not with enticing words of man's wisdom, but in demonstration of the Spirit and of power: That your faith should not stand in the wisdom of men, but in the power of God (1 Corinthians 2:4-5, KJV).

30.8 This is what we speak, not in words taught us by human wisdom but in words taught by the Spirit, expressing spiritual truths in spiritual words. The man without the Spirit does not accept the things that come from the Spirit of God, for they are foolishness to him, and he cannot understand them, because they are spiritually discerned (1 Corinthians 2:13-14, NIV).

30.9 You were bought with a price [purchased with a preciousness and paid for by Christ]; then do not yield yourselves up to become [in your own estimation] slaves to men [but consider yourselves slaves to Christ] (1 Corinthians 7:23, AMP).

30.10 Paul, an apostle (not sent from men nor through the agency of man, but through Jesus Christ and God the Father, who raised Him from the dead) (Galatians 1:1, NASB).

30.11 Am I now trying to win the approval of men, or of God? Or am I trying to please men? If I were still trying to please men, I would not be a servant of Christ. I want you to know, brothers, that the gospel I preached is not something that man made up. I did not receive it from any man, nor was I taught it; rather, I received it by revelation from Jesus Christ (Galatians 1:10-12, NIV).

30.12 But from those who were of high reputation (what they were makes no difference to me; God shows no partiality)—well, those who were of reputation contributed nothing to me (Galatians 2:6, NASB).

30.13 Moreover, [no new requirements were made] by those who were reputed to be something—though what was their individual position and whether they really were of importance or not makes no difference to me; God is not impressed with the positions that men hold and He is not partial and recognizes no external distinctions—those [I say] who were of repute imposed no new requirements upon me [had nothing to add to my Gospel, and from them I received no new suggestions] (Galatians 2:6 AMP

30.14 That we henceforth be no more children, tossed to and fro, and carried about with every wind of doctrine, by the sleight of men, and cunning craftiness, whereby they lie in wait to deceive (Ephesians 4:14, KJV).

30.15 Let no man deceive you with vain words: for because of these things cometh the wrath of God upon the children of disobedience (Ephesians 5:6, KJV).

30.16 Beware lest any man spoil you through philosophy and vain deceit, after the tradition of men, after the rudiments of the world, and not after Christ (Colossians 2:8, KJV).

30.17 See to it that no one carries you off as spoil or makes you yourselves captive by his so-called philosophy and intellectualism and vain deceit (idle fancies and plain nonsense), following human tradition (men's ideas of the material rather than the spiritual world), just crude notions following the rudimentary and elemental teachings of the universe and disregarding [the teachings of] Christ (the Messiah) (Colossians 2:8, AMP).

30.18 But as we were allowed of God to be put in trust with the gospel, even so we speak; not as pleasing men, but God, which trieth our hearts (1 Thessalonians 2:4, KJV).

30.19 But wicked men and imposters will go on from bad to worse, deceiving and leading astray others and being deceived and led astray themselves (2 Timothy 3:13, AMP).

30.20 These are grumblers, finding fault, following after their own lusts; they speak arrogantly, flattering people for the sake of gaining an advantage (Jude 1:16, NASB).

REFERENCE 31 — Worship and Obey God in Spirit and in Truth

31.1 If ye then, being evil, know how to give good gifts unto your children: how much more shall your heavenly Father give the Holy Spirit to them that ask him? (Luke 11:13, KJV).

31.2 For the Holy Ghost shall teach you in the same hour what ye ought to say (Luke 12:12, KJV).

31.3 The wind blows where it wishes and you hear the sound of it, but do not know where it comes from and where it is going; so is everyone who is born of the Spirit (John 3:8, NASB).

31.4 But the hour cometh, and now is, when the true worshippers shall worship the Father in spirit and in truth: for the Father seeketh such to worship him. God is a Spirit: and they that worship him must worship him in spirit and in truth (John 4:23-24, KJV).

31.5 It is the Spirit who gives life; the flesh profits nothing; the words that I have spoken to you are spirit and are life (John 6:63, NASB).

31.6 But the Comforter (Counselor, Helper, Intercessor, Advocate, Strengthener, Standby), the Holy Spirit, Whom the Father will send in My name [in My place, to represent Me and act on My behalf], He will teach you all things. And He will cause you to recall (will remind you of, bring to your remembrance) everything I have told you (John 14:26, AMP).

31.7 And when he had said this, he breathed on them, and saith unto them, Receive ye the Holy Ghost. (John 20:22, KJV).

31.8 The first account I composed, Theophilus, about all that Jesus began to do and teach, until the day when He was taken up to heaven, after He had by the Holy Spirit given orders to the apostles whom He had chosen (Acts 1:1-2, NASB).

31.9 But you shall receive power (ability, efficiency, and might) when the Holy Spirit has come upon you, and you shall be My witnesses in Jerusalem and all Judea and Samaria and to the ends (the very bounds) of the earth (Acts 1:8, AMP).

31.10 All of them were filled with the Holy Spirit and began to speak in other tongues as the Spirit enabled them (Acts 2:4, NIV).

31.11 And they were all filled (diffused throughout their souls) with the Holy Spirit and began to speak in other (different, foreign) languages (tongues), as the Spirit kept giving them clear and loud expression [in each tongue in appropriate words] (Acts 2:4, AMP).

31.12 And Peter answered them, Repent (change your views and purpose to accept the will of God in your inner selves instead of rejecting it) and be baptized, every one of you, in the name of Jesus Christ for the forgiveness of and release from your sins; and you shall receive the gift of the Holy Spirit. For the promise [of the Holy Spirit] is to and for you and your children, and to and for all that are far away, [even] to and for as many as the Lord our God invites and bids to come to Himself (Acts 2:38-39, AMP).

31.13 And we are his witnesses of these things; and so is also the Holy Ghost, whom God hath given to them that obey him (Acts 5:32, KJV).

31.14 So the church throughout the whole of Judea and Galilee and Samaria had peace and was edified [growing in wisdom, virtue, and piety] and walking in the respect and reverential fear of the Lord and in the consolation and exhortation of the Holy Spirit, continued to increase and was multiplied (Acts 9:31, AMP).

31.15 And God, who knows the heart, testified to them giving them the Holy Spirit, just as He also did to us (Acts 15:8, NASB).

31.16 When Paul placed his hands on them, the Holy Spirit came on them, and they spoke in tongues and prophesied (Acts 19:6, NIV).

31.17 Keep watch over yourselves and all the flock of which the Holy Spirit has made you overseers. Be shepherds of the church of God, which he bought with his own blood (Acts 20:28, NIV).

21.18 And hope does not disappoint, because the love of God has been poured out within our hearts through the Holy Spirit who was given to us (Romans 5:5, NASB).

31.19 However, you are not in the flesh but in the Spirit, if indeed the Spirit of God dwells in you. But if anyone does not have the Spirit of Christ, he does not belong to Him (Romans 8:9, NASB).

31.20 For if you live according to [the dictates of] the flesh, you will surely die. But if through the power of the [Holy] Spirit you are [habitually] putting to death (making extinct, deadening) the [evil] deeds prompted by the body, you shall [really and genuinely] live forever. For all who are led by the Spirit of God are sons of God (Romans 8:13-14, AMP).

31.21 For the kingdom of God is not a matter of eating and drinking, but of righteousness, peace and joy in the Holy Spirit (Romans 14:17, NIV).

31.22 May the God of hope fill you with all joy and peace as you trust in him, so that you may overflow with hope by the power of the Holy Spirit (Romans 15:13, NIV).

31.23 This is what we speak, not in words taught us by human wisdom but in words taught by the Spirit, expressing spiritual truths in spiritual words. The man without the Spirit does not accept the things that come from the Spirit of God, for they are foolishness to him, and he cannot understand them, because they are spiritually discerned (1 Corinthians 2:13-14, NIV).

31.24 And we, who with unveiled faces all reflect the Lord's glory, are being transformed into his likeness with ever-increasing glory, which comes from the Lord, who is the Spirit (2 Corinthians 3:18, NIV).

31.25 May the grace of the Lord Jesus Christ, and the love of God, and the fellowship of the Holy Spirit be with you all (2 Corinthians 13:14, NIV).

31.26 Are ye so foolish? having begun in the Spirit, are ye now made perfect by the flesh? (Galatians 3:3, KJV).

31.27 For he that soweth to his flesh shall of the flesh reap corruption; but he that soweth to the Spirit shall of the Spirit reap life everlasting (Galatians 6:8, KJV).

31.28 And do not grieve the Holy Spirit of God [do not offend or vex or sadden Him], by Whom you were sealed (marked, branded as God's own, secured) for the day of redemption (of final deliverance through Christ from evil and the consequences of sin) (Ephesians 4:30, AMP).

31.29 Because our gospel came to you not simply with words, but also with power, with the Holy Spirit and with deep conviction. You know how we lived among you for your sake (1 Thessalonians 1:5, NIV).

31.30 Therefore, he who rejects this instruction does not reject man but God, who gives you his Holy Spirit (1 Thessalonians 4:8, NIV).

31.31 Guard and keep [with the greatest care] the precious and excellently adapted [Truth] which has been entrusted [to you], by the [help of the] Holy Spirit Who makes His home in us (2 Timothy 1:14, AMP).

31.32 He saved us, not on the basis of deeds which we have done in righteousness, but according to His mercy, by the washing of regeneration and renewing by the Holy Spirit, whom He poured out upon us richly through Jesus Christ our Savior (Titus 3:5-6, NASB).

31.33 God also testified to it by signs, wonders and various miracles, and gifts of the Holy Spirit distributed according to his will (Hebrews 2:4, NIV).

31.34 [Yet] first [you must] understand this, that no prophecy of Scripture is [a matter] of any personal or private or special interpretation (loosening, solving). For no prophecy ever originated because some man willed it [to do so—it never came by human impulse], but men spoke from God who were borne along (moved and impelled) by the Holy Spirit (2 Peter 1:20-21, AMP).

31.35 But you, beloved, building yourselves up on your most holy faith, praying in the Holy Spirit, keep yourselves in the love of God, waiting anxiously for the mercy of our Lord Jesus Christ to eternal life (Jude 1:20-21, NASB).

31.36 "All this I will give you," he said, "if you will bow down and worship me." Jesus said to him, "Away from me, Satan! For it is written: 'Worship the Lord your God, and serve him only.'" (Matthew 4:9-10, NIV).

REFERENCE 32 — Honor the Gifts and Fruit of the Holy Spirit

32.1 I indeed have baptized you with water: but he shall baptize you with the Holy Ghost (Mark 1:8, KJV).

32.2 If you then, though you are evil, know how to give good gifts to your children, how much more will your Father in heaven give the Holy Spirit to those who ask him! (Luke 11:13, NIV).

32.3 And when he had said this, he breathed on them, and saith unto them, Receive ye the Holy Ghost (John 20:22, KJV).

32.4 For John truly baptized with water; but ye shall be baptized with the Holy Ghost not many days hence (Acts 1:5, KJV).

32.5 Suddenly a sound like the blowing of a violent wind came from heaven and filled the whole house where they were sitting. They saw what seemed to be tongues of fire that separated and came to rest on each of them. All of them were filled with the Holy Spirit and began to speak in other tongues as the Spirit enabled them (Acts 2:2-4, KJV).

32.6 And they came down and prayed for them that the Samaritans might receive the Holy Spirit; For He had not yet fallen upon any of them, but they had only been baptized into the name of the Lord Jesus. Then [the apostles] laid their hands on them one by one, and they received the Holy Spirit (Acts 8:15-17, AMP).

32.7 And as I began to speak, the Holy Spirit fell upon them just as He did upon us at the beginning And I remembered the word of the Lord, how He used to say, "John baptized with water, but you will be baptized with the Holy Spirit. Therefore if God gave to them the same gift as He gave to us also after believing in the Lord Jesus Christ, who was I that I could stand in God's way? (Acts 11:15-17, NASB).

32.8 And the believers from among the circumcised [the Jews] who came with Peter were surprised and amazed, because the free gift of the Holy Spirit had been bestowed and poured out largely even on the Gentiles (Acts 10:45, AMP).

32.9 And when Paul had laid his hands upon them, the Holy Ghost came on them; and they spake with tongues, and prophesied (Acts 19:6, KJV).

32.10 Now concerning spiritual gifts, brethren, I do not want you to be unaware. You know that when you were pagans, you were led astray to the mute idols, however you were led. Therefore I make known to you that no one speaking by the Spirit of God says, "Jesus is accursed"; and no one can say, "Jesus is Lord," except by the Holy Spirit. Now there are varieties of gifts, but the same Spirit. And there are varieties of ministries, and the same Lord. There are varieties of effects, but the same God who works all things in all persons. But to each one is given the manifestation of the Spirit for the common good. For to one is given the word of wisdom through the Spirit, and to another the word of knowledge according to the same Spirit; to another faith by the same Spirit, and to another gifts of healing by the one Spirit, and to another the effecting of miracles, and to another prophecy, and to another the distinguishing of spirits, to another various kinds of tongues, and to another the interpretation of tongues. But one and the same Spirit works all these things, distributing to each one individually just as He wills (1 Corinthians 12:1-11, NASB).

32.11 So it is with you. Since you are eager to have spiritual gifts, try to excel in gifts that build up the church (1 Corinthians 14:12, NIV).

32.12 But the fruit of the Spirit is love, joy, peace, patience, kindness, goodness, faithfulness, gentleness, self-control; against such things there is no law (Galatians 5:22-23

32.13 For the fruit (the effect, the product) of the Light or the Spirit [consists] in every form of kindly goodness, uprightness of heart, and trueness of life (Ephesians 5:9, AMP).

REFERENCE 33 — Crucify the Flesh and the Carnal Mind and Walk in the Spirit

33.1 He went on: "What comes out of a man is what makes him 'unclean.' For from within, out of men's hearts, come evil thoughts, sexual immorality, theft, murder, adultery, greed, malice, deceit, lewdness, envy, slander, arrogance and folly. All these evils come from inside and make a man 'unclean' (Mark 7:20-23 NIV; also see Matthew 15:18-20).

33.2 And he said unto them, Ye are they which justify yourselves before men; but God knoweth your hearts: for that which is highly esteemed among men is abomination in the sight of God (Luke 16:15, KJV).

33.3 They have become filled with every kind of wickedness, evil, greed and depravity. They are full of envy, murder, strife, deceit and malice. They are gossips, slanderers, God-haters, insolent, arrogant and boastful; they invent ways of doing evil; they disobey their parents; they are senseless, faithless, heartless, ruthless. Although they know God's righteous decree that those who do such things deserve death, they not only continue to do these very things but also approve of those who practice them (Romans 1:29-32, NIV).

33.4 Let not sin therefore rule as king in your mortal (short-lived, perishable) bodies, to make you yield to its cravings and be subject to its lusts and evil passions. Do not continue offering or yielding your bodily members [and faculties] to sin as instruments (tools) of wickedness. But offer and yield yourselves to God as though you have been raised from the dead to [perpetual] life, and your bodily members [and faculties] to God, presenting them as implements of righteousness (Romans 6:12-13, AMP).

33.5 Those who live according to the sinful nature have their minds set on what that nature desires; but those who live in accordance with the Spirit have their minds set on what the Spirit desires. The mind of sinful man is death, but the mind controlled by the Spirit is life and peace; the sinful mind is hostile to God. It does not submit to God's law, nor can it do so. Those controlled by the sinful nature cannot please God. You, however, are controlled not by the sinful nature but by the Spirit, if the Spirit of God lives in you. And if anyone does not have the Spirit of Christ, he does not belong to Christ (Romans 8:5-9, NIV).

33.6 For if ye live after the flesh, ye shall die: but if ye through the Spirit do mortify the deeds of the body, ye shall live. For as many as are led by the Spirit of God, they are the sons of God (Romans 8:13-14, KJV).

33.7 I appeal to you therefore, brethren, and beg of you in view of [all] the mercies of God, to make a decisive dedication of your bodies [presenting all your members and faculties] as a living sacrifice, holy (devoted, consecrated) and well pleasing to God, which is your reasonable (rational, intelligent) service and spiritual worship. Do not be conformed to this world (this age), [fashioned after and adapted to its external, superficial customs], but be transformed (changed) by the [entire] renewal of your mind [by its new ideals and its new attitude], so that you may prove [for yourselves] what is the good and acceptable and perfect will of God, even the thing which is good and acceptable and perfect [in His sight for you] (Romans 12:1-2, AMP).

33.8 The night is almost gone, and the day is near. Therefore let us lay aside the deeds of darkness and put on the armor of light. Let us behave properly as in the day, not in carousing and drunkenness, not in sexual promiscuity and sensuality, not in strife and jealousy. But put on the Lord Jesus Christ, and make no provision for the flesh in regard to its lusts (Romans 13:12-14, NASB).

33.9 The man without the Spirit does not accept the things that come from the Spirit of God, for they are foolishness to him, and he cannot understand them, because they are spiritually discerned (1 Corinthians 2:14, NIV).

33.10 Do you not know that the unrighteous and the wrongdoers will not inherit or have any share in the kingdom of God? Do not be deceived (misled): neither the impure and immoral, nor idolaters, nor adulterers, nor those who participate in homosexuality, Nor cheats (swindlers and thieves), nor greedy graspers, nor drunkards, nor foulmouthed revilers and slanderers, nor extortioners and robbers will inherit or have any share in the kingdom of God. And such some of you were [once]. But you were washed clean (purified by a complete atonement for sin and made free from the guilt of sin), and you were consecrated (set apart, hallowed), and you were justified [pronounced righteous, by trusting] in the name of the Lord Jesus Christ and in the [Holy] Spirit of our God (1 Corinthians 6:9-11, AMP).

33.11 Shun immorality and all sexual looseness [flee from impurity in thought, word, or deed]. Any other sin which a man commits is one outside the body, but he who commits sexual immorality sins against his own body (1 Corinthians 6:18, AMP).

33.12 For ye are bought with a price: therefore glorify God in your body, and in your spirit, which are God's (1 Corinthians 6:20, KJV).

33.13 Who gave himself for our sins, that he might deliver us from this present evil world according to the will of God and our Father (Galatians 1:4, KJV).

33.14 But I say, walk and live [habitually] in the [Holy] Spirit [responsive to and controlled and guided by the Spirit]; then you will certainly not gratify the cravings and desires of the flesh (of human nature without God). For the desires of the flesh are opposed to the [Holy] Spirit, and the [desires of the] Spirit are opposed to the flesh (godless human nature); for these are antagonistic to each other [continually withstanding and in conflict with each other], so that you are not free but are prevented from doing what you desire to do (Galatians 5:16-17, AMP).

33.15 Now the works of the flesh are manifest, which are these; Adultery, fornication, uncleanness, lasciviousness, Idolatry, witchcraft, hatred, variance, emulations, wrath, strife, seditions, heresies, Envyings, murders, drunkenness, revellings, and such like: of the which I tell you before, as I have also told you in time past, that they which do such things shall not inherit the kingdom of God. But the fruit of the Spirit is love, joy, peace, longsuffering, gentleness, goodness, faith, Meekness, temperance: against such there is no law. And they that are Christ's have crucified the flesh with the affections and lusts (Galatians 5:19-24, KJV).

33.16 Strip yourselves of your former nature [put off and discard your old unrenewed self] which characterized your previous manner of life and becomes corrupt through lusts and desires that spring from delusion; And be constantly renewed in the spirit of your mind [having a fresh mental and spiritual attitude], And put on the new nature (the regenerate self) created in God's image, [Godlike] in true righteousness and holiness (Ephesians 4:22-24, AMP).

33.17 But immorality (sexual vice) and all impurity [of lustful, rich, wasteful living] or greediness must not even be named among you, as is fitting and proper among saints (God's consecrated people). Let there be no filthiness (obscenity, indecency) nor foolish and sinful (silly and corrupt) talk, nor coarse jesting, which are not fitting or becoming; but instead voice your thankfulness [to God]. For be sure of this: that no person practicing sexual vice or impurity in thought or in life, or one who is covetous [who has lustful desire for the property of others and is greedy for gain]—for he [in effect] is an idolater—has any inheritance in the kingdom of Christ and of God. Let no one delude and deceive you with empty excuses and groundless arguments [for these sins], for through these things the wrath of God comes upon the sons of rebellion and disobedience (Ephesians 5:3-6, AMP).

33.18 Therefore be careful how you walk, not as unwise men but as wise, making the most of your time, because the days are evil (Ephesians 5:15-16, NASB).

33.19 Yes, furthermore, I count everything as loss compared to the possession of the priceless privilege (the overwhelming preciousness, the surpassing worth, and supreme advantage) of knowing Christ Jesus my Lord and of progressively becoming more deeply and intimately acquainted with Him [of perceiving and recognizing and understanding Him more fully and clearly]. For His sake I have lost everything and consider it all to be mere rubbish (refuse, dregs), in order that I may win (gain) Christ (the Anointed One) (Philippians 3:8, AMP).

33.20 Put to death, therefore, whatever belongs to your earthly nature: sexual immorality, impurity, lust, evil desires and greed, which is idolatry. Because of these, the wrath of God is coming. You used to walk in these ways, in the life you once lived. But now you must rid yourselves of all such things as these: anger, rage, malice, slander, and filthy language from your lips (Colossians 3:5-8, NIV).

33.21 Teaching us that, denying ungodliness and worldly lusts, we should live soberly, righteously, and godly, in this present world (Titus 2:12, KJV).

33.22 You [are like] unfaithful wives [having illicit love affairs with the world and breaking your marriage vow to God]! Do you not know that being the world's friend is being God's enemy? So whoever chooses to be a friend of the world takes his stand as an enemy of God (James 4:4, AMP).

33.23 Beloved, I implore you as aliens and strangers and exiles [in this world] to abstain from the sensual urges (the evil desires, the passions of the flesh, your lower nature) that wage war against the soul (1 Peter 2:11, AMP).

33.24 So as to live the rest of the time in the flesh no longer for the lusts of men, but for the will of God. For the time already past is sufficient for you to have carried out the desire of the Gentiles, having pursued a course of sensuality, lusts, drunkenness, carousing, drinking parties and abominable idolatries (1 Peter 4:2-3, NASB).

33.25 Whereby are given unto us exceeding great and precious promises: that by these ye might be partakers of the divine nature, having escaped the corruption that is in the world through lust (2 Peter 1:4, KJV).

33.26 Do not love or cherish the world or the things that are in the world. If anyone loves the world, love for the Father is not in him. For all that is in the world—the lust of the flesh [craving for sensual gratification] and the lust of the eyes [greedy longings of the mind] and the pride of life [assurance in one's own resources or in the stability of earthly things]—these do not come from the Father but are from the world [itself]. And the world passes away and disappears, and with it the forbidden cravings (the passionate desires, the lust) of it; but he who does the will of God and carries out His purposes in his life abides (remains) forever (1 John 2:15-17, AMP).

REFERENCE 34 — Pray Always

34.1 Truly I tell you, whatever you forbid and declare to be improper and unlawful on earth must be what is already forbidden in heaven, and whatever you permit and declare proper and lawful on earth must be what is already permitted in heaven. Again I tell you, if two of you on earth agree (harmonize together, make a symphony together) about whatever [anything and everything] they may ask, it will come to pass and be done for them by My Father in heaven. For wherever two or three are gathered (drawn together as My followers) in (into) My name, there I AM in the midst of them (Matthew 18:18-20, AMP).

34.2 And all things you ask in prayer, believing, you will receive (Matthew 21:22, NASB).

34.3 For this reason I am telling you, whatever you ask for in prayer, believe (trust and be confident) that it is granted to you, and you will [get it]. And whenever you stand praying, if you have anything against anyone, forgive him and let it drop (leave it, let it go), in order that your Father Who is in heaven may also forgive you your [own] failings and shortcomings and let them drop (Mark 11:24-25, AMP).

34.4 Also [Jesus] told them a parable to the effect that they ought always to pray and not to turn coward (faint, lose heart, and give up) (Luke 18:1, AMP).

34.5 Keep awake then and watch at all times [be discreet, attentive, and ready], praying that you may have the full strength and ability and be accounted worthy to escape all these things [taken together] that will take place, and to stand in the presence of the Son of Man (Luke 21:36, AMP).

34.6 And in the same way the Spirit also helps our weakness; for we do not know how to pray as we should, but the Spirit Himself intercedes for us with groanings too deep for words (Romans 8:26, NASB).

34.7 Rejoicing in hope, persevering in tribulation, devoted to prayer (Romans 12:12, NASB).

34.8 Pray at all times (on every occasion, in every season) in the Spirit, with all [manner of] prayer and entreaty. To that end keep alert and watch with strong purpose and perseverance, interceding in behalf of all the saints (God's consecrated people) (Ephesians 6:18, AMP).

34.9 Do not be anxious about anything, but in everything, by prayer and petition, with thanksgiving, present your requests to God. And the peace of God, which transcends all understanding, will guard your hearts and your minds in Christ Jesus (Philippians 4:6-7, NIV).

34.10 Rejoice always; pray without ceasing; in everything give thanks; for this is God's will for you in Christ Jesus (1 Thessalonians 5:16-18 (NASB)

34.11 Therefore, confess your sins to one another, and pray for one another so that you may be healed. The effective prayer of a righteous man can accomplish much (James 5:16, NASB).

34.12 I desire therefore that in every place men should pray, without anger or quarreling or resentment or doubt [in their minds], lifting up holy hands (1 Timothy 2:8, NASB).

34.13 For the eyes of the Lord are over the righteous, and his ears are open unto their prayers: but the face of the Lord is against them that do evil (1 Peter 3:12, KJV).

34.14 And this is the confidence that we have in him, that, if we ask any thing according to his will, he heareth us: And if we know that he hear us, whatsoever we ask, we know that we have the petitions that we desired of him (1 John 5:14-15, KJV).

REFERENCE 35 — Utilize the Weapons and Armor of the Holy Spirit for Readiness

35.1 And He said to them, I saw Satan falling like a lightning [flash] from heaven. Behold! I have given you authority and power to trample upon serpents and scorpions, and [physical and mental strength and ability] over all the power that the enemy [possesses]; and nothing shall in any way harm you. Nevertheless, do not rejoice at this, that the spirits are subject to you, but rejoice that your names are enrolled in heaven (Luke 10:18-29, AMP).

35.2 For though we live in the world, we do not wage war as the world does. The weapons we fight with are not the weapons of the world. On the contrary, they have divine power to demolish strongholds. We demolish arguments and every pretension that sets itself up against the knowledge of God, and we take captive every thought to make it obedient to Christ (2 Corinthians 10:3-5, NIV).

35.3 Finally, be strong in the Lord and in his mighty power. Put on the full armor of God so that you can take your stand against the devil's schemes. For our struggle is not against flesh and blood, but against the rulers, against the authorities, against the powers of this dark world and against the spiritual forces of evil in the heavenly realms. Therefore put on the full armor of God, so that when the day of evil comes, you may be able to stand your ground, and after you have done everything, to stand. Stand firm then, with the belt of truth buckled around your waist, with the breastplate of righteousness in place, and with your feet fitted with the readiness that comes from the gospel of peace. In addition to all this, take up the shield of faith, with which you can extinguish all the flaming arrows of the evil one. Take the helmet of salvation and the sword of the Spirit, which is the word of God. And pray in the Spirit on all occasions with all kinds of prayers and requests. With this in mind, be alert and always keep on praying for all the saints (Ephesians 6:10-18, NIV).

35.4 Fight the good fight of faith; take hold of the eternal life to which you were called, and you made the good confession in the presence of many witnesses (1 Timothy 6:12, NASB).

35.5 Suffer hardship with me, as a good soldier of Christ Jesus. No soldier in active service entangles himself in the affairs of everyday life, so that he may please the one who enlisted him as a soldier (2 Timothy 2:3-4, NASB).

35.6 Beloved, I implore you as aliens and strangers and exiles [in this world] to abstain from the sensual urges (the evil desires, the passions of the flesh, your lower nature) that wage war against the soul (1 Peter 2:11, AMP).

REFERENCE 36 — Believe in Miracles, Signs, and Wonders

36.1 The Lord said to Moses, "How long will these people treat me with contempt? How long will they refuse to believe in me, in spite of all the miraculous signs I have performed among them? (Numbers 14:11, NIV).

36.2 And the Lord said, I have pardoned according to your word. But truly as I live and as all the earth shall be filled with the glory of the Lord, [Isa. 6:3; 11:9] Because all those men who have seen My glory and My [miraculous] signs which I performed in Egypt and in the wilderness, yet have tested and proved Me these ten times and have not heeded My voice, Surely they shall not see the land which I swore to give to their fathers; nor shall any who provoked (spurned, despised) Me see it (Numbers 14:20-23, AMP).

36.3 Ask now about the former days, long before your time, from the day God created man on the earth; ask from one end of the heavens to the other. Has anything so great as this ever happened, or has anything like it ever been heard of? Has any other people heard the voice of God speaking out of fire, as you have, and lived? Has any god ever tried to take for himself one nation out of another nation, by testings, by miraculous signs and wonders, by war, by a mighty hand and an outstretched arm, or by great and awesome deeds, like all the things the Lord your God did for you in Egypt before your very eyes? You were shown these things so that you might know that the Lord is God; besides him there is no other (Deuteronomy 4:32-35, NIV).

36.4 Before our eyes the Lord sent miraculous signs and wonders—great and terrible—upon Egypt and Pharaoh and his whole household. But he brought us out from there to bring us in and give us the land that he promised on oath to our forefathers (Deuteronomy 6:22-23, NIV).

36.5 Thou shalt not be afraid of them: but shalt well remember what the Lord thy God did unto Pharaoh, and unto all Egypt; The great temptations which thine eyes saw, and the signs, and the wonders, and the mighty hand, and the stretched out arm, whereby the Lord thy God brought thee out: so shall the Lord thy God do unto all the people of whom thou art afraid (Deuteronomy 7:18-19, KJV).

36.6 And know ye this day: for I speak not with your children which have not known, and which have not seen the chastisement of the Lord your God, his greatness, his mighty hand, and his stretched out arm, And his miracles, and his acts, which he did in the midst of Egypt unto Pharaoh the king of Egypt, and unto all his land (Deuteronomy 11:2-3, KJV).

36.7 If a prophet, or one who foretells by dreams, appears among you and announces to you a miraculous sign or wonder, and if the sign or wonder of which he has spoken takes place, and he says, "Let us follow other gods (gods you have not known) "and let us worship them," you must not listen to the words of that prophet or dreamer. The Lord your God is testing you to find out whether you love him with all your heart and with all your soul. It is the Lord your God you must follow, and him you must revere. Keep his commands and obey him; serve him and hold fast to him (Deuteronomy 13:1-4, NIV).

36.8 And the Lord brought us forth out of Egypt with a mighty hand and with an outstretched arm, and with great (awesome) power and with signs and with wonders; And He brought us into this place and gave us this land, a land flowing with milk and honey (Deuteronomy 26:8-9, AMP).

36.9 Moses summoned all the Israelites and said to them: Your eyes have seen all that the Lord did in Egypt to Pharaoh, to all his officials and to all his land. With your own eyes you saw those great trials, those miraculous signs and great wonders. But to this day the Lord has not given you a mind that understands or eyes that see or ears that hear (Deuteronomy 29:2-4, NIV).

36.10 And there arose not a prophet since in Israel like unto Moses, whom the Lord knew face to face, In all the signs and the wonders, which the Lord sent him to do in the land of Egypt to Pharaoh, and to all his servants, and to all his land (Deuteronomy 34:10-11, KJV).

36.11 Then Gideon said to him, "O my Lord, if the Lord is with us, why then has all this happened to us? And where are all His miracles which our fathers told us about, saying, 'Did not the Lord bring us up from Egypt?' But now the Lord has abandoned us and given us into the hand of Midian." The Lord looked at him and said, "Go in this your strength and deliver Israel from the hand of Midian. Have I not sent you?" (Judges 6:13-14, NASB).

36.12 And showedst signs and wonders upon Pharaoh, and on all his servants, and on all the people of his land: for thou knewest that they dealt proudly against them. So didst thou get thee a name, as it is this day (Nehemiah 9:10, KJV).

36.13 He performs wonders that cannot be fathomed, miracles that cannot be counted (Job 5:9, NIV).

36.14 You are the God who performs miracles; you display your power among the peoples (Psalm 77:14, NIV).

36.15 They did not remember his power—the day he redeemed them from the oppressor, the day he displayed his miraculous signs in Egypt, his wonders in the region of Zoan (Psalm 78:42, NIV).

36.16 You performed miraculous signs and wonders in Egypt and have continued them to this day, both in Israel and among all mankind, and have gained the renown that is still yours. You brought your people Israel out of Egypt with signs and wonders, by a mighty hand and an outstretched arm and with great terror (Jeremiah 32:20-21, NIV).

36.17 Then He began to denounce the cities in which most of His miracles were done, because they did not repent. "Woe to you, Chorazin! Woe to you, Bethsaida! For if the miracles had occurred in Tyre and Sidon which occurred in you, they would have repented long ago in sackcloth and ashes. Nevertheless I say to you, it will be more tolerable for Tyre and Sidon in the day of judgment than for you. And you, Capernaum, will not be exalted to heaven, will you? You will descend to Hades; for if the miracles had occurred in Sodom which occurred in you, it would have remained to this day. Nevertheless I say to you that it will be more tolerable for the land of Sodom in the day of judgment, than for you" (Matthew 11:20-24, NASB).

36.18 "Do not stop him," Jesus said. "No one who does a miracle in my name can in the next moment say anything bad about me (Mark 9:39, NIV).

36.19 When he came near the place where the road goes down the Mount of Olives, the whole crowd of disciples began joyfully to praise God in loud voices for all the miracles they had seen (Luke 19:37, NIV).

36.20 This, the first of His signs (miracles, wonderworks), Jesus performed in Cana of Galilee, and manifested His glory [by it He displayed His greatness and His power openly], and His disciples believed in Him [adhered to, trusted in, and relied on Him] (John 2:11, AMP).

36.21 Now when he was in Jerusalem at the passover, in the feast day, many believed in his name, when they saw the miracles which he did (John 2:23, KJV).

36.22 Now there was a man of the Pharisees named Nicodemus, a member of the Jewish ruling council. He came to Jesus at night and said, "Rabbi, we know you are a teacher who has come from God. For no one could perform the miraculous signs you are doing if God were not with him (John 3:1-2, NIV).

36.23 Then Jesus said to him, Unless you see signs and miracles happen, you [people] never will believe (trust, have faith) at all (John 4:48, AMP).

36.24 And a great crowd was following Him because they had seen the signs (miracles) which He [continually] performed upon those who were sick (John 6:2, AMP).

36.25 Jesus answered them and said, Verily, verily, I say unto you, Ye seek me, not because ye saw the miracles, but because ye did eat of the loaves, and were filled (John 6:26, KJV).

36.26 Still, many in the crowd put their faith in him. They said, "When the Christ comes, will he do more miraculous signs than this man?" (John 7:31, NIV).

36.27 Therefore said some of the Pharisees, This man is not of God, because he keepeth not the sabbath day. Others said, How can a man that is a sinner do such miracles? And there was a division among them (John 9:16, KJV).

36.28 Then gathered the chief priests and the Pharisees a council, and said, What do we? for this man doeth many miracles (John 11:47, KJV).

36.29 Even after Jesus had done all these miraculous signs in their presence, they still would not believe in him (John 12:37, NIV).

36.30 There are also many other signs and miracles which Jesus performed in the presence of the disciples which are not written in this book (John 20:30, NIV).

36.31 Men of Israel, listen to these words: Jesus the Nazarene, a man attested to you by God with miracles and wonders and signs which God performed through Him in your midst, just as you yourselves know (Acts 2:22, NASB).

36.32 Everyone kept feeling a sense of awe; and many wonders and signs were taking place through the apostles (Acts 2:43, NASB).

36.33 Now, Lord, consider their threats and enable your servants to speak your word with great boldness. Stretch out your hand to heal and perform miraculous signs and wonders through the name of your holy servant Jesus (Acts 4:29-30, NIV).

36.34 And Stephen, full of faith and power, did great wonders and miracles among the people (Acts 6:8, KJV).

36.35 When the crowds heard Philip and saw the miraculous signs he did, they all paid close attention to what he said (Acts 8:6, NIV).

36.36 Therefore they spent a long time there speaking boldly with reliance upon the Lord, who was testifying to the word of His grace, granting that signs and wonders be done by their hands (Acts 14:3, NASB).

36.37 The whole assembly became silent as they listened to Barnabas and Paul telling about the miraculous signs and wonders God had done among the Gentiles through them (Acts 15:12, NIV).

36.38 I will not venture to speak of anything except what Christ has accomplished through me in leading the Gentiles to obey God by what I have said and done— by the power of signs and miracles, through the power of the Spirit. So from Jerusalem all the way around to Illyricum, I have fully proclaimed the gospel of Christ (Romans 15:18-19, NIV).

36.39 To another the working of miracles; to another prophecy; to another discerning of spirits; to another divers kinds of tongues; to another the interpretation of tongues (1 Corinthians 12:10, KJV).

36.40 And in the church God has appointed first of all apostles, second prophets, third teachers, then workers of miracles, also those having gifts of healing, those able to help others, those with gifts of administration, and those speaking in different kinds of tongues (1 Corinthians 12:28, NIV).

36.41 The signs of a true apostle were performed among you with all perseverance, by signs and wonders and miracles (2 Corinthians 12:12, NASB).

36.42 Does God give you his Spirit and work miracles among you because you observe the law, or because you believe what you heard? (Galatians 3:5, NIV).

36.43 How shall we escape [appropriate retribution] if we neglect and refuse to pay attention to such a great salvation [as is now offered to us, letting it drift past us forever]? For it was declared at first by the Lord [Himself], and it was confirmed to us and proved to be real and genuine by those who personally heard [Him speak]. [Besides this evidence] it was also established and plainly endorsed by God, Who showed His approval of it by signs and wonders and various miraculous manifestations of [His] power and by imparting the gifts of the Holy Spirit [to the believers] according to His own will (Hebrews 2:3-4, AMP).

36.44 Having a form of godliness but denying its power. Have nothing to do with them (2 Timothy 3:5, NIV).

REFERENCE 37 — Avoid Pride and Stay Humble

37.1 If my people, which are called by my name, shall humble themselves, and pray, and seek my face, and turn from their wicked ways; then will I hear from heaven, and will forgive their sin, and will heal their land (2 Chroni-cles 7:14, KJV).

37.2 Lord, You have heard the desire of the humble; You will strengthen their heart, You will incline Your ear (Psalm 10:17, NASB).

37.3 The Lord is close to those who are of a broken heart and saves such as are crushed with sorrow for sin and are humbly and thoroughly penitent (Psalm 34:18, AMP).

Part IV - Scripture References

37.4 The sacrifices of God are a broken spirit: a broken and a contrite heart, O God, thou wilt not despise (Psalm 51:17, KJV).

37.5 The reverent fear and worshipful awe of the Lord [includes] the hatred of evil; pride, arrogance, the evil way, and perverted and twisted speech I hate (Proverbs 8:13, AMP).

37.6 When swelling and pride come, then emptiness and shame come also, but with the humble (those who are lowly, who have been pruned or chiseled by trial, and renounce self) are skillful and godly Wisdom and soundness (Proverbs 11:2, AMP).

37.7 Pride only breeds quarrels, but wisdom is found in those who take advice (Proverbs 13:10, NIV)

37.8 The fear of the Lord teaches a man wisdom, and humility comes before honor (Proverbs 15:33, NIV).

37.9 Pride goeth before destruction, and an haughty spirit before a fall (Proverbs 16:18, KJV).

37.10 Better it is to be of an humble spirit with the lowly, than to divide the spoil with the proud (Proverbs 16:19, KJV).

37.11 Before his downfall a man's heart is proud, but humility comes before honor (Proverbs 18:12, NIV).

37.12 The reward of humility and the fear of the Lord Are riches, honor and life (Proverbs 22:4, NASB).

37.13 A man's pride will bring him low, But a humble spirit will obtain honor (Proverbs 29:23, NASB).

37.14 The lofty looks of man shall be humbled, and the haughtiness of men shall be bowed down, and the Lord alone shall be exalted in that day. For the day of the Lord of hosts shall be upon every one that is proud and lofty, and upon every one that is lifted up; and he shall be brought low (Isaiah 2:11-12, KJV).

37.15 The Lord of hosts has purposed it [in accordance with a fixed principle of His government], to defile the pride of all glory and to bring into dishonor and contempt all the honored of the earth (Isaiah 23:9, AMP).

37.16 For thus saith the high and lofty One that inhabiteth eternity, whose name is Holy; I dwell in the high and holy place, with him also that is of a contrite and humble spirit, to revive the spirit of the humble, and to revive the heart of the contrite ones (Isaiah 57:15, KJV).

37.17 For all these things My hand has made, and so all these things have come into being [by and for Me], says the Lord. But this is the man to whom I will look and have regard: he who is humble and of a broken or wounded spirit, and who trembles at My word and reveres My commands (Isaiah 66:2, AMP).

37.18 He hath shown thee, O man, what is good; and what doth the Lord require of thee, but to do justly, and to love mercy, and to walk humbly with thy God? (Micah 6:8, KJV).

37.19 And said, Truly I say to you, unless you repent (change, turn about) and become like little children [trusting, lowly, loving, forgiving], you can never enter the kingdom of heaven [at all]. Whoever will humble himself therefore and become like this little child [trusting, lowly, loving, forgiving] is greatest in the kingdom of heaven (Matthew 18:3-4, AMP).

37.20 And whosoever shall exalt himself shall be abased; and he that shall humble himself shall be exalted (Matthew 23:12, KJV).

37.21 He went on: "What comes out of a man is what makes him 'unclean.' For from within, out of men's hearts, come evil thoughts, sexual immorality, theft, murder, adultery, greed, malice, deceit, lewdness, envy, slander, arrogance and folly. All these evils come from inside and make a man 'unclean.' (Mark 7:20-23, NIV).

37.22 So, as those who have been chosen of God, holy and beloved, put on a heart of compassion, kindness, humility, gentleness and patience; bearing with one another, and forgiving each other, whoever has a complaint against anyone; just as the Lord forgave you, so also should you. Beyond all these things put on love, which is the perfect bond of unity (Colossians 3:12-14, NASB).

37.23 He must not be a recent convert, or he may become conceited and fall under the same judgment as the devil (1 Timothy 3:6, NIV).

37.24 But he gives us more grace. That is why Scripture says: "God opposes the proud but gives grace to the humble (James 4:6, NIV).

37.25 Humble yourselves [feeling very insignificant] in the presence of the Lord, and He will exalt you [He will lift you up and make your lives significant] (James 4:10, AMP).

37.26 Likewise, you who are younger and of lesser rank, be subject to the elders (the ministers and spiritual guides of the church)—[giving them due respect and yielding to their counsel]. Clothe (apron) yourselves, all of you, with humility [as the garb of a servant, so that its covering cannot possibly be stripped from you, with freedom from pride and arrogance] toward one another. For God sets Himself against the proud (the insolent, the overbearing, the disdainful, the presumptuous, the boastful)—[and He opposes, frustrates, and defeats them], but gives grace (favor, blessing) to the humble. [Prov. 3:34] Therefore humble yourselves [demote, lower yourselves in your own estimation] under the mighty hand of God, that in due time He may exalt you (1 Peter 5:5-6, AMP).

37.27 For all that is in the world—the lust of the flesh [craving for sensual gratification] and the lust of the eyes [greedy longings of the mind] and the pride of life [assurance in one's own resources or in the stability of earthly things]—these do not come from the Father but are from the world [itself] (1 John 2:16, AMP).

REFERENCE 38 — Expect Trials and Persecution

38.1 Many are the afflictions of the righteous: but the Lord delivereth him out of them all (Psalm 34:19, KJV).

38.2 My son, do not despise the Lord's discipline and do not resent his rebuke, because the Lord disciplines those he loves, as a father the son he delights in (Proverbs 3:11-12, NIV).

38.3 Behold, I have refined thee, but not with silver; I have chosen thee in the furnace of affliction (Isaiah 48:10, KJV).

38.4 And I will bring the third part through the fire, and will refine them as silver is refined, and will try them as gold is tried: they shall call on my name, and I will hear them: I will say, It is my people: and they shall say, The Lord is my God (Zechariah 13:9, KJV).

38.5 Blessed are those who are persecuted because of righteousness, for theirs is the kingdom of heaven. Blessed are you when people insult you, persecute you and falsely say all kinds of evil against you because of me. Rejoice and be glad, because great is your reward in heaven, for in the same way they persecuted the prophets who were before you (Matthew 5:10-12, NIV).

38.6 You will be betrayed even by parents, brothers, relatives and friends, and they will put some of you to death. All men will hate you because of me. But not a hair of your head will perish. By standing firm you will gain life (Luke 21:16-19, NIV).

38.7 If the world hates you, keep in mind that it hated me first. If you belonged to the world, it would love you as its own. As it is, you do not belong to the world, but I have chosen you out of the world. That is why the world hates you. Remember the words I spoke to you: "No servant is greater than his master." If they persecuted me, they will persecute you also. If they obeyed my teaching, they will obey yours also. They will treat you this way because of my name, for they do not know the One who sent me (John 15:18-21, NIV).

38.8 I have told you these things, so that in Me you may have [perfect] peace and confidence. In the world you have tribulation and trials and distress and frustration; but be of good cheer [take courage; be confident, certain, undaunted]! For I have overcome the world. [I have deprived it of power to harm you and have conquered it for you.] (John 16:33, AMP).

38.9 And they departed from the presence of the council, rejoicing that they were counted worthy to suffer shame for his name (Acts 5:41, KJV).

38.10 Establishing and strengthening the souls and the hearts of the disciples, urging and warning and encouraging them to stand firm in the faith, and [telling them] that it is through many hardships and tribulations we must enter the kingdom of God (Acts 14:22, AMP).

38.11 Moreover [let us also be full of joy now!] let us exult and triumph in our troubles and rejoice in our sufferings, knowing that pressure and affliction and hardship produce patient and unswerving endurance. And endurance (fortitude) develops maturity of character (approved faith and tried integrity). And character [of this sort] produces [the habit of] joyful and confident hope of eternal salvation (Romans 5:3-4, AMP).

38.12 Now if we are children, then we are heirs—heirs of God and co-heirs with Christ, if indeed we share in his sufferings in order that we may also share in his glory. I consider that our present sufferings are not worth comparing with the glory that will be revealed in us (Romans 8:17-18, NIV).

38.13 Who shall separate us from the love of Christ? Shall trouble or hardship or persecution or famine or nakedness or danger or sword? As it is written: "For your sake we face death all day long; we are considered as sheep to be slaughtered." No, in all these things we are more than conquerors through him who loved us. For I am convinced that neither death nor life, neither angels nor demons, neither the present nor the future, nor any powers, neither height nor depth, nor anything else in all creation, will be able to separate us from the love of God that is in Christ Jesus our Lord (Romans 8:35-39, NIV).

38.14 We are troubled on every side, yet not distressed; we are perplexed, but not in despair; Persecuted, but not forsaken; cast down, but not destroyed; Always bearing about in the body the dying of the Lord Jesus, that the life also of Jesus might be made manifest in our body. For we which live are always delivered unto death for Jesus's sake, that the life also of Jesus might be made manifest in our mortal flesh (2 Corinthians 4:8-11, KJV).

38.15 For you have been granted [the privilege] for Christ's sake not only to believe in (adhere to, rely on, and trust in) Him, but also to suffer in His behalf (Philippians 1:29, AMP).

38.16 Yea, and all that will live godly in Christ Jesus shall suffer persecution (2 Timothy 3:12, KJV).

38.17 As many as I love, I rebuke and chasten: be zealous therefore, and repent (Revelation 3:19, KJV).

REFERENCE 39 — Overcome and Obtain Your Inheritance

39.1 Then Caleb quieted the people before Moses and said, "We should by all means go up and take possession of it, for we will surely overcome it" (Numbers 13:30, NASB).

39.2 Enter through the narrow gate. For wide is the gate and broad is the road that leads to destruction, and many enter through it. But small is the gate and narrow the road that leads to life, and only a few find it (Matthew 7:13-14, NIV).

39.3 And you will be hated by all for My name's sake, but he who perseveres and endures to the end will be saved [from spiritual disease and death in the world to come] (Matthew 10:22, AMP).

39.4 But he that shall endure unto the end, the same shall be saved (Matthew 24:13, KJV).

39.5 And you will be hated and detested by everybody for My name's sake, but he who patiently perseveres and endures to the end will be saved (made a partaker of the salvation by Christ, and delivered from spiritual death) (Mark 13:13, AMP).

39.6 Be not overcome of evil, but overcome evil with good (Romans 12:21, KJV).

39.7 Do you not know that those who run in a race all run, but only one receives the prize? Run in such a way that you may win (1 Corinthians 9:24, NASB).

39.8 I press toward the mark for the prize of the high calling of God in Christ Jesus (Philippians 3:14, KJV).

39.9 [As to what remains] henceforth there is laid up for me the [victor's] crown of righteousness [for being right with God and doing right], which the Lord, the righteous Judge, will award to me and recompense me on that [great] day—and not to me only, but also to all those who have loved and yearned for and welcomed His appearing (His return) (2 Timothy 4:8, AMP).

39.10 Therefore then, since we are surrounded by so great a cloud of witnesses [who have borne testimony to the Truth], let us strip off and throw aside every encumbrance (unnecessary weight) and that sin which so readily (deftly and cleverly) clings to and entangles us, and let us run with patient endurance and steady and active persistence the appointed course of the race that is set before us (Hebrews 12:1, AMP).

39.11 Blessed (happy, to be envied) is the man who is patient under trial and stands up under temptation, for when he has stood the test and been approved, he will receive [the victor's] crown of life which God has promised to those who love Him (James 1:12, AMP).

39.12 And when the Chief Shepherd appears, you will receive the unfading crown of glory (1 Peter 5:4, NASB).

39.13 I am writing to you, fathers, because you know Him who has been from the beginning. I am writing to you, young men, because you have overcome the evil one. I have written to you, children (1 John 2:13, NASB).

39.14 Little children, you are of God [you belong to Him] and have [already] defeated and overcome them [the agents of the antichrist], because He Who lives in you is greater (mightier) than he who is in the world (1 John 4:4, AMP).

39.15 for everyone born of God overcomes the world. This is the victory that has overcome the world, even our faith. is it that overcomes the world? Only he who believes that Jesus is the Son of God (1 John 5:4-5, NIV).

39.16 He who has an ear, let him hear what the Spirit says to the churches. To him who overcomes, I will grant to eat of the tree of life which is in the Paradise of God (Revelation 2:7, NASB).

39.17 He who has an ear, let him hear what the Spirit says to the churches. He who overcomes will not be hurt by the second death (Revelation 2:11, NASB).

39.18 He who has an ear, let him hear what the Spirit says to the churches. To him who overcomes, to him I will give some of the hidden manna, and I will give him a white stone, and a new name written on the stone which no one knows but he who receives it (Revelation 2:17, NASB).

39.19 He who overcomes, and he who keeps My deeds until the end, to him I will give authority over the nations (Revelation 2:26, NASB).

39.20 He who overcomes will thus be clothed in white garments; and I will not erase his name from the book of life, and I will confess his name before My Father and before His angels (Revelation 3:5, NASB).

39.21 He who overcomes, I will make him a pillar in the temple of My God, and he will not go out from it anymore; and I will write on him the name of My God, and the name of the city of My God, the new Jerusalem, which comes down out of heaven from My God, and My new name (Revelation 3:12, NASB).

39.22 He who overcomes, I will grant to him to sit down with Me on My throne, as I also overcame and sat down with My Father on His throne (Revelation 3:21, NASB).

39.23 He who overcomes will inherit these things, and I will be his God and he will be My son (Revelation 21:7, NASB).

REFERENCE 40 — Fear God, Not Man

40.1 Hearken unto me, ye that know righteousness, the people in whose heart is my law; fear ye not the reproach of men, neither be ye afraid of their reviling (Isaiah 51:7, KJV).

40.2 Yea, though I walk through the valley of the shadow of death, I will fear no evil: for thou art with me; thy rod and thy staff they comfort me (Psalm 23:4, KJV).

40.3 I sought the Lord, and he heard me, and delivered me from all my fears (Psalm 34:4, KJV).

40.4 In God I trust; I will not be afraid. What can man do to me? (Psalm 56:11, NIV).

40.5 The Lord is on my side; I will not fear: what can man do unto me? (Psalm 118:6, KJV).

40.6 Do not be afraid of those who kill the body but cannot kill the soul. Rather, be afraid of the One who can destroy both soul and body in hell. Are not two sparrows sold for a penny ? Yet not one of them will fall to the ground apart from the will of your Father. And even the very hairs of your head are all numbered. So don't be afraid; you are worth more than many sparrows (Matthew 10:28-31, NIV).

40.7 For God hath not given us the spirit of fear; but of power, and of love, and of a sound mind (2 Timothy 1:7, KJV).

40.8 For God did not give us a spirit of timidity (of cowardice, of craven and cringing and fawning fear), but [He has given us a spirit] of power and of love and of calm and well-balanced mind and discipline and self-control (2 Timothy 1:7, KJV).

40.9 So that we may boldly say, The Lord is my helper, and I will not fear what man shall do unto me (Hebrews 13:6, KJV).

40.10 There is no fear in love; but perfect love casteth out fear: because fear hath torment. He that feareth is not made perfect in love (1 John 4:18, KJV).

40.11 But as for the cowards and the ignoble and the contemptible and the cravenly lacking in courage and the cowardly submissive, and as for the unbelieving and faithless, and as for the depraved and defiled with abominations, and as for murderers and the lewd and adulterous and the practicers of magic arts and the idolaters (those who give supreme devotion to anyone or anything other than God) and all liars (those who knowingly convey untruth by word or deed)—[all of these shall have] their part in the lake that blazes with fire and brimstone. This is the second death (Revelation 21:8, AMP).

40.12 Readiness is fear of the Lord. The fear of the Lord is clean, enduring for ever? (Psalm 19:9, KJV).

40.13 The secret of the Lord is with them that fear him; and he will show them his covenant (Psalm 25:14, KJV).

40.14 The angel of the Lord encampeth round about them that fear him, and delivereth them. taste and see that the Lord is good: blessed is the man that trusteth in him. O fear the Lord, ye his saints: for there is no want to them that fear him (Psalm 34:7-9, KJV).

40.15 The fear of the Lord is the beginning of wisdom: a good understanding have all they that do his commandments: his praise endureth for ever (Psalm 111:10, KJV).

40.16 The Lord taketh pleasure in them that fear him, in those that hope in his mercy (Psalm 147:11, KJV).

40.17 The fear of the Lord is the beginning of knowledge: but fools despise wisdom and instruction (Proverbs 1:7, KJV).

40.18 The fear of the Lord is the beginning of wisdom: and the knowledge of the holy is understanding (Proverbs 9:10, KJV).

40.19 Let us hear the conclusion of the whole matter: Fear God, and keep his commandments: for this is the whole duty of man (Ecclesiastes 12:13, KJV).

40.20 Ye are bought with a price; be not ye the servants of men (1 Corinthians 7:23, KJV).

40.21 Having therefore these promises, dearly beloved, let us cleanse ourselves from all filthiness of the flesh and spirit, perfecting holiness in the fear of God (2 Corinthians 7:1, KJV).

40.22 Be subject to one another out of reverence for Christ (the Messiah, the Anointed One) (Ephesians 5:21, AMP).

40.23 Wherefore we receiving a kingdom which cannot be moved, let us have grace, whereby we may serve God acceptably with reverence and godly fear (Hebrews 12:28, KJV).

REFERENCE 41 — Trust in the Lord and Surrender Everything to Him

41.1 The Lord redeemeth the soul of his servants: and none of them that trust in him shall be desolate (Psalm 34:22, KJV).

41.2 Truly my soul waiteth upon God: from him cometh my salvation. He only is my rock and my salvation; he is my defense; I shall not be greatly moved (Psalm 62:1-2, KJV).

41.3 My soul, wait thou only upon God; for my expectation is from him. He only is my rock and my salvation: he is my defence; I shall not be moved. In God is my salvation and my glory: the rock of my strength, and my refuge, is in God. Trust in him at all times; ye people, pour out your heart before him: God is a refuge for us. Selah (Psalm 62:5-8, KJV).

41.4 Trust in the Lord with all thine heart; and lean not unto thine own understanding. In all thy ways acknowledge him, and he shall direct thy paths (Proverbs 3:5-6, KJV).

41.5 The fear of man bringeth a snare: but whoso putteth his trust in the Lord shall be safe (Proverbs 29:25, KJV).

41.6 Therefore I tell you, stop being perpetually uneasy (anxious and worried) about your life, what you shall eat or what you shall drink; or about your body, what you shall put on. Is not life greater [in quality] than food, and the body [far above and more excellent] than clothing? Look at the birds of the air; they neither sow nor reap nor gather into barns, and yet your heavenly Father keeps feeding them. Are you not worth much more than they? And who of you by worrying and being anxious can add one unit of measure (cubit) to his stature or to the span of his life? [Ps. 39:5-7] And why should you be anxious about clothes? Consider the lilies of the field and learn thoroughly how they grow; they neither toil nor spin. Yet I tell you, even Solomon in all his magnificence (excellence, dignity, and grace) was not arrayed like one of these. [1 Kings 10:4-7] But if God so clothes the grass of the field, which today is alive and green and tomorrow is tossed into the furnace, will He not much more surely clothe you, O you of little faith? Therefore do not worry and be anxious, saying, What are we going to have to eat? or, What are we going to have to drink? or, What are we going to have to wear? For the Gentiles (heathen) wish for and crave and diligently seek all these things, and your heavenly Father knows well that you need them all. But seek (aim at and strive after) first of all His kingdom and His righteousness (His way of doing and being right), and then all these things taken together will be given you besides. So do not worry or be anxious about tomorrow, for tomorrow will have worries and anxieties of its own. Sufficient for each day is its own trouble (Matthew 6:25-34, AMP).

41.7 Come unto me, all ye that labour and are heavy laden, and I will give you rest. Take my yoke upon you, and learn of me; for I am meek and lowly in heart: and ye shall find rest unto your souls. For my yoke is easy, and my burden is light (Matthew 11:28-30, KJV).

41.8 Teaching them to observe everything that I have commanded you, and behold, I am with you all the days (perpetually, uniformly, and on every occasion), to the [very] close and consummation of the age. Amen (so let it be) (Matthew 28:20, AMP).

41.9 And Jesus answering saith unto them, Have faith in God (Mark 11:22, KJV).

41.10 And I will ask the Father, and He will give you another Comforter (Counselor, Helper, Intercessor, Advocate, Strengthener, and Standby), that He may remain with you forever—The Spirit of Truth, Whom the world cannot receive (welcome, take to its heart), because it does not see Him or know and recognize Him. But you know and recognize Him, for He lives with you [constantly] and will be in you. I will not leave you as orphans [comfortless, desolate, bereaved, forlorn, helpless]; I will come [back] to you (John 14:16-18, AMP).

41.11 Jesus answered and said unto him, If a man love me, he will keep my words: and my Father will love him, and we will come unto him, and make our abode with him (John 14:23, KJV).

41.12 Abide in me, and I in you. As the branch cannot bear fruit of itself, except it abide in the vine; no more can ye, except ye abide in me I am the vine, ye are the branches: He that abideth in me, and I in him, the same bringeth forth much fruit: for without me ye can do nothing (John 15:4-5,, KJV).

41.13 For I am convinced that neither death nor life, neither angels nor demons, neither the present nor the future, nor any powers, neither height nor depth, nor anything else in all creation, will be able to separate us from the love of God that is in Christ Jesus our Lord (Romans 8:38-39, NIV).

41.14 For we walk by faith, not by sight (2 Corinthians 5:7, KJV).

41.15 Let your conversation be without covetousness; and be content with such things as ye have: for he hath said, I will never leave thee, nor forsake thee (Hebrews 13:5, KJV).

41.16 Let your character or moral disposition be free from love of money [including greed, avarice, lust, and craving for earthly possessions] and be satisfied with your present [circumstances and with what you have]; for He [God] Himself has said, I will not in any way fail you nor give you up nor leave you without support. [I will] not, [I will] not, [I will] not in any degree leave you helpless nor forsake nor let [you] down (relax My hold on you)! [Assuredly not!] [Josh. 1:5] So we take comfort and are encouraged and confidently and boldly say, The Lord is my Helper; I will not be seized with alarm [I will not fear or dread or be terrified]. What can man do to me? (Hebrews 13:5, AMP).

The End

www.ingramcontent.com/pod-product-compliance
Lightning Source LLC
Chambersburg PA
CBHW031616160426
43196CB00006B/152